SMALL STEPS, HUGE CHANGES

*The Extraordinary Moments
of an Ordinary Life*

PHYLLIS REED

iUniverse, Inc.
Bloomington

iUniverse books may be ordered through booksellers or by contacting:

iUniverse
1663 Liberty Drive
Bloomington, IN 47403
www.iuniverse.com
1-800-Authors (1-800-288-4677)

ISBN: 978-1-4620-0057-9 (sc)
ISBN: 978-1-4620-0058-6 (hc)
ISBN: 978-1-4620-0056-2 (ebook)

Printed in the United States of America

iUniverse rev. date: 03/21/2011

For
DeAnna Lynne Colglazier
Michael, Matthew, and Thomas Colglazier

And

In Memory of
Gregory Loren Gardner

If you bring forth that which is in you, that which is in you will save you. If you do not bring forth that which is within you, that which is in you will destroy you.

Gnostic Gospels, The Gospel of Thomas, Verse 70 in some translations.

TABLE OF CONTENTS

Poems of Remembrance   175

PREFACE

Each of us in every moment has the opportunity to create our life with the choices we make as we experience it. Each of us can choose to see our self as a victim of our experiences or as the co-creator of our life. Whether it is to recover from a major blow such as: the loss of a child, the betrayal of one person by another, the loss of physical or mental health, or some day-to-day change that could alter life, it seems that one person grows out of a desperation to survive and another gets stuck in the despair of his or her current circumstance. At different times, the same person may have both responses to what he or she is experiencing. My experiences and my responses to them have transformed me from an angry frightened person to a more joyful and loving one. My intention is to share my experiences and my recorded memories of them with the hope that they may support others who have or will have similar experiences in their lives.

It has taken me years to see that the drama of big events and the excitement of big leaps have not been my growth patterns. My healing has begun more often with the urge to make one small desperate step when life seemed overwhelming, and it seemed that nothing could possibly make a difference. Each courageous small step born out of a need to just survive has brought me back to health and to huge changes.

My guidance during difficult times has come from within me. I have wondered if others have had the same experience; and if some did, why some did not. When the pain of feeling powerless has been present within me a voice has simply said, "get up." Some source of strength pulsed through me, and I could not "not get up." While reviewing the recorded history of my life experiences, my writings began to morph into this collection of essays, poems, thoughts, feelings, and letters that you now hold. It is my hope that by sharing my thoughts and feelings about my non-physical determined energy to survive, it could support others in finding their answers within themselves. Friends and family have said that my recorded experiences often express our common human struggles and our basic need to share them in order to heal.

My collective small steps recorded in sacred moments have created this huge step of sharing the deepest parts of me with you. It is my tribute to all of us humans that have rallied and lived joyously when it appeared the odds were against us. It is my deepest intention to encourage others, who read my words here, to do the same. You may find that you are deeply afraid, that you are overwhelmed with hurt, that the pain of loss is unbearable, and then suddenly know that you can take one small courageous step. In that moment, it is possible to discover that you have the potential to heal by choosing each small step one at a time. Through the intimate sharing of our deepest fears and greatest joys, we can connect and support each other in our efforts to co-create a more meaningful, less fearful life. In your life and mine, may whatever arises serve to awaken compassion first for ourselves and then for all others.

Namaste

Phyllis Reed

A Gift No One Else Can Give

For as long as I can remember, I have been given sacred moments without understanding them and without giving them that label. My sacred moments of clarity have been vivid and distinct. It has not mattered whether they awakened me in the middle of the night, came as a realization about the day before, or arrived as a vision inside my mind and soul, I wanted to write them down so that they could be captured in the now and their feeling never forgotten. These moments of creation seemed to exist apart from everything else but me. As I began to write, my words took on a life of their own and what I had intended to write and what I actually wrote were poles apart. Later it could seem as if someone else must have been the author.

In my youth, I thought I should write the great novel, but didn't feel as if I had lived long enough to write about life—mine or anyone's. Later, my dreams of writing anything other than vignettes of my own experiences were overcome by the events of just living. Since my life could be tagged as "classic normal," I felt my ramblings would not be of much interest to anyone except maybe my children. Often some of my best writings were created as letters to my children. The subject matter was stimulated by a deep need to express my heartfelt believes and longings to them and often about them. I wanted to get it right. I wanted them to hear the integrity within my words. I did not want to debate some obscure point of contention and lose the essence of the message. So I wrote, and gave them a gift no one else could give them.

Sometimes it was not a letter, but only an idea about life that needed to be expressed through the wiser voice that lived inside my writings. These writings about my experiences, ideals, visions, and memories grew in number. Each cherished one represented a time in my life when the only thing that mattered was to write it down. In many ways these writings when placed together, became a photo album filled with words instead of pictures about hope, despair, happiness, and longing. I took it out and relived the moments exactly as they were, but from the perception of this new person I was becoming with each new experience.

Over time I added to the album, and it slowly has grown into a collection of thoughts that have taken on a deeper meaning than each one has expressed individually. When a circumstance seemed to call to me to share it, I invited others to read what I had written. Often they found beauty in my thoughts. They generously offered that they found comfort, inspiration, and resonance about their own lives between my lines. My word album became a collection of sacred moments that somehow expressed the universal experience of those of us who consider ourselves "classic normal." Our lives have been filled with ups and downs, tears and happiness, anger and forgiveness, and love and fear. These daily experiences have not caused major earthquakes or volcanic eruptions around the world. They have merely been the common ordinary, extraordinary experiences of life, death, disappointments, accomplishments, losses, and gains. Mysteriously, they have shaken our core, given us insight, and shaped our lives. Strung together the sacred moments of each day have created our sacred lives.

During one of my own sacred days, a kind and caring Universe called to me. It suggested that it was time to share my combined experiences more freely. I felt unworthy and yet, I trusted the wise voice of the woman within me who writes about her life. Each of the writings from my sacred album, which I share here, is a sacred part of me that I now entrust to the sacred part of you.

LEARNING FROM NATURE

Today I experienced an awesome sacred moment, the birth of a Monarch butterfly. I tagged her (MLJ825) and fed her sugar water. I held her, named her Zoe, and released her. She flew directly to a beautiful purple flower. It was an amazing opportunity to experience nature unobstructed by fear.

Overlooking the James River

I See Me

Each year as autumn comes, I feel a sense of balance that somehow reminds me of the complexity of the changes that will occur or that I want to create. Deng Ming-Dao[1] wrote: *It is not a simple, smooth continuum from summer into autumn. There is complexity and counterpoint. If nature is full of subtlety and even false appearances, how wise must we be in order to follow life's rhythms unerringly?* Recently, I told a friend that change is not easy. I said it with assurance, authenticity, and passion as we discussed the changes that are or could be part of our lives in 2010 and beyond. And yet, there is a part of me that longs for the changes I want to come with a snap of my fingers. Change is gradual and acceptance of change within me is complex at times.

So today I'm asking myself, "What is there about autumn that renews me and restores my balance?" Perhaps it is the freshness of the air, the clear bright night sky, the scurrying of animals as they prepare for winter, or perhaps it's just nature's way of brilliantly reminding me to move toward what surely will follow—the cold quiet season of winter. More than all these things, I feel it is the beginning of my assessment of how I have spent my time so far this year. That assessment will require a choice to be with "what is" today and to relax into my feelings about it instead of my thoughts.

Last winter was cold and snowy wet. I suffered loneliness that I had not suffered for a long time. I traveled to warmer climates, but carried the loneliness with me—the longing for more in other words. I hiked the snow-covered streets of my community and soaked up its beauty and discovered my angels, known and unknown, that surround me. But I cannot deny that for much of winter the choice to suffer in loneliness came more often than I care to admit even to myself. I gave up an unfulfilling romance and regained a friendship. I meditated, found solace in chosen silences, connected with my soul's essence, and deepened my connection to the Earth and the Universe. It was a time of amazing quiet introspection, but not of deep peace.

---

1   Deng Ming-Dao wrote in *365 TAO Daily Meditations*

Spring found me reaching out from a different place with a changing perspective that would not have been possible without the wintertime aloneness and the wisdom that came through that less than peaceful silence. Spring like autumn brings balance to me at times, but it is filled with energy and I have a need for new and exciting learning. Last spring brought theatre back into my life, and a renewed need to understand the life that exists upon the Earth around me. Biking became my old-new form of exercise and golf matches fell by the wayside. I hiked the mountains and valleys with people I love and expanded my lungs to hold my soaring spirit. Although short lived because of an injury, tennis called to me again. I volunteered to support others in learning about the earth, and my world was filled with the colors of music. I was offered an opportunity to support the youth of my community in the coming school year; something I love to do.

Summer brought surprises. During a weeklong visit by my daughter, we hiked and talked and slept and ate and enjoyed being together. Then out of the blue, or out of the green, I slipped on a blade of grass and found myself on crutches. The injury slowed down my movements, but did not lessen my joy of being with my family. I did not rail against it or wish for something more. Without undue suffering, I accepted it and decided what I would do next. My summer energy is like that, no time to anguish over what is not. The sun is out, the air is hot, the activity level busy. Rainbows are frequent and I am present in my life and relationships (old and new); I laugh often and feel lazy at times without judgment. I sing, I dance, and I rush around in joy! I don't seem to notice what is missing.

Then comes autumn with its visible, complex, and tangible changes. Somehow I receive a message from my soul that it is time to harvest what I've planted and contemplate what will be needed as winter comes. It is not a longing for change, but more a knowing that change is inevitable, and that I welcome it. Often I voice to others that I am a winter child and that I love the contemplative nature of winter. This year my daughter reminded me that my birthday is really the end of fall. Of course I knew that at some level, but when she said it I paused to really take it in. Each year I watch the trees change their color and marvel at their beauty. I watch the skies clear and feel the beginning of Indian summer. I relish the cool breeze that holds a gentle chill. I begin to want to come indoors and to read more. I buy a new puzzle for cold-day activity. I write more and become more disciplined in choosing how I will spend my time. In short, I begin to prepare for the cold more-solitary days to come.

Perhaps this year has brought me to this new perspective that I am an autumn child filled with the complexity that is required to live my life fully until its end this time around. As is true each time the opportunity arrives, I'm remembering to choose life as it is in this moment. I see me! I am simple and I am complex. My life contains the beauty and the ability to change demonstrated in autumn energy. In autumn I see all of me and accept what I see—knowing that change is and will be constant.

My Tree Outside My Window

For years I dreamed of a tree just outside my window. Its branches glowed with sunlight and filled my window with shapes and images that brought me peace. After I woke from that dream, I had a knowing that I would one day live in sight of that amazing tree. As life changed and moved, I remembered the tree and always watched hoping that it would appear with a message for me about where and how I was to live.

Since that dream, many trees have stood outside my windows, but in my mind and heart they were not "my" tree of knowledge. Then a few years ago, I chose to build a retirement home here in the Blue Ridge Mountains of Virginia. I purchased a lot that was filled with trees, but none of them seemed like my dream tree and many would be cut down to make room for my house. But it was a beautiful spot on the top of a hill nestled in the valley and surrounded by the larger mountains. The wind blew up from the valley below and the trees danced with delight—so did I. The breeze moved my hair, gently rushed across my skin, and brought a feeling of deep peace to my heart.

When I first moved into my cute little blue-and-white house, my furniture had not yet arrived. I created a pallet on the floor surrounded by my books and pillows. I was so grateful for what I had created. The room was a robin egg blue with white trim, and it had windows from floor to ceiling along one wall and three more transom windows high on the wall where my bed would eventually go. The sun rose into the windows from over the mountain. I had positioned my house to take advantage of the open space view and morning light.

I was really tired from all the move preparations, my sleep was deep, peaceful, and long. When I awoke the room was already filled with hues of changing light. As I turned my gaze toward the window, there it was, "my" dream tree glowing with sunlight and filling my eyes with the wonder of the Universe. I lay on the floor wondering if I had been sleeping in my high bed instead of sleeping on the floor, would I have been at the right angle to recognize what I was now seeing? I laughed out loud and hugged and congratulated myself for having the courage to begin this new life.

This new life has had many surprises along with pleasant and difficult experiences, but I celebrate my choice each day and know it was the right one for me. Today during my morning reading and meditation as I felt this gratitude in my heart, I glanced up and the tiny windows around and across my front door jumped into view, but not in the way they usually did. What I saw was each small pane of the window as a work of art, a different angle of the tree branches framed within each. I felt a surge of joy about my choice to live in this quiet place, and also I began to look around the room with a different eye.

This cute little blue-and-white house is filled with windows, and no matter where I look I see the wonder and art of nature reflected there. Sometimes it is a large view of the distant mountains, sometimes it a small branch, or one tiny leaf of a tree branch, and sometimes it's a curved image reflected in the mirror on the other side of the room, slightly distorted, but just as amazing. I sat in awe at the beauty of life in nature that now surrounds my own life.

My "tree" of knowledge has had a difficult year. The valley suffered a drought last summer and the building of my house may have damaged part of its root system. The top third of the tree's branches seem to have died at the end of summer. Sometimes during a drought, a tree will pull energy into its core and a few branches will be sacrificed so that it can survive another year. So I refused last fall to have it removed. For the past few months, I have watched it, given it Reiki treatments, and prayed for its survival. It seemed so important for it to be here with me. But this morning, I have a new vision of what that tree symbolizes within me, and I have realized that it has never belonged to me. It is not and never was "my" tree.

At first the tree represented the hope of finding the perfect place to retire. Then it represented the courage it took for me to create a new life. Then it represented the centeredness I was beginning to discover deep within me. Now it represents the strength that is needed to let go of what is no longer necessary and to live with joy. For all living things, survival is a strong instinct during the time of physical existence. As I gaze into each small window here, I see separate pieces of that total existence. Some living things will thrive for another season, but as I watch them grow or fail to grow, my view of them from my windows will alter everyday. We do not belong to each other; we are simply a part of each other sharing the same life connecting force.

Unencumbered by a busy mind, this knowing comes from seeing clearly each small window with its partial view, seeing clearly the whole tree surrounded by the mountains, and seeing with the same clarity the continuous changes in both. Physical existence changes and ends. I trust the Universal force that holds us together through all the beginnings and endings here upon this Earth and beyond. For this moment in time, the beautiful symbol of a dream tree outside my bedroom window reminds me we are sharing physical life, and we can choose to embrace that sharing by just being present with what is. For me at least, that is an amazing change of perspective, and the most joyful part is that I am grateful for the view. In each and every moment, my intention is to be present and align my personality with the authentic needs of my soul. It is in this state of gratitude, that I am choosing life!

Butterflies Have Returned

Years ago I sat under trees reading a lot, and it seemed I was part of the life that surrounded me. Butterflies buzzed around me and represented the energy of connection that I felt. Sometimes to my amazement, one would land and sit upon me for a few seconds. It was a bit heavier than air, but not much. Somehow that tiny presence got my attention in a way that much more dramatic experiences couldn't quite capture.

As I grew, butterflies continued to be a visual source of spirit for me. They followed me on paths as I walked. They flew in circles around my head as I read. They flashed their color and caught my attention especially when I was hurrying here or there. I would stop to gaze in wonder at their beauty in flight and at their stillness as they gathered their nectar. It occurred to me even then that the butterfly didn't seem confused about its purpose. After it outgrew its cocoon, it simply was attracted to bright colors and flowers, it gathered nectar, it fluttered about, and it gave beauty back to the earth and to me.

One day on King's Mountain in North Carolina, while walking an historical battle trail with a friend, a butterfly kept darting in and out around me. We laughed and I said it was one of my ancestors trying to contact me. A few steps further and we found the grave of Colonel Ferguson, a British soldier of Scottish descent during the civil war, who had lost his life in that battle. My father's name was Ferguson too. Coincidence you say? Maybe! Anyway I told my friend that sometimes butterflies landed on me for a visit. He didn't believe me so I said that I would sit quietly on the bench to see if this butterfly wanted to make a deeper connection. I knew it had to be the butterfly's choice! I no sooner sat down than the butterfly landed on my open palm, and just stayed there as if waiting for my friend to capture a picture. I still have the picture for all you non-believers.

About ten years ago, I began to lose sight of the beauty of my own life. People died and people left, I didn't always get what I wanted or I thought I needed, my days seemed dark even when the sun was shining, and I felt as though I had no power to create differently. I lived in the past or the future, because the "now" was just too painful. I began to cry and feel that deep powerlessness inside my body and to question whether or not I deserved to exist at all. As unbelievable at it may sound, no butterflies ever fluttered near me anymore.

I continued to think of butterflies as a symbol of life connecting to life, but my energy seemed to repel them. I began to watch and to hope for them everywhere. When I did see one, I would freeze and inwardly whisper, please oh please land on me again. They didn't! Their absence became a huge symbol for how disconnected I felt from my own spirit.

I began to look inside me at the suppressed emotions that had numbed my life. I found the pain of sadness, anger, jealousy, vengefulness, and more. Under those emotions, I found the energy of a victim within my own life. I slowly began to accept those painful emotions, to feel them deeply, and to choose differently by making responsible choices to cultivate the healthy parts of me that were generous, kind, and loving, and which would support what I felt my spirit wanted me to do. I began to live in the moment as best I could from the healthiest part of me I could find. I found compassion for me and then for others and joy began to return to my life little by little.

Six summers ago I was feeling light and free, and I walked up to a fence by the trail where I was hiking. What I saw there triggered me to cry softly and then to giggle with joy. There on some incredibly radiant yellow and purple flowers were hundreds of butterflies. They fluttered, they soared on the wind, and they glided to a stop on the flowers, and they caressed each other in flight. Their presence stopped all my thoughts, and I forgot to urge them to land upon me. It seemed like all the butterflies that I had not seen of late had gathered and were waiting there to greet me upon my Path. It felt like a miracle just to be near them on a day glorious with sunshine.

I have continued my Path toward *harmony, cooperation, sharing, and reverence[2] for life* by continuing to examine what is happening inside me with the help of great teachers and other spiritual partners. I know that my purpose of spiritual growth is more in alignment with the needs of my soul than it has ever been. I love my life and I see beauty in my days, even the most difficult of them. I see butterflies scurrying around everywhere. Sometimes they fly in a circle to say a quick hello. At the golf course one landed on my car. It was black with blue on the tips of its wings. I felt so

2   Gary Zukav's, author of Seat of the Soul, view of our soul's needs.

grateful for its presence there. I had no need for it to come closer; nearby was near enough.

Later, I was planting flowers, which a friend had given me the day before. He said the flowers, bright yellow miniature mums, were a bowl of sunshine to lighten a rainy day. We both laughed and paused to take in their glow of color. I was contentedly planting our bowl of sunshine in the earth just outside my bedroom window along with a lavender plant I had bought for myself. I was hot and sweaty and my spirit was in residence. Something buzzed and caught in my hair. I jumped and swung my arm in fear because I thought it might be a wasp. As I shook my hair and looked up, a giant monarch butterfly was waving hello and goodbye at the same time as it sailed away toward the flowers I had just planted. It had touched down upon my hair perhaps drawn by the fragrance of lavender. I danced a circle of gratitude around the flowers, because butterflies had returned to me without me longing for them to do so. It was a precious symbolic gift that came without attachment, theirs or mine. I already was feeling the joy of living and the butterfly skipping through my hair was just more nectar on my petals.

For me butterflies have always been a symbol of the fragility, shortness, and beauty of this physical existence. They struggle and spring from their cocoon and do what butterflies do. I love that and want to keep evolving from my own cocoon of remembered pain toward just being me in each moment. I know that being truly present in each moment and growing spiritually through the most loving part I can find within me is my primary purpose. The young man who landscaped my new yard felt butterfly bushes were just the right thing. They're purple; I love that!

Exploration

Today I took part in the chemical testing for safe water of one of Wintergreen Resort's creeks with my Volunteer Naturalist Group. I came to this project with a small base of knowledge and so I was eager to experiment and learn. The scientist leading the experiment divided us into five teams of two people each. One team was to measure nitrates in the water, another to measure phosphates, another ph level, another oxygen and temperature levels, and another the turbidity of the creek water. We gathered our instructions and our test tubes, put on our waders, and entered the creek at different spots. Each team had a particular job to do, and then we were asked to meet at the edge of the creek to report what we had done, how we had done it, and what we had learned about the water's health.

For ten minutes or so, each team focused on its particular task and gave little attention to the other teams' activities. My partner and I were measuring phosphate levels, and we took it seriously—each supporting the other, first holding the tube, then making sure of the amount of water in the test tube, putting in the chemical tablet, waiting the prescribed time, watching for color change, and comparing the color to the chart we were given. It was fun, concentrated, cooperative, and informative, without judgment.

We headed back to the table where the other teams were gathering with the results of their experiments. As we exchanged information and what that meant about the health of the water in the creek, we all started to get the whole picture. We trusted each other's findings and soon began to see the importance of each of the tests. I could see how the strength of each test was supported by the results from the others and how important it was to integrate the knowledge we had gained about the water.

We went on to gather the life from the creek into nets from areas of clear water, leaf filled water, and water under heavy rocks. We took our specimens and put them into ice cube trays filled with creek water so we could identify them. Because the water tested very clean, we expected to see mayflies, stoneflies, salamander newts, etc; life that could not exist in contaminated or polluted streams. What we found collectively and shared grew our knowledge base of the water.

Later as I drove home down the mountain, I began to see how this same kind of experiment could be supportive of my creation of authentic power. I could choose to see each fearful part of me as an explorer that gathers experiences by becoming active and creating pain in my body. If I did not give power to the fearful part that resists it, I could trust its findings. I could integrate it into my base knowledge of other fearful and healthy parts of my *Earthsuit*[3]. I could see where an unhealthy imbalance existed. I could choose responsibly how to create a more healthy inner landscape, and I could create authentic power to support my soul's intentions. I could do so without judgment of my inner landscape as eternally flawed. If my intention was to create a healthy and loving existence, I could choose an action to do that. If I shared my experiences with others, I could better co-create health and it might not take as long or be as difficult as it could alone.

It was good to see all this. I could have stood on the edge of the creek and just watched what appeared to be clean water flowing over the rocks, felt the wind in my hair, smelled the moistness of the earth and never wondered about the actual content of the water. Eventually, the turbidity of the water I could see and smell would have shouted "contamination," but it might have been too late to support the life that depended on it. By exploring the content of the water more deeply with the support of others, I could make early discoveries, take actions, and insure the health of the water for generations.

If I could apply this shift in perspective to my own fearful parts, I could utilize exploration and experimentation to heal them, and I could insure that I do not add to the fear of the human collective for generations. The result of experimenting, sharing what I have learned, and changing what I have found that co-creates pain and/or pollution within me could change my life from fearful and powerless to loving and authentically powerful. What a worthy and exciting exploration that could be! And so I begin again!

---

3   Gary Zukav's, author of Seat of the Soul, term for our physical body.

A Soul's View

Slowly this morning, my eyes open to the familiar abstract art that is my transom window at the top of my bedroom shades. Only a small portion of that beautiful old tree is visible. The sun is shining and I squint against the brightness. Part of one limb of that old tree seems different as I shake off the marvelous warmth of recent sleep. There perched on the limb almost as big as the limb itself is a hawk. It is huddled on the limb looking very cold, but it sits in complete stillness. I let my mind wonder "when did it come and where is it going?" Is it searching for prey or is it resting from the winter wind?

Into the quietness comes the flapping of giant wings. It is another hawk coming to rest on the same limb. It nudges gently at the first hawk and flutters and drops with great strength from the sky. The first hawk does not move so the second hawk nudges again. It is hard to tell if it is an invitation to mate or a demand to give up the spot. For one moment, they both are in complete stillness; so am I watching with the curiosity of a child. They do not know I am there nor how much energy their presence brings to my soul. This energy calls to me, and I begin to wiggle and awaken in gratitude for this new day and the vision of life happening just outside my window.

Suddenly from its stillness, the first hawk flaps its wings and takes flight. It is enormous and its fleeting shadow covers my window on route to its next destination. After it passes, my eyes are drawn back to the top of the tree where the second hawk now occupies fully the frozen space of the first. It is totally unmoving. It is as if one bird was there, then it split into two birds; one took flight, and the one that remains continued the vigil of watching. Intellectually I know there have been two hawks, but my soul knows they are somehow connected and my soul is part of that same connection. I smile and come fully awake.

Something unseen nudges me from my own stillness as I think about the duality of being a physical body inhabiting this beautiful collective soul. I glance back at my seemingly empty bed and witness the part of me that is watching in stillness. My heart soars and I, like the hawk, go in search of breakfast.

Moon Dancing With My Shadows

I went to a workshop at Omega Institute, Rhinebeck, New York, and I had a few early morning hours dancing seemingly alone in the moonlight, which will stay with me. It was so incredible that I tried to write about it, because it was the perfect topic for an essay. But the words did not flow on to the page. It needed editing. But from what I had written, the reader would most certainly understand the essence of my experience. During the remainder of the week there, I edited the essay several times and eventually it morphed into a short surreal poem. It seemed better—it captured the light of my mood—but somehow did not convey the importance of that few hours of Moon Dancing with my Shadows. Yes I said "shadows." Now a week later I am at home and awake in the early hours of morning and I know it is time to write.

It was 4:00 am on that other morning, and I had slept soundly and felt rested and excited about the learning that was occurring in me, but I also felt completely alone. My room was a dorm room about seven-feet square, and I shared a bath with several men and women in similar rooms. It reminded me of when I was a child and shared one bath with three sisters and a brother. It was a fond memory that warmed my spirit. But at this hour, all was very quiet. As I gazed out into the darkness, I had the urge to take a walk, but felt frightened that I would be walking in an unfamiliar place in that darkness, and it might not be wise. Unsafe even! But the urge to "just go" seemed to come from a fearless peaceful place inside me. So I opened the door. It creaked. I jumped and then giggled softly about the fact that my fearlessness was short lived. It was very dark and I moved slowly off the porch alert to every sound. Not fearless perhaps, but feeling the moist peaceful brush of the air on my face. It had the slight chill of autumn, and I could imagine the burst of color that would soon fill the trees.

I headed down the path my eyes adjusting to the darkness. Into my night vision came murky images in shadow. Under each tree and beneath each bush, there seemed to be an aurora of light that painted a distorted picture of each bush upon the ground below. My feet picked up speed, my fear lessened, and I began to explore the light that broke the shadows. It was everywhere as I went everywhere with a shadowed yet opening heart. As I entered the garden, it was a cascade of silence punctuated with the crunching sounds of my footsteps upon the path. Now and then something would move in the silence and take my attention away from the shapes and forms of the plants that lined the walkway. I would feel uneasy, but would return quickly to the joy building inside me. I had forgotten this feeling of freedom that has moved my spirit since I was a child, the love of nighttime, and the magic of moonlight.

As I meandered here and there, I began to notice the source of the shadows of light. The stars were vivid and above me hung a luminous quarter moon. It called to me and I followed. It led me down a path aglow with white splashes from a nearby streetlamp or two. This time when movement caught my senses, I saw on the side of the Main Hall at Omega two shadows. I stopped abruptly! Could they both be me, one a giant shadow and the other much smaller? The giant shadow seemed to want something; perhaps it had the answer to my questions. So I stood with it toe to toe and asked aloud, "Do you have a message for me?" No message came so I asked again, twice. Twice more no message came, but I did remember a few songs from my childhood, and I began to sing: *When You Wish Upon a Star*, *Catch a Falling Star*, and *Would You Like to Swing on a Star*. I began to twirl and twist and jump and skip and dance as I sang with abandonment. I forgot that darkness was nearby. Of course, as shadows do, they joined the dance. I welcomed their company and the aloneness that I felt seemed to lift with the sound and movements of our Moon Dance. The small shadow seemed especially present not to mention a graceful dancer. The freedom of childhood was mine with my shadows. As I glanced up, I noticed that the stars were vanishing from the sky and the moon had moved toward the lake so I let my feet dance after it. I remembered one of my favorite childhood poems, *I Have A Little Shadow That Goes In and Out With Me*. I remembered how much I loved giving it to my grandchildren!

As the moon and I danced toward the lake, I began to hear more sounds. Animals began to scurry and the charcoal sky was turning a soft silver hue. And then I saw it, the view that will hold my memory captive. The lake lay in stillness and hovering above it was a wall of mist, kind of stringy, but not transparent, and above all that hung the moon spreading its final visible glow before dawn arrived with the sunrise. The stillness of that view became stillness within me. I stood in awe at the beauty only a few here at Omega would see today. My earlier fears had been challenged with my love of adventure. Out of that stillness a rabbit hopped, two deer walked slowly behind me, and the early birds of morning began to chirp. I had become a part of nature. Just when I could hardly believe the vision my courage had co-created with the moon, a flock of wild geese cut the mist of the lake as they winged their way across in perfect formation. I could hear the harmony their wings played against their bodies. Then as if a powerful director had taken over the scene, a fish danced to the ice-like surface of the lake. I turned to find a circle of life rippling the water and the dancing fish no longer visible.

Earlier when I left the dorm, how could I have believed that I was alone? Life was hidden in the shadows and difficult to see, but it had completely surrounded me as I danced. I turned to head back to the dorm, a little wet, a little cold, and covered with the glow of *Moon Dancing with my Shadows*. Maybe my shadow did give me a message. If I could remember to challenge my fearful thoughts, Moon Dancing would always be possible. I hummed *Que Sa Ra Sa Ra, what ever will be will be,* all the way back to the dorm and into the shower. I'm still humming!

A Walk With Zoe

Is Zoe real I asked the wind, and think I'll write a poem. Is Zoe real I asked the tree and think I'll write a poem. Is Zoe real I asked a rock and remember a children's chant that comes to me on the wind, through the trees, and up from the rocks: *Zoe, Zoe, Zoe, rock is my home.* This is not the poem I imagined when first I sat down to write.

At noon, feeling a bit disconnected I went for a walk. As has happened only a few times before, I ran into the owner of Zoe, a neighborhood pup! Zoe quietly walked up to me stopped and waited for my hand to caress her, which I do because she has come to represent my connectedness here and she is so cute. Then she just wanders around very present and patient as I discuss her with her owner. She is a Schnauzer, but not quite a Schnauzer—her ears are too long, her body is too long, and she is not yippy at all. In fact, her owner says she came that way although her mother and father were indeed both Schnauzers. Zoe is from Canada and her owner feels sure that there is a larger dog living in her DNA. Within me it doesn't matter—she is part of me in some mysterious way.

A different Zoe is an angel that I've only seen through my heart. I sometimes say she's a thought, but not quite a thought—she's too kind, too compassionate, and not yippy at all. Zoe comes from love, and she sometimes rides on the wind. Sometimes I don't notice her, but always, she is patient and present when I do. She has been around for a very long time now and I trust her healing essence. I have not always known her name, but she consults with another angel of mine, Grandmother Reed. Somehow they are connected, love together, and watch over me as I struggle and learn during this incarnation. They seem most accessible when experiences become difficult. Of late, they have been arriving in my dreams during experiences of peacefulness. Their message is clear, "I do not have to learn how to live my life; I am life."

Zoe is the Greek word for *life*; and since 1970, it has had a major resurgence as the first name given to baby girls. There is something meaningful about this to me, and I'm grateful for it, because it seems like a good omen for the evolution of the human race here on Earth. But is "my angel, Zoe" real? The answer is in the wind that shakes and caresses the trees. And especially, the answer comes bubbling up through the rocky cliffs and sandy pebbles surrounding me as I walk with Zoe. Sometimes the sounds from the rocks catch the wind and become a chant I can hear and identify with soulfulness. It is the children's chant I heard long ago calling out to me: *Zoe Zoe Zoe. Rock is my home.*

It happened at a museum in Canada, and the sound resonated throughout the museum from a group of children who only met on that specific day—a day I remember being filled with love. I have carried the children's haunting melody with me to this day believing that it held a message that would one day reveal itself. So today I asked and listened! "Is my angel, Zoe, real?" I asked the wind, the trees, and the rocks, and something deep in me giggled with the knowing that this Earth, this rock is my home. And, as many times before, I sang within my heart this precious jingle that holds for me a truth beyond thought. Zoe is Life manifested though my choices; she is my essence; she brings me balance; she is my Love.

Zoe Zoe Zoe! I am filled with gratitude and reverence for life, everyone's, and especially mine, which raises another question: isn't it all the same life? Zoe Zoe Zoe?

Drought and Sweet Rain

In the midst of a drought, I have almost forgotten the feeling of the gentle caress of a summer shower upon my skin. Then in the early hours of morning, I hear it, the falling of water through my drainpipe at the edge of my bedroom. It grows louder and before I fully realize I've been awake, I've fallen back to sleep rocked by its rhythm. A few hours later the sound returns to my consciousness, and I roll over to look at the time. It's 9:30 am and I've missed my tennis match.

At the window, it seems the grass has turned green overnight and the trees drip with raindrops and their heavy leaves droop. They seem to be deep in prayer thanking the Universe for this much needed drink. In awe now, I stand somewhere between a pout that the rain means no tennis and a deep sense of gratitude for the peacefulness I sense just outside my window. A ring of downy soft white clouds surrounds the mountain in the distance while its summit reaches up to feel the moist breeze that moans with pleasure through its treetops.

From deep within comes a longing to be outside, but my mind overrides it saying, "you're hungry, fix breakfast, and let the rain settle down a bit." So breakfast becomes my focus. The phone rings and its my daughter. She sounds a bit nervous and shares about a health issue that she has decided needs some action to bring healing. I listen without opinion for a change knowing that she must choose her experiences. The sound of her voice warms my heart, and I feel our connected loving energy within me. Now wanting my coffee because it is late morning, I make it and choose a movie to enjoy while I sip it. Again the phone rings, it is an old friend, and his laughter reminds me of a walk we once took. He too has choices to make to create his life experiences, which he will do physically apart from me, but always energetically connected.

But now I can resist it no longer. My previous urge to be outside returns. My new hiking boots need to be broken in and the rain is now just a mist. Before I leave the porch, I feel the sweet rain's moisture upon my bare arms, legs, and face. I check the sky and it is several shades of color, ranging from the lightest blue to the darkest charcoal, but my longing must be given its space. The birds are noisy, the path is wet, the squirrels scamper about, the trees dance quietly, and oh the magic of the rain kissing my skin; I love the sense of freedom the supple touch of wetness brings. My spirit begins a heart song as my thoughts warn of a deep soaking if I linger here. So I give both what they want: I don't linger here, and I head out toward the lake walking briskly and allowing the damp pliable massage of the Universe to surround and protect me.

As I return to my doorstep, my skin feels renewed, my spirit feels buoyed, and my thoughts are peaceful. I remember all the times that a summer shower has befriended me and given me a sense of belonging. Einstein once said, that the answer to just one question could decide how we experience life. The question is: *Is the Universe friendly?* Today the answer for me comes with the feeling of sweet rain after a drought. Perhaps it is a symbol to remind me of the ever-changing experiences of this sweet physical existence.

Morning On The Bay

My eyes open full of slumber from deep sleep and the memory of lovemaking and I see it. It is framed in the window, but nothing can contain the promise of life within my vision. The silence is so complete that it shouts and fills my heart and my mind with its presence. Ever now and then this remarkable and penetrating silence is interrupted with a distant sound. The sky becomes a backdrop for translucent color. Without moving, I watch in awe and see within my frame all the colors of a rainbow but so much more vibrant and deep. At their depth they are orange, coral, canary yellow, cobalt blue—made more vivid by the pastels at their edges. They float in the softest most peaceful purple. A thin film of tissue-clouds, which ripples through creates the purple float in wave-like patterns. There must be a slight wind blowing and as I watch, it changes each hue of color slightly and the change is mirrored in the glass-like water below. I can see its effect but I can't hear it.

My slumber calls me back. My eyes close for only a second and as they reopen, another picture magically has formed, just as beautiful and just as still. The Universe and I are waking together. The sunrise is mounting in the sky and a lone bird follows the paths of color and soars outside my framed image, then another, and then another. Their calls are getting more frequent, more urgent, and they reverberate against the quietness. I wish I could name them and return their greeting. I smile and remember a different morning of walking and bird watching.

I look through my frame more closely now for I am awake. The colored ripples of the sky have entered the water and have surrounded a family of ducks that swim inside a tiny triangle of turbulence of their own creation. For a moment their smallness dominates my picture, and I marvel that they have survived another night in nature.

Without a sound, a single fishing boat has appeared unannounced. Who is in it and how did I miss its coming? I blink again and the silence is less pronounced. My frame has filled with many birds and the tree leaves have come into focus. They dance among the sparkles of light upon the moving water. The sun's bright shape is visible. The wind hits the chimes and they sing to me. I hear a dog bark and the murmur of a human voice from across the water. I can't make out the words. I notice the boats around the dock and invite my full awareness to enter. The world outside the window is brimming with visible and invisible life, but the silence is still there punctuating each breath. I hear my own, then his.

It is morning on the Bay.

Unexpected Splendor

It had been raining for several days and for one who loves the outdoors that can have its difficulties. As I rose this morning, the windows were smeared wet and gray, and the sun was hidden by the heavy cloud cover of two stalled autumn-storm systems colliding. As I meditated about my day and how to make it the most productive, I felt the peace that comes from trusting that whatever the day held, I would be fully present with it. I also felt the fearful tug that insisted that I needed to be outside and to feel the warmth of sun upon my skin.

All in all, this seemed like a good day to clean my house and catch up with emails to old friends. Later I would enjoy my Thursday afternoon yoga class and prepare a dish for tomorrow evening's dinner theatre gathering at the Nature Foundation. But first I wanted to catch up with what was happening on Facebook. Before I turned on my computer, I decided to lift the blind of my front window to see if the mountain was completely invisible—expecting this to be the case. To my surprise, instead the splendor of color snapped into view. Just outside my window was my Japanese maple tree. Yesterday it had been green, but not this morning. This morning it was a brilliant red of changing autumn hues. So I rushed outside to my front porch to truly take it in. I wanted to be fully present with its splendor against the gray backdrop of mountain ranges that seemed more like giant dark clouds in the distance.

Stepping outside, I was greeted with a cold brisk wind that surprised and delighted my senses. It carried the smell of moist soil, dry leaves, and a hint of mint from who knows where. There on the other side of my porch steps was even more splendor, the row of burning bushes had turned bright red to light the path of the autumn storms. I stood in silent gratitude for their warmth and grace. I could feel deep warmth spread through my body as my outer skin turned cool and damp with the air's soft caress.

I marveled at how much nature supported my authentic need of warmth and nurturing on this third overcast day. Sometimes the sun is hidden, sometimes the air is heavy with rain and mist, and sometimes a different kind of warmth just for the soul can be provided and experienced. All it took was an intention to be truly present with whatever came. Today what surrounded and hugged me was the unexpected splendor of this compassionate Universe with which I co-create life.

Different Perspectives

The far corner of my back yard seems like the perfect spot for a place to sit. It is shady in the morning and evening. It has a beautiful view of the third hole of the golf course. In the distance is a compelling mountain sunrise that transforms into many different hues of blue each evening as sunset comes into the valley. When I moved in, I placed a stone path into the space with the intention of placing a wooden bench in this perfect spot at the end of the stones. I wanted to create a restful and contemplative garden spot for friends, relatives, and me.

Since that time, I've put a hammock in that spot. That didn't work for no one used it and it collected bird droppings if I left it out. So each evening, I would take it down and each morning put it back. Each morning I grumbled at myself for continuing to make such a useless effort. So I put the hammock in the middle of the yard for a time, but the space in the corner seemed so empty and the middle of the yard was too hot to rest there. I still continued to put the hammock out, take it in, put it out—you get the drift. Finally, I tired of the process and put the hammock away.

Then I felt sure I had the answer. I would put a swing out in the corner—the idea seemed perfect. So I did. It was wooden, could hold two people, and gave a pleasing touch to my garden. Only one problem—no one sat out there—not even me. I tried it a few times, but I was bitten my mosquitoes and from out there the screened porch became much more appealing. The porch also had the same view so I would be drawn back to cover. After looking out each morning at the swing no one sat in, I brought it onto the deck and again my perfect spot for sitting at the end of my stone walk returned to empty.

A few months ago a friend brought me an unfinished Anarondike chair for my garden spot, because I mentioned that two separate chairs would probably work better than a swing. It was a gift of love that the students at his school had built in their workshop. I appreciated the gift, but kept looking at it with a critical eye each day—I really thought I needed two. One chair alone in the woods seemed out of place, and it sat at a strange tilt no matter where I placed it. It needed painting, but to paint a chair that didn't fit and that no one sat in seemed absurd. My motivation was badly lacking, the unfinished unprotected wood was beginning to crack, and my procrastination made me itchy. Each morning as I looked out, I felt it was a useless chair that served no purpose. Then I began to ask myself an important question: Where do I really need a chair?

That's when my perspective jolted toward change. That was three weeks ago and that lonely looking, out of place chair that no one ever used has been transformed. It sits proudly on my front porch with a fresh new coat of blue paint welcoming my visitors. Painting it was therapeutic in a good way. The chair seems to say, "sit a while, take your shoes off, you're welcome here." I love how it looks and feels. I sit there for a few minutes each day, sometimes just to change my shoes or read the mail, sometimes to watch the sunset over the back of Wintergreen mountain, sometimes just to enjoy waving at my neighbors walking past on their way to the lake, and sometimes to just feel grateful for the life that surrounds me.

My perspective about the sitting area at the back corner of my yard has also undergone transformation. I'm here to report; it is definitely NOT nor never was a perfect spot to sit! This fall and next spring, I will fill my corner garden with colorful flowers that will brighten my view each morning. It will be ideal with the rolling hills of the golf course framing it, and the mountain in the distance will still call and sooth my spirit each evening.

Sometimes simply changing perspective can be the catalyst for the creation of something wonderful and useful. Just seeing a circumstance or an object in a new way can make all the difference. Krishnamurti once wrote: *When you live within a concept, you cannot learn.* I have always loved learning and intend to shift my perspective as often as needed to continue to create purpose.

Unseen Dimensions of Life

It is Christmas Day, but not the "white" Christmas of fabled songs. It is sixty degrees and the sun is shining brightly and the air is clear and smells of pine and earth. The north wind howled during the long night and brought with it this extraordinarily spring-like day. The trees are tall and appear barren against the backdrop of a brown and gray mountain. The rains of the past few days have been heavy and so the pine trees are rich and green, their life so apparent. They seem to stand out as the only living plants in this colorless landscape of seemingly dead things.

Neighbors are walking their dogs, enjoying their holiday guests, or watching their children whoop and holler toward the treetops. I'm having a hard time staying present with the beauty of the surrounding nature. I stop and chat. I get lost in thought about the beautiful presents I have received. One gift is a picture book of nature and each photo is accompanied by a poem of connection that pulls human life into images that seem at first glance to be void of it. It is from my daughter and her family. When I opened it, I was grateful that a book of such beauty could awaken a thought of me within them.

As I round the corner of the clubhouse, I remind myself to "stay present" as the bookmark my grandson sent admonished me to do. The golf course lay before me. Last year the management of the golf course had planted something they called "Florida" grass. It is a hardy grass that turns yellowish brown in winter. I didn't like it the first time I saw it, but today the contrast between it and the regular grass is much like the pine trees against the lifeless trees lining the path. I hear the thought, *lifeless*, and know deep inside me that it is just a thought. The trees are not lifeless; they are in a phase of resting and preparing for spring. It is a powerful, necessary, and sometimes unseen dimension of life's re-creation.

Suddenly, I am truly present in nature. I see this phase of life clearly and my heart opens to its beauty. I kneel to touch the yellowish grass and it is soft and moist against my fingertips and filled with life. Leaves and twigs surround me on the ground. These broken twigs will not bear new leaves in the spring. As I pick one up, it still feels warm and supple. It is the evidence of nature trimming and nurturing the remaining limbs. It will feed the soil as it withers; and if I don't take time to notice, it will happen anyway. For an instant, I notice my aging hand holding it. It is no longer the hand of a young vibrant girl, and it too seems filled with life and beauty of another kind.

It can be thornier to see life as winter comes. It takes staying in the present and observing the smallest of events and knowing that spring begins here. How many phases and dimensions of life go unseen as I journey through it? A longtime ago on a different winter day, an old and crippled man told me that he was incredibly grateful for this time of his life. He said he was especially grateful for the part of him that accepts and relishes what he can't know. On that day, through a veil of tears, I knew intuitively he was on to something. Today I discover what it was and there is no need for tears. With joy I pick up a few large scattered twigs and carry them home. Who knows why?

A Small Avalanche

StoneyCreek is a quiet valley community at the foothills of the Wintergreen Resort in Virginia, and today it is covered with a powdery blanket of snow. The sun shining across the ground makes the earth seem soft and inviting like clouds floating across the sky in spring. As I gaze in awe from my window, a small avalanche of white soars down from a tree branch to a cushiony mound of snow that covers a tree stump below. The earth welcomed and absorbed it completely. If I had not witnessed it, I would not have known it had happened, and yet the earth was changed. I thought about how many changes go unnoticed and unappreciated by those of us that walk upon the earth as it welcomes and absorbs our footsteps.

Message from StoneyCreek

Today I walked in the brisk cold air of StoneyCreek. I was bundled in multiple coats, hoods, gloves, and hats. Fortunately, no one could have recognized who I was. As I walked, I decided to pick up a rock from a mound of rocks that I had visited before. I've been slowly moving some of the smaller rocks to my garden. It has brought me joy to watch them accumulate under my window. Today a larger rock seemed to say, "Take me"; so I tried to pick it up. I thought, "not too heavy," asked permission from the earth to move it, and started my climb up the path toward home. After about one hundred yards, I began to feel the weight of the rock. I dropped it on the ground, but I couldn't leave it behind. So I decided no matter how long it took I would get that rock to my house, about a half-mile. So I picked it up again and walked another one hundred yards before I dropped it again.

As I repeated this process, I thought about commitment, something that had been on my mind a lot during the past week. I was fully committed to taking the rock to my home; it seemed we had made a contract. So I looked for the shortest distance, sometimes staying on the path and other times walking in the grass and dirt. I got more and more tired, but the beauty of the pink and gray in the rock encouraged my effort. When I had repeated this process for about nine-tenths of the way home, two workers stopped as I dropped it to the ground. They asked me if I needed help, and my first response was, "No—I'm almost there." One of them said, "That's a forty-pound rock!" I laughed and said, "If I had known that, I couldn't have carried it so far." He said, "Let us help." In that moment, I realized that I was fully committed to getting the rock to my home, but that didn't mean I had to do it alone. I gratefully surrendered the rock to the back of their cart. It is in my garden now, and it is seems content to be there. When I stand looking out my window, it reminds me that a "limited commitment" would not have accomplished the task. As snow begins to fall, I set an intention to look at all the places in my life that are constrained by limited commitment. And now thanks to a message delivered by a rock from StoneyCreek, I am fully committed to receiving help with gratitude from wherever it comes.

Suns Outside My Window

The clouds slip by as I watch and wonder what life I can't see from this place. The giant sun appears on the horizon that is straight and bright white at the top of my small oval window. I'm flying. Also there is much blue out there in varying pastel shades. Each cloud layer creates a different depth of white. Within the second layer of clouds is a slightly elongated morning sun outlined with the purest of white spikes that round out along their edges and create a prism of diffused weightless illumination back into the clouds. Now and then a small string of thinning clouds appear and change the shape of this reflected illusion of light.

We are traveling forward and south very fast, but within my illusion the clouds are moving slowly and steadily backward and northeast. I blink and the blues have darkened and the sun reflection has shortened into a disk of brilliance totally absent of color. Is that the Earth breaking through? No, just more dark clouds below, which is now a vision of white cotton-like softness connected by uneven lines of cobalt blue sky—it attaches to my window.

I imagine life on Earth beyond the clouds and suns. People in Florida are waking up, going to work, walking the dog, or kissing their children. They have no knowledge of the airplane filled with life above them. If they chance to look up, they will see only the thick cloud cover and wonder if the entire day will be dark around them. They may be slightly aware of a distant roar, but give it no notice. They won't see my two suns connected by floating white-mountain clouds. They won't see the pillows of blue and white shadows that dance in rhythm with the moving plane. They won't see me here in my seat, head bent sometimes and sometimes head turning as I observe and write.

Through the clouds, I see a body of water that sends a glowing canary-yellow image up toward our wings. It spreads and fads and fills my small window. It is a kaleidoscope of irregular indescribable blotches of sunlight from yet another sun. I can't see the life moving on Florida's soil, but I know it is there. They can't see the world I inhabit at this moment here in my canister in flight, and they don't even know I'm here.

My thoughts travel to other places and other worlds I can only imagine. I don't see them. And yet, some voice inside me says they do exist. What an amazing adventure is life—the seen and the unseen. My window turns pure white, a canvas for my imagination. The suns, all of them, begin to set on the horizon—it's only 9:00 a.m. How strange to see suns setting instead of rising at this hour. Perhaps there is no difference. The pilot cheerfully announces our arrival, and I've returned to Earth. Here Florida weather is overcast and threatening rain, but I will carry throughout this day the brightness of that other world—now unseen but so very very real.

Standing on the Beach

Witness a flight into fantasy. Soaring like a seagull over the ocean, I look down upon the beach. It is truly I; but I can fly freely anywhere I want to go. The ocean with its gigantic waves beckons me into its depths, and I go. Diving down, the cold dark water contacts my skin, and deeper and deeper, darker and darker it becomes. My vision, like magic, adjusts and I am transported out of darkness into a world of color. Before me the fish scamper around green-leafed octopus-like plants. The greens are olive, lime, forest, and emerald colored. The majestic blue and brilliant orange of the wiggly things around me seem to glow. The cool touch of the water plays upon my fingertips and toes. A strange-shaped object slithers in my direction; I stand transfixed.

His hair is the color of apples, his mouth moist like dew; he walks in light with a perfect blend of strength and balance. As he moves within my reach, he spreads his wings and sails upward trailed by an overpowering light. The darker arena left behind draws my curiosity as I shield my eyes. The ocean floor covered with moss is filled with diamond shaped stars. I shake my head—has my flight taken me to the depths of the ocean or to the outer realms of space? The freedom to fly overcomes me again, and I drift searching for the unknown as yet adventure. The mist around me turns into a kaleidoscope of soft blues and grays. The colors calm me and I rest peacefully content in these quiet surroundings of nothingness. As my body becomes one with the sea, only my mind takes flight. I wonder if true freedom is death when our souls leave our bodies and fly into the unknown afterlife. Is that the only freedom, the one we search for each day of our lives? The melancholy becomes too great; I must fly while I can. Up, up like the unidentified image before me, I break through the waters edge. The world is as I left it, but I have experienced a flight into fantasy, and I can never be the same.

The Place I Live Most Fully

There is a place so special that it is difficult to describe, because to be able to live there, you must feel what I feel there. It is a place where brooks babble, leaves hold tight to tree branches, snow clings on bushes, birds flutter their feathers, and the wind makes everything dance. In "Nature" is not the only place I live, but I am by far more alive there than any other place.

I live on the beach when the salt and air burn my sun-drenched skin and a sudden shift in the wind sends a cold touch and make "goose bumps" appear. The feel of the hot sand on my bare feet makes me move quickly, but there is a feeling of calm and wellbeing inside my soul. The seagulls keep watch over me, and dauphins jump and promenade in the early morning just for me.

I live in the mountains when the mist is so thick it seems like you could step off the rock and walk to the other mountaintops. A small animal may come for a short visit, but it senses my need to be alone and scampers to his own private place in Nature. The coldness of the mountain makes me shiver, and I know I'm alive because I can see my breath as I climb upon a rock so sturdy it has endured for thousands of years. Some would say a rock is not alive, but they have obviously not looked closely where I live.

I live in a spring shower in a small park. The rain is warm like sunshine, and you can feel the shrubs and trees drink it in. The puddles form and are then absorbed into the hard cracks in the ground. Hills turn red or black and all the ants run for cover. Small children turn their faces up to greet the raindrops, as I do. Most grown-ups tuck their heads down to stay dry and safe. Have they forgotten how it feels when the moisture touches their eyelids and drips in streams off their noses? And then a miracle occurs in my home in Nature just as I begin to feel a chill. The sun announces its presence even before all the raindrops have vanished, and the sky rejoices with stripes of vivid color we call a rainbow. It fills my heart with laughter, and I can't stop smiling for there is music everywhere.

My place in Nature is not always easy and serene. Sometimes there is thunder and lightening and earthquakes. If you choose to feel its presence instead of being afraid, or as well as being afraid, you will know that you are truly a part of this wild and glorious place called Nature.

Today when I walk out onto my balcony, the air, be it hot or cold, wet or dry will play upon my skin and revive me to face a new day. This place where I live is dependable and always reminds me that I am a part of the Universe. Nature—the place I live most fully.

Knowing

It beckons from a distance, reaching out with its solemn and calm exterior. Its shade cools the area surrounding its girth. What secret does it hide beneath its craggy skin? How does it withstand the elements that torment and threaten its life? From a distance, it speaks of serenity among the forces of nature. Approached more closely, its scars become visible: a knot caused from a sudden wind when it was young as it twisted to hold its footing, a hole deep inside it wears the markings of an animal's claw, lovers' initials carve deep scratches and mar its beauty, bark torn away by a careless passerby leaves a permanent blemish, but still it stands undaunted.

Nearer, come nearer it calls. Suddenly, it appears battered from the rain as its leaves fall to the earth or hang limp and tattered. Its Herculean branches, snarled from exposure, shout in agony, but possess undying power; they no longer shiver or shake during the storm. Touching reveals a tremor within its soul as its roots bulge and shove the earth nearby in their quest for life. Reaching, expanding, it grows more stable with time; and yet, in the recesses of its old and wandering anchors almost unnoticed a small tender sprig whispers and springs forth. Will it survive? Does it already know the secret?

Old Oak—you must tell, I must know.

The Cemetery

As I stood in the cemetery surrounded with the vivid colors of the cut flowers, the gray sky, and the raindrops on my umbrella, how much death of loved ones and cut flowers seemed to have in common. The flowers were torn away from their roots as people were torn from their lives leaving behind new growth, old soil, and a scar upon the stalks.

The cycle of existence displayed upon the hillside among the grieving relatives, the recent dead, the greening and leafy trees, and the soon-to-die cut flowers is so filled with happy and painful memories. Rain can be so very quiet; and me here alone but not quite alone, softly demands my own attention.

Sadness, hope, love, memories, change—what to make of it? The flowers were of every color and the lush trees hung heavy with water, their leaves turned upside down to protect them against the gray and shadowy sky.

Almost without notice, I was reaching for new order as I looked to the future. The past could not hold me forever. One grows tired and must seek to renew an altered life.

TRANSFORMATIVE RELATIONSHIPS

Everything that I understand, I understand only because I love.

Leo Tolstoy

Fragmented and Whole Hearts Joined Together

Without An Image, Who Am I?

Recently some of my spiritual partners have suggested that when I've interacted with them, they have felt guardedness in me—that something about me did not seem real. Each time that has occurred, I've felt confused. I have felt that I was being real and that I was being in my integrity, so the guardedness had to be in them. Right?

Today as I studied the *Heart of the Soul* by Gary Zukav, I was drawn to the chapter called *Idol Worship*. In that chapter it said, "The broken container is her image of herself." In that moment, I realized at a deeper level than ever before that I do not know who I am without an image. The image is different in different settings, but an image never the less. Because I could not admit this even to myself, I have at times chosen to remain alone so that no image would be necessary. Today I realized that "solitary contentment" has become the image I have of myself when I'm alone so that I will not feel the pain of the separateness I have created.

On this day, I asked myself—if I had no pre-conceived image of myself, no need for admiration from others, no role I had to play—what would I be and/or do today? No image was present within me and no answer came. The pain in my chest, solar plexus, and second energy center was immense. Incredibly, I felt no need to be courageous, or strong, or wise, or thoughtful, or tearful or anything; I just sat. After a while, my pain lessened and breathing became easier. I realized that all of my images have been created to protect myself from rejection of myself as well as from the rejection of others.

In that moment of lesser pain, I chose to love the emptiness I was feeling. No bells rang, no birds chirped, no one cheered, no message called to me, no judgmental thoughts invaded my mind; there was nothing to be and nothing to do. There was no image to maintain. I was just a soul in the deep process of knowing it and of exploring deep intimacy within myself. To truly create a relationship with another, I discovered that I must know all the parts of me—the fearful and the loving. So I began again with gratitude.

Middle Child or Link Between Worlds

Being borne a middle child has formed my thoughts and perceptions for a long time. In many ways, I have come to know that I have recreated that feeling of being in the middle and not actually belonging for some sixty-six years. Here a brief history of my current incarnation could be helpful to understanding this latest realization.

I was borne into a family of five living children, a mother, a father, and one deceased younger brother. My oldest sister was seven years my senior and had a different father. My older and only living brother was two years older, and I had two living younger sisters that were four years and six years my junior. My deceased younger brother was rarely if at all mentioned, but he existed always in my awareness as I grew.

My family members were born-again Christians with very fundamental believes about God and sin. At a young age, I decided that I was not like them. I could not believe in a God that punished in one minute and was said to be all knowing and loving in the next. I also could not believe that my family's God provided the only Path to "heaven" or goodness. So not only was I the "middle child," I was the "sinful child." I chose early to see myself as a part of this large family, but separate from it in very fundamental ways of my own choosing.

Also I viewed myself as very different in other ways. I was the only one in my family to want to be educated in the ways of the world. All my siblings as well as my parents did not finish high school. The part of me that did not feel as if I belonged in this family began to feel admirably unique and superior to my family members. I loved them; they loved me, but we were different. My sisters had much in common, and often I felt I was on the outside looking into their shared world. It was liberating for some parts of me and painful for other parts. I felt I could not truly belong to my family without sacrificing my freedom of expression—I chose to live on the edges of the love I observed within its center.

Now as I look back on that first choice to live on the edge, I see other examples of that same choice in my life and the consequences they created.

I chose to have two children instead of three so I would not create a middle child. One of my children has died, which leaves my daughter an only child. For years, I chose to join lots of clubs and organizations, but was only content if I held a controlling function. Once I felt I had lost the ability to influence, I looked for another organization, but always under the guise of growth. In other words, I kept the connection, but did not remain a part. In unawareness of the fact, I became an outsider observing the organizations I helped to create.

In my work life, I took jobs where I became the head of the administrative functions of the organization. I worked for management at very high levels. I represented the administrative needs to them. The administrative staff viewed me as management and the management staff viewed me as a "unique" member of the administrative staff. They trusted and confided in me as if I was a member of the management staff, but I did not view myself in that way. Again, I was the observer. Within the administrative staff, I was viewed as a member with connections to high-management, and therefore, not truly a part of the administrative staff. I viewed myself the same; a part, but different; the middle role again.

Since retiring, I have moved to a small mountain community that I love. It is smack in the middle of the Bible belt, and I consider myself non-Christian, but spiritual. Sound familiar? The community is made up primarily of married couples, and I am single. They have accepted and welcomed me, but my feeling is that I am different and on the edges of their shared lives as couples and Christians. It is sometimes both joyful and painful to be with them, and as the evening ends to know that I am the one going home alone. They do not create this separateness; it is within me. This separateness also exists in my thoughts about being a grandmother. I have two beautiful grandsons. My daughter and son-in-law are very loving. My son-in-law's parents are still together. When my daughter chose the custodian of her children should something happen to her and her husband, she chose her husband's parents. From my separateness perspective, I have viewed them as the grandparents and myself as the "other" grandparent watching their closeness grow. It was and still is at times both joyful and painful although my child, her husband, and my grandson's are very loving.

My primary man/woman relationships have been with one man seven years older and one man younger by five years. In my own way, I loved them both, but the one common thread is that they were different from me in very fundamental ways. I learned a lot about the different generations through them and often have considered myself apart from their lives; loved but separate yet again.

For eight years, I was a member of a spiritual group whose sole purpose is to create internal authentic power. I have been working to do that—create harmony, cooperation, sharing, and reverence for life. And yet, I did not always feel a sense of belonging and have indulged an angry part of me in some of my actions with them. Afterwards, I'm not sure why; and then have questioned why I remained in the group. Now I have taken a break from the group with support from its leaders. At first I blamed the group leaders and others. Now I see that it was my unconscious choice to be separate again, because I felt my choices would be limited if I embraced the group and its purpose completely.

Now I'm beginning to ask a different question. Within my life's purpose, am I a middle child that does not belong or a soul whose purpose is to become the link between worlds? Time will tell; and how I see my life then, as it is now, is a choice to view my life through love or fear. What will I choose? Are we all one collective soul, and if so, our purpose may be to rediscover that fact?

My Old Soul Story of Long Ago

I have begun and discarded this "old soul" story three times. In truth I'm not sure I have one. After rejecting the organized religion of my parents, I began to live only in my head. So it seems my soul has been in hibernation during most of my story. In my mind, I saw the logic and natural order of the things in nature; this order became my religion. My heart beats fast when I watch a sunset. My eyes sometimes tear at the sight of a rainbow. I feel small when I stand at the base of a giant oak tree or by the ocean. My chest rises and falls with the lightening storms that cross the sky, and I am filled with the knowledge that all these things are a part of me. I know that if I want a shade plant to grow strong I must find a shady corner, and if I want sunflowers to grow, they must have open sunny spaces to prosper. This seems true of people as well: assess their needs, provide their needs, and they grow.

This all worked well for many years. I was reasonably happy and successful. I put away a lot of "needless" emotions, particularly anger and sorrow. Anger and sorrow were things I did not want in my life. In fact, they sometimes frightened me. I told myself that things here and there did make me angry and sad, but they were not important enough to acknowledge. So I didn't. The problem with intellectualizing emotions was that after a while there was little that was important enough to cause me to have any reaction. I didn't experience much anger, jealousy, or sorrow, but I also began to notice that joy didn't come around very often either. I put on a good face to my friends. I was the apparent model of well adjustment and stability—even to myself.

Things began to happen: My marriage was empty so I left it. I learned that my son was an alcoholic. I fell in love head over hills with someone for the first time. He betrayed me. I clung to him. My former husband died. I began to be tearful. I began to carry sadness even when I pretended outwardly that I was happy. I began to isolate. A friend suggested a workshop at National Training Laboratory called *The Human Interaction Laboratory*. I attended and I cried for seven days. Soon afterwards, my robust Mother died unexpectedly of a brain tumor. But like always, I told myself bad things happen and loss at my age was the natural order of things; I would choose not to suffer. I tried, but I couldn't stop crying. Frightened, I sought counseling and other things. I got better, cried less often, and was more in touch with my feelings, but there was still this indecision about the right Path to attain deep inner spiritual peace. It was a painful indecision I had carried since childhood. If my parents were wrong, what was right? The living things around me demonstrated everyday that something more than me was at work here, and I committed to finding it. Studying books, sharing with friends, and meditating helped; yoga helped, acupuncture helped, counseling helped, and then…I read *Seat of the Soul* by Gary Zukav and for the first time, the Universal force that I knew existed within me—but which I did not know how to access—came into focus. I knew that the right Path for me must include feeling as well as thinking. I was not very good at it, and I was often overwhelmed with the magnitude of the task. After I saw Gary Zukav and Linda Francis' WETA special and learned about their web site, I registered for the "emotional awareness" workshop immediately; no analysis required. I had to go.

At about that time, I went to a movie called *Four White Feathers* and one of the characters said to another, *why are you helping me, when you could save yourself?* The other character responded *you are in my Path so I have no choice.* Emotional awareness clearly has to lead my spiritual quest. It is painful sometimes, but I feel certain that it is my "natural order." Growing spiritually in this way is my Path—so I have no choice. As each of us needs support during our journey; I will notice with an opening heart those who cross my Path.

Calling Back Spirit

Recently, I read a story about a Native American Indian that participated in World War II and was wounded and eventually sent to a prisoner-of-war camp. He experienced many things that he could not have imagined when he entered military service. After his release, he came home to his tribe with a broken body that could not walk or heal. He was saddened by what he had seen and done as a soldier and he felt very depressed and withdrawn. His tribe nursed him and encouraged him to no avail. He did not respond to the loving care they gave him and his condition continued to worsen. Finally, the elders of the tribe decided they must do something. They removed him from his wheelchair and they removed his bandages; they threw him into the river with the instruction to "call back his spirit or die." It was the most difficult experience of his life. He somehow pulled himself to shore and his recovery began. His open wounds healed, his depression lifted, and he eventually was able to walk with a cane and contribute greatly to the expansion of wisdom within his tribe through a loving heart.

This story has stayed with me for days. Although I have not participated in a war, I have co-created experiences that have been very painful during the last fifteen years. My healing from those emotional wounds has been hard and long and filled with resistance to the pain. In so many ways, I had become an emotional cripple—quietly without my full awareness—blaming others, circumstances, and the Universe for all the imperfections in my life. Love surrounded me, but I couldn't seem to feel worthy of taking it in, and the more I learned about myself the less I felt worthy of even this most imperfect life.

Then my heart began to soften and my experiences began to show me how disconnected I had become from my spirit. I began an inward search of understanding the experiences of my life; not as a judge of them, but as a student in the "Earthschool."[4] What I discovered and now know for sure is that it is all up to me to see my experiences not as punishment or reward, but as my "unique" Path to healing, if I choose. No one threw me in a river

---

4 Gary Zukav's, author of Seat of the Soul, calls our environment during our physical incarnation the Earthschool.

and demanded that I call back my spirit! It was my choice to go deeply into the painful emotions within me, find the messages contained there, and bring my learning into the Present. Looking at both the beautiful and not so beautiful parts of me without attachment, but with appreciation and compassion for the lessons they have delivered from the Universe has been the most difficult task of my life to date.

My healing continues as I observe my emotions and the pains they create within my body, look at the thoughts that support the pain they create, and then choose to change me! Carolyn Myss states in her book, *Anatomy of the Spirit,* that ...*choice is the process of creation itself.*

Without fully understanding the process of learning I undertook, I have set an intention to heal or you might say, *call back my spirit or die.* I have chosen life and have begun the co-creative journey of loving and caring—first for me and now for many others.

The Honor of Sharing a Life

This week my daughter and I attended the celebration of life for her friend's Mom. The service was held in an Episcopalian church. At first I had many judgments about the message of the service and it's focus on an external God. My heart hurt deep inside and my lower back ached. Here were all her friends and family saying good-bye from a fearful part of their personality; at least, that was my fearful perspective. Then I began to really see each person in the service as a soul, and I began to see something more. I saw the love and devotion they had for her and how many lives she had touched. Instead of resisting the fearful pain in my body, I challenged my judgments, and I began to feel gratitude for the connectedness I felt with this woman who had died, which I knew only through her daughter.

Had I stayed locked in my judging, I would not have been present and aware of all the love that surrounded me and flowed from me to everyone there. I was able to be gentle with the part of me that judges and to feel compassion for everyone who chooses to be fearful of the differences of others' chosen paths. That compassion began with compassion for me. I feel no one should or even could judge another's spiritual path, and yet I have many times. I could see that a belief in a God outside of me is not my experience, but I could also see that how another chooses to believe no longer threatens my own believes. I felt liberated from a past of needing to see eye-to-eye in order to feel connected. The choice to feel separate stems from my fearful part that wants other's to admire and believe that I am doing the "right" thing. When they choose something different or voice to me that I should choose something different, my fearful part can choose to see my own actions in a diminished light.

What I've learned is that my actions and my challenges to my fear must come from a source within me, and then the consequences of those actions must be fully accepted by only me. Whether or not I choose to feel separate because of another person's thoughts, actions, or judgments is my full responsibility. The difference my action made within me was that I felt humbled by the fact that I have had the honor of sharing the *Earthschool* with all those who are here with me, those who believe as I do, and those who do not.

The Bigger Picture

It had been thirty-six years since I left Ohio to live in a different part of the country. Each time I had visited since leaving, I had begun the thought judgments before I arrived of how I would never choose to return there to live. This trip was different. I had set the intention to be present in each moment rather than project judgmental thought over my coming experiences. As I drove into Ohio, I saw its flatness, big skies, and the wind blowing through the tall cornfields; the leaves on the trees were already beginning to turn as mums bloomed everywhere. It was beautiful.

During my stay, my niece created an experience on Labor Day that involved the entire family. She came into the bathroom as I prepared for the day. She told me of a seemingly abusive occurrence between her and her husband and began to sob. I looked into her face that was filled with pain; I just held her until she stopped crying. When she stopped crying, my fearful part that feels it can fix things wanted to tell her just what she should do; but not this time. Instead I listened as she shared her perspective of what had happened, and what I heard was a soul shattering in pain. Nothing in her spiritual upbringing had prepared her to see herself as a creator rather than as a victim. Later she talked about her options and what different choices she might consider. My only intention was to be present, and I believe that was supportive of her in that moment. When she asked a question, I answered her as simply and directly as I could. I was surprised that I felt no attachment to her choices, which would not have been possible without my own growing knowledge of her and myself as creators of our own lives. It is only possible for me to change me. Only she can change what she no longer wants in her life through her choices. My job is only to love her.

When I drove away this morning, I was grateful that I had been there and perhaps supported her in seeing that a different perspective could be possible. I also saw that my own different perspective had allowed me to see my family's fearful parts with less judgment and with less need to have them be different. It was an enlightening visit.

Without judging whether or not it was a good thing, I saw the bigger picture of why I had moved away. My own spiritual growth had depended on me making that choice. I was humbled by the wisdom of a Universe I don't fully understand. I also knew for sure that Ohio was exactly the place I was supposed to be. I was filled with appreciation for my commitment and courage to take risks, to grow spiritually even when it was difficult, and for all those who have supported me along my Path just by loving me.

Exploration Comes With Healing Pain

Since I was young I've looked to men to be my support and at different times they have been, but in the final analyses, I more often took care of them. For a long time, I saw myself as a victim of their weaknesses. Today I can see better that it was through my interactions and choices with them that I have discovered and have come to appreciate my own strength. Many of the women in my family suffer in silent sadness, which seems addictive to me. It covers the anger they feel for life not turning out the way they wanted.

I have not been immune to this sadness/anger/shame pattern. For years, I believed that if everyone else (especially the men) in my life would get his or her act together, I could be happy. I now see that as a Story this belief has kept me safely confined in my own addictive pattern of handling problems intellectually and moving on with life without challenging the fearful parts of my personality that have kept me stuck.

As of late, I have been going into that pain, exploring it, and challenging it by shifting my perspective from victim to scientist. It has enabled me to be more objective and less analytical about the choices I have made. What I've noticed again this week is that when I am feeling deep pain with the intention to heal, I take good care of myself. When I am indulging the fearful part of my personality that feels alone, sad, angry, etc. in the moment, I bake a frozen pizza or eat more sugar treats or salsa and chips. I'm not sure if this is an addiction; it feels more like a way to vacate from my feelings in the moment. I don't crave sugar continuously and I don't eat between meals—it's more situational and meals become less healthy and nutrition becomes less important to the fearful part I'm indulging. I've challenged it this week by noticing when this is happening and choosing to make myself a more nourishing meal instead. Sometimes I am able to do that and sometimes I eat the pizza and my fearful part tells me it is a matter of convenience. Even my fearful part can see that I am not in my integrity when I numb myself with junk food. It is a way to avoid looking deeply at what my choices have created. For me, there is a fine line between intellualizing and exploring. What I've learned is that exploration comes with some healing pain, and intellualizing takes me away from the pain and is resistance to "what is." It's been a painful week, and it has supported my intention to learn about addictions and my own unhealthy choices.

Last night we had a horrific storm. When the storm was coming across the valley, I wanted to turn on my CD player and not feel alone. Instead I sat on my meditation cushion and watched the storm and my feelings come toward me without resistance. It was scary and it was beautiful. I loved the learning that was carried to me by the wind and rain and lightning when I challenged my fear and just felt completely present with the storm. It demonstrated to me once again that I have the courage needed to live from my most healthy places, and it is always my choice.

This morning I am filled with gratitude for all that I've learned.

Energetic Power Struggles

My most common power struggles are silent and energetic. Much of the time the other person isn't aware it is happening unless that person is a spiritual partner with developed awareness of the energy around him/her. My most vivid awareness came this week when I was co-leading a short hike for five-year olds at Monocan Lake. The other leader had been a kindergarten teacher and had led similar hikes before. This was my first time since taking my Volunteer Naturalist Training. We had four different groups and for me each of the groups was very different energy. My co-leader, however, thought our first group went so well that she wanted to replicate the exact order again with each group. I could feel my back tightening, and I was certainly not totally present with the children as I judged her methods and energetically sent her silent messages about how I was feeling. I felt she was being too structured and attached to things being as she expected them.

During the second group, I realized that I too was attached to "unstructured" in this case. After the second group, I used my courage to share that I thought each of the groups was different, and that I would like to try to be more spontaneous during my interactions. She was not very open, but I had said what I needed to say, and it was about me not her. Although she didn't change her need to control the group, I was able to just be present with the children and let go of needing my co-leader to be different. At the end of the day, she shared that she feared for the children's safety if she allowed too much freedom. My heart melted as I saw the accumulation of her fear over her lifetime. We shared lunch and discussed how teaching methods have changed over the years. Sharing what was difficult for me had freed her to share openly with me about her own experiences.

This sounds kind of goofy, but my second example is small but familiar. During our Friday group hike to Jones Run, I took a pretty spectacular fall on the slippery rocks at one of the many falls that were rushing with high spring water. I cut my hand, and I got a few bruises. I was not seriously hurt, just a bit stunned by the unexpected. At first my knee hurt and then my wrist as my fellow hikers gathered around. Each one seemed to want me to do or say something, to assure them I was okay, and I was just sitting silently on the ground—taking inventory of what hurt the most—unsure if I was okay.

At first I felt embarrassed and guarded and resisted their attention and help energetically. Then I felt a deeper pain than any of the pain caused by the physical fall. It was deep in my heart on the left side. I had activated a fearful part of me that wants always to look okay, and it told me to resist letting anyone know what I was really feeling. In an instant, I chose to challenge that need; said I was mostly okay, but could use a Band-Aid for my hand. It was so easy and they immediately relaxed and helped me to my feet. I could see their emotional pain and fear dissipate as did mine. I wasn't hurt much, but the love and caring I felt lifted me off the ground easily. I was receiving compassion and giving compassion at the same time. We continued up the trail. It was a wonderful hike, and we saw the first Trout Lilly of spring. To me its beauty was much more spectacular than my flying through the air earlier had been. Again the group shared the joy of learning and sharing our experiences together.

My silent power struggles have diminished as they have given way to learning about my own fears instead of attempting to change the circumstances and the people outside me.

Fly Fishing

It is amazing how my learning about "Life" comes from my experience of living "it." The experience this time was learning to fly-fish with a new friend. At the beginning, I was nervous walking down the street to meet him, but his smile of acceptance immediately put me at ease. He was preparing to fly-fish and was totally present in the process. A small knot in the fishing line needed undoing, and in that moment, it was totally absorbing him, and then, me. Silently I asked what would help and gently put my hand under the weight at the end of the line so the string was less rigid and more easily maneuvered. It seemed to help, and soon we were off to the pond, poles in hand.

The path toward the pond is laden with overhanging shrubs and trees, and on that day the leaves were filled with the colors of autumn. As we walked along, my heart felt at peace and my earlier fear had vanished. Being there with this person was pleasant and the day glorious; for me, that was enough. I was going fly fishing unexpectedly! Yum! The pond is familiar for I walk around it often, but today it seemed to glow orange, gold, and pink, and deep in its center was a blue sky, dotted frequently with white clouds. It reflected my excitement. My clothing was too warm so I threw scarf and jacket on the ground as my new friend readied the poles for action. He stood quietly near the pond. The fishing pole rocked back and forth in his hand with seemingly little effort; and yet, the line danced in the air and floated out to his perfectly chosen spot upon the water. He spoke of wind direction and technique. His action was repeated, and it was as if the line's dance represented the Universe celebrating fall. I approached him and we kissed gently. It seemed the most natural of small acts, and yet that feeling lingers for me yet.

As he placed his pole into my hands for a try, there was a sudden tug on the line. We had caught a small golden fish. We laughed and I took the credit, which he graciously allowed. It wiggled on the line; he expertly unhooked it and threw it back. Now it was my turn to hold the pole and throw in the line; it looked easy. However, my wrist seemed stiff, my arm disconnected, my movements too jerky, and the line twisted in a knot many times. Each time, with patience and presence, he untangled the line for me. His actions seemed to transmit that this too was part of the learning process. It occurred to me that when there is a knot in a fishing line, or in Life, calm perseverance and presence are needed to remove it. My lesson continued. My friend taught me to dance the line without landing it; I loved the movement and the grace of it as it hummed overhead. His steady eyes observed without critical judgment as he encouraged me to throw it over and over again, and to slow down the motion. I caught three small golden fish, and I tried to take them off the hook. Each time they jumped and wiggled, I jumped and squealed, and my friend completed my task and threw the fish back in the pond.

Then unbelievably, I caught another fish, my fourth! I was determined to unhook it and throw it back myself. My teacher of the day said the fish was scared, because I was scared. In that moment, my fear of hurting the fish vanished, and I reached out calmly, and held the tiny fish as it came to complete stillness and cooperated in its own freedom. As I stood and connected with the tiny scale-covered body, I advised the fish to swim toward the middle of the pond so he wouldn't be caught again. His eyes seemed to register that he heard me so I sailed him high into the air and out into the pond! Part of me wanted to hold him forever, but for his Life, he needed the pond.

That blissful moment will stay with me: me without fear, the fish without fear, the man without judgment, and the day filled with learning. Some of the moments of that remarkable day were captured in photographs, but that rare moment could not be captured; it was a sacred experience of deep energetic connection that could only be felt, shared, and remembered. As I turned toward the bank and my new friend fisherman, my joy was reflected in his cheerful, steady, blue gaze! The lesson continued.

Love Remembered

I am in a circle of people. I have agreed to remain silent and through that silence to give and/or to receive love. Since my deepest feelings of connection have come during silence, I think, "finally I can freely demonstrate the incredible caring I have for all who are a part of this kind and gentle group."

As the eyes looking back into mine pass by one after the other, I send love to each of them so easily and I feel as light as a cool mountain breeze. A soft refrain about worthiness carries my love and my heart sings. I feel joyful. I hold onto each set of eyes for as long as I can before I move on to the next. Some are blue, some are brown, some wear glasses, some twinkle with merriment, some are full of tears like mine. All of them look brighter and deeper than I have noticed them being before.

With a jolt in my chest like an electric charge, I remember that I have agreed to do something more than give love; I have also agreed to receive theirs. Now, not unexpectedly, my chest is tight, breathing is all but impossible. One set of eyes passes and the pain intensifies, and then another, and then another. The pain builds. I know this fear; it is familiar. I feel unworthy of the love that is flowing like a soft spring rain into the deepest crevices and cracks of my broken and sorrowful heart.

As the eyes of reflected love continue to pass, I know without a doubt that it is not their love that I cannot receive—it is my own. The pain in my chest bursts and flows into my stomach, my heart is a vast and empty wasteland of rigidity. Tears pool in the corners of my eyes and drop like small rocks upon my face. My compulsive need for my tears to stop kicks in immediately, but I cannot wipe them away. On each side someone who loves me is holding my hand. Their warmth penetrates my fingers and scurries up my arms and into my opening heart. With each set of moving eyes, my heart awakens a bit more. The energy of received love transforms my inner pain, and I feel joyful peace.

The tears continue and I do not resist their raindrop softness upon my cheeks. As the music ends, I stand and look with loving eyes into loving eyes. They are the same eyes with which I began the circle, but I have changed. There is no confusion only clarity. I do not feel fear; I feel only love. It is my own and it feels familiar. In this shared moment, it is mirrored in the sparkling moist eyes of my spiritual partners. I feel blessed and a melody sings in my head as I move out of the circle: *Some people wait a lifetime for a moment like this.* I know with certainty, it is the voice of my soul expressing gratitude for this experience and all the others that have created my Life during this incarnation.

Why Have a Child?

It is my child that asks the question and the feeling of why blocks my thoughts. And I, a person of many words, cannot speak to her logically. Why a child? Why a child?

Are the words not coming because I've never asked myself the question honestly? Or, are the words not coming because logic rarely enters into the love and need for a child? Or is it just fear of revealing how deeply a parent loves, because that love makes us vulnerable? Or, is it because the feelings of hurt and love one experiences in childbearing and childrearing are so deep within us that they have become a part of us—much like the child? So now hours later, I sit alone and ask, "Why have a child?"

Why did I have a child? Let's start with basics. I was in love with a man that treated me like a princess. We were married and more affluent than most of our friends. We wanted to be together for always. One way of doing that was to recreate us in the body of our child. He gave me so much; I wanted to give him a gift no one else could match. I wanted to give him a child–not just any child—my child! Even now the feeling I had then warms me and touches some need deep inside me. It is the same unexplained tug at the heart as when my daughter looked across the table, and her eyes moist with an intensity she herself did not quite understand, spoke the question, "Why have a child?"

If I had been clever, like I want her to believe I am, I could have said, "It is an action to preserve our species and just nature's "survival instinct." Perhaps it is true and logical that our survival instinct is the only reason at certain ages we fall in love, become one through sex, and produce a "miracle," a child. Because only "instinct" can tell us what a child can mean in our lives. We have no way of knowing that from the instant of birth, we have begun a journey of love from which we can never eradicate ourselves. We have no way of knowing the level of emotion we are capable of feeling. The fear, joy, pride, sorrow—yes, even at times—the disappointment, the jealousy, the anger laced with tenderness, and the helplessness we are allowed and fortunate enough to know deep in the fiber of our beings as parents are feelings so precious they cannot be express in anything so ordinary as words. Through the life and eyes of our child, we are reborn over and over and over again. The pleasure of conception, the pain of birth, the pleasure of successes, the pain of failures are a part of the cycle of life, as is the pain of old age and the pleasure of death because of a belief in an afterlife.

More than anything I wish I could have given my child a logical answer for she is so much more logical than me. I cannot! I do not really know why I had a child any more than I know the meaning of life itself. I only know that I chose to have two children and the depth of feeling I have for them is not something I would have wanted to miss. There are no words that can answer my child, but there are feelings inside her as there were inside me so many years ago that will not be denied.

Why have a child? If she could have been inside my mind when she looked longingly to me for an answer, she would know there are no logical answers only an extraordinary feeling of love that needs expression, but no explanation.

Tale of Two Children

16 February 2000

Dear Greg and DeAnna,

This year, for your birthdays, I give to you a present no one else can give— the memories of seven years compiled in this video. The quality of the film is old and sometimes dark, the skill of the photographers was pitiful (lots of heads partially or wholly missing), the focus of the editor distracted by her emotional attachment to the subjects, but the main characters of the film are star quality. Later on you can scan through and find the parts you like, but for this first-time viewing, sit down with a snack, give yourself two hours, and watch every single minute so that you miss none of the love that is pictured here. I call this epic:

A Tale of Two Children - The Early Years

Once upon a time and long ago your father and mother stopped at Cypress Gardens on their way home from their honeymoon. The story opens here with the flags of the skiers flying as if they are celebrating what is to come. Then you will witness a great flood, the name and place of which has been lost, but the energy of the aftermath of the storm cannot compare with the energy of the children that are to arrive later. A trip to Disney Land comes in the early part of the story before the children are born. This part of the story drags a bit, but stay with it because the children will arrive soon. The mother and father of the story make an appearance at an old farm in Kentucky. As it turns out, this old farm is where the father was born, and the mother is about two months pregnant with the first child. Then the first child appears and is overwhelming in his magnetism. You will sit spellbound for about forty minutes while this child goes from his first trip home, his first cereal, his first Christmas, his first birthday, to many other firsts; he was called Greg and he made the editor laugh. The movie cameras in those days needed flood lights to illuminate the subjects, and the subjects wouldn't look at the camera if all the lights were on. So the photographer used only two of the four lights. You will see that time and darkness do not enhance the subjects. But watch closely, because the subjects themselves are compelling.

As time passes, Greg grows older and the second subject finally appears on screen. You will note that she does not look at the camera often, and her life is presented out of sequence. You will see her having her first cereal and walking, and then her mother-to-be will appear in a maternity smock (how could the editor let that happen). However, the small creature is adorable, curious, and always climbing on something. She is later to be called monkey face by her mother and she is fetching in this appearance. You will see her as an infant, then as a lively little girl of two, her fourth birthday before her first birthday, climbing on the back of a car, climbing on a rock, climbing on a swing; her name is DeAnna, and she is an outstanding beauty.

The highlights of the film come when the two children are seen together in a sandbox. The editor laughed and cried as she watched the children learn to eat, play, walk, laugh, and grow. I hope you will forgive the quality of the film itself and cherish the memories it represents.

The principal photographer loved the children more than he was able to express in words, but in his rare appearances here you will see love in his eyes. The editor is in the film throughout, but mostly as hands and half a face as birthdays and Christmases come and go. Always her love is evident. This is as it should be, after all it is a *Tale of Two Children*.

I love you and hope all your birthdays are filled with as much love as they were when you were children. You have been a source of joy to a lot of people, especially me. DeAnna, you will receive this gift first for your birthday in February and must not tell Greg about it, because his copy will not come to him until his birthday in April. Greg when you receive this gift in April, call DeAnna and talk about how bad the quality of the film is and how much you liked it. Stay close always.

Now—Go watch the movie! Happy Birthdays.

Letter of Spirit to My Children

Dear Greg and DeAnna,

This letter will come as a surprise and maybe not a welcome one because I have never been a spiritual teacher for you directly. I feel as though in many areas of your lives, I have been a good and reliable—and don't forget funny—teacher and mentor to you. I may not have always been as compassionate as was possible, but I was sincere in my attempts to prepare you to stand on your own, make your own decisions, and take your lumps. There are a few lumps that I wished I had helped out with, but that's another letter. The main reason I didn't guide you directly with spiritual teaching is because I didn't know myself where to find the answers that I needed about spiritual things. I was fearful to embrace the God of my Mother because it seemed to close all the doors I felt should be opened. It seemed to limit freedom of thought and action so much that from my perspective it made prisoners of those that chose that path. So I chose as my mantra "the natural order of things;" my logical mind could see the connection of all things there. Because I did not articulate clearly what that meant because I did not know, I expressed doubts about the existence of a God. Those doubts may be a legacy that I have passed on to you indirectly through my actions.

During the years—as is my habit when I want to learn something about any subject—I read the words written by others who have studied for a long time what I wanted to know. Then I made decisions about what I believed and that was that until more information was presented. Spiritual study has been no different. The last four or five years, because of my experiences, I have questioned and read and questioned and read and questioned and read; well you get the drift. It was not until a few years ago at a workshop that I discovered that spiritualism is not about intellectual thought, but about the feelings of the soul. Since I wasn't sure if I had a soul, in the religious sense, I was in a bit of trouble.

So surprise, surprise, I became depressed—me who rules my life through the natural order of things. This was not good—nothing inside me seemed in any kind of order. The more I thought about it the more confused it became. With great embarrassment, I looked for help—I found it, rejected it, found it, rejected it, found it, rejected it; well you get the drift. There is still much confusion in this process of growing into what I will be. But now I know a couple of things: there is a force among us that connects us all; it is different for each of us; it is different for each of us at different times; it does not have to limit our ability to learn; it does not solve all our problems. We each have a soul that speaks to us through our intellect if we pause to listen. We must not judge someone else's believes as wrong because they are different from our own. And perhaps the most important thing I know is this, the Paths we choose are co-created to teach us what we have taken physical form to learn. Each of the paths is different because our lessons are based on what we have learned to this point, So with added experience, our truth changes about the spiritual as well as the physical.

I found this little book (*Seat of the Soul* by Gary Zukav) when I needed it and now hesitantly ask you to at least read a few words. I'm not saying I believe everything this person has to say, and I'm certainly not asking you to embrace this as your truth. Why did I hesitate? It has not been the natural order of our lives for me to give you spiritual guidance, and it may never be again. But at this moment, the part of me that I have discovered over the last few painful and exciting years (my soul) seeks this expression. I believe that we all have a soul that is connected to something bigger in a way that supports the Universe in which we live. I believe it does not matter whether we call it God, Jesus Christ, Buddha or the natural order of things—it is real. And if we are sincere in our quest for the knowledge of our soul, we will eventually know how to achieve our purpose for this lifetime.

I miss my Mother and Father today, because they are a huge part of who I have become to date. We often disagreed and sometimes were disagreeable in the process. It was the natural order of things. They were my first spiritual teachers.

I love both of you for the contributions you have made to my life on your journey to yours, and I thought inquiring minds would like to know that you have and will be surrounded by love all of your life as are we all. The limit to receive it, or not, rests within us. My mom and dad called it "free will." I call it choosing responsibly.

My Mother – My Daughter – A Wedding

It has taken me months to write about my Mother's attendance at my daughter's wedding. You see my Mother died in March and my daughter got married in September of that same year. I can see you scratching your head and wondering how that could be—they were very close. I believe that my daughter viewed my Mother as her spiritual teacher. My last vivid memory of my Mother is when the two of them were sitting in my Mother's hospital bed. My daughter had brought my Mother a small white stuffed lamb. The closeness I observed between them filled my chest with heaviness for I had never experienced that closeness with my Mother. Some said we were too much alike while others expressed that we had very different ideologies. Both of those things seem true to me. But that's a different story.

On the morning of my daughter's wedding, I hosted a breakfast for just the members of our family. It was small, informal, intimate, and at my home. I had written an essay entitled, *Things That You Might Not Know About DeAnna* to share with those who had not lived with my daughter as I had. In the essay, I relayed a story about her that talked about her yearlong infatuation with monkeys when she was a small child. It caused everyone to laugh as I had hoped that it would. She is anything but a monkey, but that year caused me to nickname her "monkey face." It was a term of endearment that has lasted into adulthood.

Unbeknownst to me, my sisters had chosen a plate from my Mother's belongings as a wedding gift for my daughter. My daughter had made and given it to my Mother during her monkey obsessed year. It was a creative child's depiction of a monkey face. My sisters said it was a gift from my Mother. When my daughter opened it, I felt a chill that started at the top of my head and moved down to the base of my spine. It seemed that my Mother's essence filled the room; tears filled my eyes—so sad was I that my Mother could not share the beauty of the moment before she died. My sisters had also decided to give my daughter the necklace my family had given my Mother on her 80th birthday; it contained all the birthstones of all my Mother's children, grandchildren, and great grandchildren. The necklace had been my daughter's idea and at my Mother's birthday party, we had called her along with the necklace a "work in progress." My daughter opened the gift, saw the necklace, and welled-up with tears. She was not alone. As I looked at all my sisters, I knew that my Mother was still a "work in progress."

The wedding was a glorious affair. After two painful losses in our life, we were ready for a celebration. Sometimes in life there is a moment that comes that is unforgettable; my daughter dancing with her new husband was that kind of moment for me. I thought of my own wedding and for some reason saw my Mother's face hovering above us. At the reception, close by the cake, was a bouquet of yellow roses. Before my husband's death he had given my daughter yellow roses for special occasions often. We questioned everyone as to who had put the bouquet on the table. No one knew. But when I touched them, I felt the chill of my Mother's presence. I put it out of my mind. Of course, I felt we would find out soon who had brought them. Right? We never did.

That night I was drifting off to sleep so thankful for the wonderful day and all it represented for the future. In the darkness but surrounded by light appeared the face of my Mother, not as an old woman, but as she had been when she was my daughter's age. She was unmistakable, and she was smiling. I was startled and sat straight up in bed. I said that I saw my Mother's face; my partner turned and said I was dreaming and that I should go back to sleep; it had been a very long day. I smiled and lay down for I knew it was not a dream, but a sacred moment of awareness. My Mother had found a way to visit us on my daughter's wedding day and give her blessing; she was very strong willed. Some say we share that trait. That seems true to me.

Some History You May Not Know About DeAnna (My Daughter)

Once upon a time and far away, a small squirmy girl was borne, 24 February 1967, to be exact. She weighed a hefty six pounds, six ounces—all muscle and a lump on her head. She came into a small family as the fourth person; she came equipped with a father (Elvie), a mother (Phyllis), and a brother, (Greg) and lots of other relatives. She was named DeAnna Lynne Gardner—capital A in DeAnna, Lynne with two Ns, and Gardner with one E. Already her life was complex. Her Grandmother Gardner came to live with the family for a few weeks to help her get a good start. DeAnna missed being born on her grandmother's birthday by only one day—she just couldn't get here any earlier than she did, which was actually 12 days before her expected arrival date. And although it appeared she was late, she was really quite early—appearances can be deceiving. As life progressed, a "tad late" became her trademark perhaps as a result of expectations stemming from that earlier misconception.

At age three, she was already showing her creative intellect. She discovered that if you put a small round object deep into your nose and tell your Mother, you could create chaos and still be treated like an angel. The only drawback was her brother's continuous prediction that she was surely "going to die." The doctor took out the rock, rain flooded the house because the open windows were forgotten in the excitement, she didn't die, and the family gave her ice cream. She learned that was just the right approach to assure success. This could have been the beginning of her career in business management and consulting.

At age four, after a family-move to Massachusetts, she began to show signs of a competitive spirit. As a new child at a neighborhood birthday party, she went last and dropped four out of five clothespins into the bottle. So the hostess decided to play the game again; DeAnna dropped in five out of six. After DeAnna annihilated the competition four times in a row, the young Mother decided it was time to completely change the game. It was obvious to her that this quietly determined child was going to keep on winning and through winning change her world.

At around the age of six or seven, this quiet determination reappeared at a piano recital. DeAnna had a small piece to play—she began, she played through to the last measure and hit an incorrect note—she began again; she played through to the last measure and hit the same incorrect note—she began again. The audience smiled, the teacher and mother held their breaths (for they knew DeAnna). Again the last measure was coming up, and the room grew silent with anticipation. DeAnna played the last measure perfectly; the applauds were deafening—it was her first reward for being persistent.

But just in case you think this young, quiet, determined girl lacked compassion or a willingness to help, let's talk about her dance recital. As the dance came to a close, all the little dancers were lined up (including DeAnna) with their right arms extended up and their left arms extended out, except for one little girl who obviously had not discovered which was left and which was right. Upon observing this poor child's confusion, DeAnna without instruction, marched to the end of the line and took the little girl's hands in her own and switched their positions. DeAnna returned to her own spot assured that the group was now putting its best foot (or hand in this case) forward. The audience loved it; we're not so sure about the child she helped.

Now you may have decided that this was one serious little girl; not always true. If you listened unobserved, you could hear DeAnna's mother calling her "monkey face," and you could believe that doing so is not very nice. However, it is a term of endearment. DeAnna's silly act of scratching her head, crossing her eyes, and making monkey noises demonstrated a sense of bazaar humor in an otherwise sensible, grown-up, kind, and gentle little girl. This money face showed up for weeks on school paintings and drawings, plates made for her grandmother, photographs with her friends, and frequently in the mirror. It was a display that indicated that underneath her serious exterior there existed the capacity for laughter and drama. It was delightful, because it was unexpected. If you meet DeAnna ask her to show you. You'll laugh, but asking does carry some risk.

All these characteristics have stayed and further developed as DeAnna has grown. She has used them to graduate with honors from high school and compete at the varsity level of sports, to graduate with honors from the University of Virginia, to be successful in business at a highly respected business-consulting firm, to receive her Masters Degree in Business from Harvard, and to land an interesting job at Walt Disney World.

DeAnna can be squirmy, quiet, determined, competitive, compassionate, helpful, persistent, stubborn, and funny. All of these things make her a loving and loyal friend, a fierce competitor, and a unique and wonderful daughter and sister. If you're smiling, you already know that the little squirmy girl has grown into a beautiful young woman not much different from the child.

Toast –Rehearsal Dinner, 25 September 1998

Along time ago, and then again recently, I read that happiness comes with the knowledge that you matter, and I believe that it is true. Your wedding announces to all of us that to each other you matter; your marriage will stay happy because you've learned to tell each other.

And so to DeAnna and Michael:

I wish for you the pure pleasure of genuine love and an adequate capacity for compromise. I wish for you the sharing of deep passion and the blessing of contentment. But especially, I wish for you the wisdom to continue to demonstrate your caring for each other.

Browning wrote:

You are all that is good and kind–you were made perfectly to be loved.

And, I believe that it is true.

May your life be filled with experience and wonder!

Mike's Birthday

Dear Mike,

DeAnna and Matthew could not have one of their totems without you having one. This is your mineral totem (azurite).

It has gentle and peaceful vibrations that make it helpful as a focal point for meditation.

It demonstrates the beauty of imperfection while containing the potential for perfection within it.

Wear or keep it close to you to connect more powerfully with earth's energy and to obtain a clearer insight into your own nature.

This mineral will help you to expand your awareness and to become more clear sighted.

Crows (of which you are one—born at this time) have a gentle side to their nature that enables them to harmonize situations in which they are involved.

You are loved as a son, and I hope you have a wonderful birthday.

Love,
MamaPhyl

First Daughter's First Mother's Day For DeAnna

It is your first Mother's Day. Yeah! Motherhood is one of those things in life that cannot be explained and must be experienced to know its wonder. Even when you plan for it, it comes unexpectedly and leaves you awe struck. It is filled with great joy and sometimes worry, and you are changed forever. Greg was only a month old on my first Mother's Day, and I have no memory of it now—sleep deprivation is not a good memory enhancer. How to be a good Mother will always be a concern for those of us who care deeply. I believe the only way to give our children what they need is to avoid losing sight of all the other things we Mothers are: mate, friend, lover, child, employee, gardener, singer, teacher, homemaker, soccer player, philosopher; the list is endless and should be. For each of us who we "are" can be viewed differently each day and each minute. Even when Motherhood is the overwhelming thing of the day, remember to save a small space in it for yourself. Someday when you are fifty-eight, you will wake early, be proud and happy about being a Mother, and still look out your window as the sun rises, see a half moon, and know wonder. You will know that the meaning of Motherhood is a mystery only to those who have never been Mothers. You are part of me, part of the sun rising, and the light that fills my moon.

I love you. Dance!

A Tale of Two Weeks with Two Boys

It all began on a foggy, rainy morning in Virginia with a phone call from Mommy to her Mom (me). It went something like this—I feel "not good." Her Mom (me) was scheduled to leave that evening to be in Orlando to wait for Tommy to be born, but the Virginia weather combined with Mommy sounding like a little girl on the phone, made her Mommy (me) take a flight in the early afternoon. Matthew and Grampy (Daddy's Dad) picked me up at the Orlando airport, and Matt (being just over two) became confused because usually Grampy and Nana were a team and Pops and Grams (also me) were a team. How did Grampy and Grams fit together here? We explained the matter and we headed for home. Nana was with Mommy at home, and Pops was working in Virginia and would come to visit later.

When we arrived at the house, lo and behold there was Mommy really feeling "not good." Not to worry, Grampy and Nana would go to dinner without her and Daddy. Daddy, Matthew, and I would stand guard waiting for Tommy to decide if he really was ready to come out. It certainly looked suspicious, but then things quieted down; I think Tommy took a nap inside Mommy's tummy. Later Daddy decided he better go register for his golf game with Grampy and Nana for the next day. They had been planning to play golf at this really terrific hotel for weeks. But alas, it was not to be.

Around two in the morning on 29 August 2002, Tommy woke up and demonstrated to your Mommy with all his might that his time had come and Daddy should cancel his golf match. Tommy was ready to meet his big brother, Matt. He wanted out! Mommy and Daddy woke me up and prepared to go to the hospital. We were delighted that I had taken an earlier flight. I stayed with Matt and let him know that Tommy was on the way. After arriving at the hospital, Mommy and Daddy began to wait for Tommy. They didn't have long to wait. Tommy was very anxious to get out, but he was a bit sleepy from being awake all night. When he dozed off, his heart rate dropped lower than the doctor wanted to allow. So activity commenced to get him out even if he was sleepy. The doctor decided to take him out through the wall of Mommy's tummy. Ouch! That's called a cesarean section by grown ups. Around 7:00 am with the help of many others, Tommy was yanked into our world. He was very little, but very strong. He cried to announce his coming and then he yawned and closed his eyes contentedly. We were so glad that he was healthy and Mommy was doing well; we didn't mind that he was very sleepy.

Daddy, Mommy, and Tommy stayed in the hospital for a couple of days, which gave Matt and me a chance to get reacquainted. At first, Matt was not too pleased that I was the only one there; he really liked having his Mommy and Daddy take care of him. I showed him pictures of himself when he was little like Tommy. I told him he was borne on 16 June 2000, and Tommy's birthday would be 29 August 2002. Those facts made him a big brother. We looked at pictures that showed Matt growing and growing. We had a great time after that. When he got lonely for his Mommy and Daddy, I whipped out some dinosaurs that looked very real, and we named them and made up games to play with them. Matt loved them and said he would share them with Tommy when Tommy got a little bigger. Matt and I really had fun. He loves cars and trucks and he shared his with me.

When Tommy was two days old, Daddy came home to take Matt to the hospital to meet his new baby brother. Matt was so excited, he kept running around and squealing. It was very exciting to watch. Into the big white truck, we climbed. Mommy and Tommy were waiting at the hospital just as excited to see us. At the hospital, big brothers are always welcomed eagerly. Daddy carried Matt through the door, and Matt's eyes were so big with wonder that his Mommy giggled. There in a tiny, tiny bed laid Tommy sound asleep. Matt knew immediately that this new baby boy was his little baby brother. He looked in and said in his biggest voice (he was the big brother after all), HELLO TOMMY! The whole family was so happy, and I took pictures to send to all the relatives. Matt gave Tommy a bunny; Tommy gave Matt a PT Cruiser and a Taxi and a video called *Bob the Builder*; Matt gave Mommy a beautiful tray; Daddy gave Mommy a beautiful bracelet. Mostly everyone gave each other hugs and love. I was so lucky to be there to take pictures and to feel the warmth surrounding us all. I have tucked the moment into my memory for all times. Anytime I feel a bit lonely, I just take out the memory, shake it off, and it will still have that same warmth stored deep within it.

That afternoon Matt came home and really missed his Mommy and Daddy after nap time. Nana, Grampy, and I watched videos with Matt and he ate the chocolate chip muffin Nana had brought to him. We had a grand time and he soon was too busy to notice he missed everyone. We also were very excited, because Pops was due to come to visit that night. He flew in from Virginia while Matt was sleeping that night. When Matt got up he ran to see Pops, and he almost forgot that this was the day that Daddy, Mommy, and Tommy were coming home. I reminded him, and we hurried to get dressed so Daddy could pick him up to go to the hospital to bring home his new little baby brother, Tommy. We made it! Matt and Daddy left, and Pops and I went grocery shopping. We also picked up all the pictures we had taken of all that was happening. Mommy and Daddy gave us a baby-sized book to put them in for safekeeping.

When Pops and I arrived with loads of groceries, there was Mommy, Daddy, Matt and Tommy. They had gotten home first even though they had stopped at McDonald's for lunch. How fun. Then we had to hustle around, because Nana and Grampy were coming for dinner. Pops and I made roast pork. It was very good, but Tommy was too little to eat it, and Matt wanted pasta. Pasta was a big part of my two weeks with two boys. Mommy cooked it, Daddy cooked it, the neighbors brought it, Grams (me) cooked it. We ate it and ate it and ate it! Two weeks with two boys generates too much pasta for me, but everyone else was deliriously happy.

Mommy got a bit sick in the afternoon, but she recovered quickly. It was so good to have her home. She and Tommy slept a lot. Pops, Nana, and Grampy took turns entertaining Matt just the way Mommy would later when she was feeling better, but Matt let us know that "Mommy's the best." Later in the two weeks, Matt let us know that "Daddy's the best." Did I mention that Matt was just over two? He loved pasta, chocolate, Daddy, Mommy, and Tommy. He also loved french-fries, pancakes, Grampy, Nana, Pops, and Grams; but not all at the same time except on rare occasions. Did I mention Matt was just over two!

Matt let us know that he thought Tommy "sleeps a lot." Tommy let us know that he did not sleep a lot when he was hungry, wet, or missing his Mommy. Mommy said she thought he liked to sleep near his food supply. No one disagreed. I got Tommy's late evening shift (~9:00 to 12:00 or 10:00 to 1:00 am), which seemed to be the time Tommy had chosen to check out the world around him. This was when Mommy, Daddy, and Matt slept peacefully. This gave me a perfect opportunity to tell Tommy all about the wonderful family he had chosen. Matt got up at 6:00 am every morning to have his milk, but he didn't want breakfast until around 9:00 am. That gave me an opportunity to watch in wonder at all his antics. Matt was very energetic and a good eater. He ate his cereal, he ate his fruit, and he ate his toast. He also loved his broccoli at dinner. Did I mention that he liked pasta and chocolate? Tommy only liked Mommy's milk and his paci—and the paci not that much!

After Nana, Grampy, and Pops went home and Daddy went back to work, Mommy, Matt, Tommy, and Grams went on our first outing to have lunch at McDonalds. We had a great time. Matt ate chocolate ice cream. Later in the week, we went out to breakfast at the Panera Bread shop. Matt liked the pumpkin muffins, but Mommy and I had bagels. We all had orange juice. Tommy just slept and was a very good little baby brother. Matt was a big brother all morning and took care of Tommy in the car. Mommy and I were very grateful for his help.

When Tommy was fourteen-days old, Mommy and Daddy had to take him to the doctor for his checkup. That meant that Matt and I could go out to lunch. Matt loved pancakes so we went to Perkins. He talked and talked. We visited the ducks. We picked up even more pictures. Tommy had a good visit at the doctor's office and weighed in at nine big pounds. This made Mommy secure that he was getting enough to eat.

Life was very busy during my two weeks with two boys. Friends and family came and went to give Matt and Tommy presents and the rest of us food. Laundry was done over and over everyday. It seemed that Tommy's diapers had sprung a leak, and he was wetting everything in sight and all things unseen. We changed diapers for Matt and Tommy so they would be "daytime dry" instead of "nighttime soggy." They liked that. We gave baths, we read books, we played race cars, we watched videos, we went out to eat, we went shopping at Walmarts, and I bought Matt an elephant shirt. Later Matt stayed with Daddy while Mommy, Tommy, and I went shopping for a chair, a toy box, and some new clothes for Matt and Tommy. We missed Matt during our trip, but he told his Daddy that night that he had "really enjoyed playing in the back yard." It had been a lovely day of activity for us all. Life was beginning to return to normal.

Orlando is hot in August and September, so we went swimming, Matt and Daddy went biking, we played Playdoh, we chatted, we cried, we hugged, we laughed, we ran, we read, we did yoga, and we talked to friends and family on the phone. We sent videos so everyone would know that Tommy had arrived and that Matt was now an official big brother. Uncle Greg said he thought Mommy and Daddy should have gotten a puppy. He was just kidding. Uncle Greg was not feeling too great and that made us a bit sad, but we hoped he would be well soon. Matt learned how to do the "down dog," and Tommy learned how to move his hands and smile at me. Some thought it was just gas, but grandmothers know better. His dimples shone brighter when it was a real smile.

The time came when Grams (me) needed to go back to Virginia to be with Pops and to get back to work. Matt knew it was time for me to go, so he invited me to do just that. He was with his Daddy and having a great time. I came into the room and he said, "Grams I want you to go home now." That made us all chuckle because Matt was just over two and very articulate about whom he preferred at the moment. We had all been subjected to his rejection at one time or another. Tommy continued to curl up in my bed and sleep each evening and to make lots of baby noises until the day actually came when I was to catch my plane back to Virginia. Mommy and Daddy gave me a beautiful butterfly and thanked me for being their butterfly during the beginning of their family of four. They also gave me a bookmark to share with Pops. We took more pictures. Daddy took me to the airport while Mommy, Matt, and Tommy were sleeping. I sat at the airport with my caramel coffee and reminded my tired-self how lucky I had been to share the moments when this new little boy, Tommy, had come to live with us. It reminded me of another time when another little boy, Matt, had come to live with us. Holding Matt and Tommy when they were new to the world gave me an incredible set of memories to take with me into old age. It allowed me time with my only daughter who has grown into a beautiful and wise Mother. It gave me the opportunity to harass my only son-in-law and get to know him as a father and husband. He is very special. Two weeks with two boys had to come to an end, but I knew it was just our beginning.

Pops met me at the airport in Virginia with a giant hug and a big kiss. He thinks he's lucky too. He promised not to feed me pasta. For that, I was grateful. The Universe is a better place after two weeks with two boys. Thanks Mommy and Daddy!

Welcome Tommy!
Glad you're here Matt!
Love *Grams*

Tom's Baptism

Dear Tom,

Today your parents began your spiritual life with baptism, and I held you in my heart. Of course, you cannot read yet but one day you will, and I hope the message of this small book (*Everything You Need to Know is Inside You*) will be with you throughout your life.

Like we did before you, you will grow through the experiences of your life. You will have many choices to make based on what your experiences teach you. And, as we did before you, you will choose your own spiritual path; it may not be the same as ours. This book says that the answers are within you. I believe that is true. The path that rings true for you, if followed, will provide the meaning and purpose of your life; listen to your heart.

Our Paths may mirror each other's or they may only cross. Your Path may be smooth or it may be bumpy, but know always that whatever Path you take and wherever it leads, you can count on my loving support.

Love *Grams*

Matthew—You Are A Deer

As you already know
Because your father has read
By your birth totem, the deer
You will always be led.

Some people will say
This is just superstition
But you must remember
It's ancient tradition.

Your symbols of nature
Are constantly near
Observe them and learn
All you can from them "Deer."

Love
Grams

I'm His Mom: A Story of the Spirit!

His name is Greg and he has lived for 37 years. He is a combination of humor and anger that leads people to wonder why he has chosen the life he leads. He came to me when I was very young and my feelings for him range from deep caring to shame for the choices he has made. He can hurt me to tears and bring me laughing joy within the same moment. He has my father's eyes and nose and a connection to me that is unexplainable. He surprised me early; I wanted a baby girl and he was a tiny little red-faced, squirmy boy; I wanted a Gerber baby and he was a long, skinny baby with colic. The love I felt for this small bird-like creature filled me with wonder and helped me to understand the depth of the universal connection I had always known exists. Although I was not religious in the traditional sense, I knew that a spiritual connection had begun that would not end, and I whispered to no one in particular, *I'm his Mom.*

He is a man now and the life he leads continues to bring me spiritual awareness—and at other times—despair. In so many ways he is like me. He has many of my attributes and faults; I must forgive him for not using the attributes as I would have liked and forgive myself for the faults that he has inherited from me. This story is a spiritual journey in progress. The ending is unclear for Greg is a final-stage alcoholic with liver disease; I do not know if he will survive. I don't even know if this story is about his spiritual journey or mine.

I need to write about this journey to cleanse away the sadness, but the words do not come. I sit and look at my computer and wonder what this story is really about. I have never been able to write except from my feelings, and these feelings are too deep to even recognize what they are, and I sit and try to get in touch with them. I think about the past.

There are memories of a young boy that loved sunsets and wanted to design cars and fly airplanes; a young boy that trudged through the snow to deliver his papers; a young boy that refused to be potty trained; a teenage boy who played hockey, loved basketball and Havechek; a young boy who practiced basketball for hours and piano for two minutes. He was a teenage boy with musical talent and not enough discipline to practice and instead created a love affair with recorded music. He was intelligent, but refused to study the things that didn't interest him. He was a leader among his friends, but was seemingly unaware of it. He loved his sister but gave her grief. He loved his father, but said he did not like him much. He seems to love me, but it was to me that he directed his anger. I see a young man in love, but selfish within the relationship. I see a young man hurting from lost love. I see the college student that didn't apply himself to study, but brought to everything he enjoyed energy and life. I see a young man who worked hard at every job he ever had. He cared about so many things, but pretended to be above it all. I see a gifted, creative young man that filled every room he occupied. I see him giggling with his first beer. I see him curled into a fetal position, too drunk to stand and filled with cramps so severe he could hardly move. I see him trying to quit drinking. I see him beginning to drink again. I see him squandering his inheritance. I see him empathetic with Matt, my grandson denying that he cares about children. I see him deeply loving DeAnna and Mike, my daughter and her husband, but not able or healthy enough to visit. I see how much his family and friends love him. I envision him alone and sick in an airport on his way to change his life. I wonder if he is as fearful as I am about his ability to do that.

I think about the present. Greg is in New York at St Jude Retreat House. He went there out of desperation because of failing health and no resources. He has been diagnosed with liver disease. One minute he says he loves me and in the next he is foul mouthed and spewing anger at some perceived wrong that has been done to him. He says he appreciates the help he is being given, but there is no real show of appreciation. He calls other people names and shows great disdain when someone else is less than perfect. He is suffering great pain and he is making jokes about his situation. He may not survive, or he may survive with continued illness. The people who love us have gathered together to show him how much he is loved. His sister has been generous in her support of him, emotionally and financially. His biggest concern seems to be having enough money to buy cigarettes. My biggest concern is that he will die without knowing that there is a connection to the Universe that protects him if he asks, or that he will not learn that being loved and loving others has a direct relationship to how much he is able to love himself.

I think about the future. Will all the love, energy, and financial investment be sufficient to keep him sober and alive? Will DeAnna and I be able to cope with the disappointment if he dies or goes back to drinking? Will I be strong enough to see this through no matter what the outcome and no matter how much support Greg needs to live? What is there to learn here? What does all this have to do with spiritual journey, his or mine? Where does that small, eager, young, tenderhearted boy of the past exist inside Greg today?

The spiritual journey has been a long one for me. Born in a traditional Christian and Southern Baptist family, I questioned early what I was being taught because it did not feel right for me. I have continued to question and read about the spiritual aspect of life. I knew deep inside that my universal connection was to be found on a different Path than the one I had been taught to follow as a child. For a while when my children were young, I tried to embrace the religion of my youth by taking my children to Sunday school and even teaching Sunday school myself. I chose not to teach religion in those classes, but instead taught what we now call "socialization" to my students. It just did not seem logical that there is only one Path to God, and I could not in good conscious teach that to anyone. Although I attended Christian churches most of my life, I taught my children through my actions that they had choices about their spiritual lives. This freedom of choice may have confused them into thinking that I did not believe in a creative force within our Universe. For that result I am sorry, but we cannot go back. Since I was unclear what my connection to the Universe was, how could I foster a belief about that connection within my children? And even if I had known, how would I have known it would be right for them. Instead I gave them a model of self-reliance and integrity that was heart felt.

As time pasted, I began to notice that wherever nature existed there was a natural order that occurred if no one interfered. The trees in the forest almost seemed to have a voice that spoke to me in concert with my own thoughts. They taught me to trust the order I saw. If a tree needed shade, to give it shade; if it needed sun, to find the brightest spot and support its health. I'm still not exactly sure where that voice exists within the Universe, but I know it exists within me and is the guide I try to follow. Someone once said, *be still and know*; so I do. The stillness of observation brings integrity of thought and if I can trust my own inner voice, I can thrive and prosper in an environment that enriches my spirit. Through inner awareness, I can deal with the sadness, disappointments, and triumphs of my life and give them equal weight. I believe that all experience serves to help me find and accomplish the purpose of this physical life.

It is my hope for Greg that he will recognize and be able to get in touch with the spiritual part of himself. It is my hope that he will learn to trust his own small voice so that he will understand that within the Universe there is a connection between all persons and all things and each of us must *be still and know* that it exists for us. And with that knowing, we give our life meaning. In his knowing, it is my hope that he will find the answers for his life.

For a while, I railed against the darkness of his drinking; searching for the right words to say to bring him back to those of us that love him so completely. Now I still try to influence him to seek a different life style, but I have come to see that his illness has been a catalyst for great learning for me. The depression I have felt over Greg's behavior and other things has caused me to look deep inside myself for the answers I need rather than endlessly searching for purpose in those around me. I have learned compassion for others as I have come to know that each is a representative form of something inside me. Greg's drinking has been a manifestation of my fearfulness that I have come to love and to understand is a part of being human in a Universe that follows a natural, visible order. The examination of my fears has created a way for me to finally forgive the perceived wrongs that have been committed by others and myself. The hurt and fear that I have felt have given me courage and an ability to "let go" of some of my own need so that I can offer help without assurance of where that help will lead. It has been a challenging journey up to now and for me it continues. I believe that this spiritual odyssey will always continue during my physical existence and is the purpose of this life.

As Greg searches for physical health, I will contribute in whatever way seems right to me. Perhaps he will find mental and spiritual health as well. If he does not, I will hope for the strength to let him live the life he chooses until its physical end. In spite of all we have gone through together with perceived failures on both sides, we make each other laugh. Regardless of how long I have Greg and in whatever circumstance that creates in my present life, I will love him. We are forever connected; *I'm his Mom!*

The Voice of God

For many years, I had celebrated Christmas half-heartedly. It was for me just a long-standing, uncomfortable tradition based on a fundamental Christian upbringing and belief; a belief that I could not accept. But this year felt different for it had been a year of great fear, great risk, great love, and great learning. My only daughter had given birth to her second son, Thomas, by emergence cesarean section and had honored me by giving him my maternal family name, Reed. My only son had recovered from his addiction and was facing two terminal illnesses. I had found a spiritual path that I knew was a true path for me, and I had embraced its principles. It had taught me to honor and revere all life whether or not it was within my personal understanding.

My children and partner love Christmas, and so I decided that I could with integrity revere Jesus as one of the great enlightened teachers of the world. My partner's son was with us this year, and we were sharing the day with my son-in-law's parents for the first time. On this wonderful day we called Christmas, I felt like the luckiest of women. It was a day of presents, laughter, teasing, music, sadness, tears, and joy. It was a day when I looked back and remembered many of my life's experiences and gave thanks for them. I had come to know that all my experiences, the joyful and difficult, were gifts from the Universe, which gave me an opportunity to heal my soul and make spiritual growth a priority through each of them.

As we sat down to the lovely dinner my daughter had prepared with a little help from each of us, I could feel a protective energy source all around us. In this environment of multiple believes, I could not imagine how we could express our spiritual connection and not leave someone feeling dissatisfied with the words we used. But as we gathered around the table surrounded by chatter and companionship, the noise level grew louder and louder with the sounds of the people I love most. We were together in a way we had not been in a really long time.

Then as it often happens in noisy family gatherings, there was a sudden gap of silence, and out of that stillness came the small and gentle voice of my two-year old grandson, Matthew. He said almost in a whisper, "Merry

Christmas Grams." No one had coached him and the sincerity of his tiny voice made us all turn toward him with the awe adults often display when faced with the purity of a child's love. In that sacred moment, he continued around the table wishing each of us by name, "Merry Christmas." After he included all of us, the sharing of stories and laughter resumed as it had been before.

I do not remember what presents were given and received earlier that day, but I will never forget the still, small voice of God that came through Matthew and made all of our individual Paths one, connected by our Love for each other.

Rocking Chair Comfort For DeAnna

Because you are who you are, you will want to know why I decided to give you a rocking chair. The reasons are not very logical, but they are mine. You are loved now and forever, and this chair is a solid and permanent symbol of that love. A rocking chair represents comfort to me; and you will think of me when you sit in it, which assures me a place near you always. As time passes, the cushions and coverings will wear and be changed, but with care the wooden rockers will go on rocking for generations. I like that!

Like this rocker, you will be given opportunities to change, but the changes must build on the strong and courageous foundation that is your inner being. You have and will always have it, we all do. You must learn to listen and trust the voice of your heart. Live today. Notice its wonder. Capture its joy. Tomorrow will come and you will deal with it, because you must. But for today, sit in your rocker and feel the extraordinary in all the ordinary things that surround you.

Share your rocker, share your memories, share your hopes for the future, but teach your children to find inspiration in their own "today's."

I love you, and hope that the New Year will find you peaceful. Enjoy your rocker.

A Gift From The Divine

About ten years ago, my former husband was dying from prostrate cancer that had moved to his spinal column; Greg, my son, was drinking heavily; and DeAnna, my daughter and I were attempting to take care of lots of stuff. I could see that DeAnna was in a lot of pain, but because she is a quiet personality I felt uncertain of the source of it. Her father was dying, but I felt there was something more going on too. I remember asking myself over and over again what I should do, what I should say. In the midst of all that, a small woman entered the picture, a social services person employed by the hospital to make visitations on the families of the terminal patients.

She took DeAnna and me to a small room at the end of the corridor, and asked if we had any questions. DeAnna's eyes were wet with tears, but she was in so many ways very composed. She asked the woman if it was common for someone not to acknowledge that he was dying. And the kind and gentlewoman asked DeAnna why she asked the question? DeAnna voiced that she was concerned about whether her Dad was okay with dying, because he had shared nothing about what he was feeling with her. Then the kind woman with such compassion, but no pity, asked another question. She asked DeAnna if when her Dad was healthy, he had shared a lot of what he was feeling with her? DeAnna barely whispered, "no" and that he had always been more interested in talking about what she was doing. Then the woman said the exact right thing to support DeAnna—she said that people were very much the same in dying as they were in living, and if DeAnna had things she wanted to say to her Dad, it would probably be a good thing to just go ahead and say them even though it seemed he couldn't hear her at this point. DeAnna's tears stopped, and she told the woman that she had told him everything she wanted him to know. I could see her pain dissolve. We thanked the woman and never saw her again, but the amount of comfort she gave us has stayed with me always.

I have felt that she was a gift from the divine sent to support us when we most needed it.

An Unsent Letter to Greg

Dear Greg,

I worry that you will die without remembering the closeness we once had before you gave your life to alcohol. I no longer feel the anger I once did, but the sadness for what might have been lingers. Your choices and your purpose in living this life as a person who sacrifices other things in order to drink will remain a mystery. Clearly your illness has brought me many lessons and has softened my heart. It has helped me to be more compassionate, more forgiving, and more tolerant; and I wonder what it has brought to you. Each of us search for meaning in life and finally discovers that creating a Life that is meaningful to ones self is perhaps our greatest purpose.

Your life has enriched mine. DeAnna's and Matthew's togetherness has reminded me of the purity of a Mother's love for her first born child; and how the growth in the child is reflected in an equal amount within the Mother. You do not remember your first glimmer of recognition of me—I do. You do not remember your first toothless smile—I do. You do not remember the first time I hugged you and you hugged me back—I do. You do not remember your first step—I do. Each step of your life has brought learning to me. I wonder if deep inside you there remains the memory of that new and precious love—your very first and my most precious. My wish for DeAnna and Matthew is that you will someday be well enough to know your new nephew; what meaning it could have in Matthew's life. You could teach him about sunsets, cars, music, and laughter, just as you taught me so long ago.

Reaching out to you should be so easy, but I hold back hoping that your need for the closeness we once had will bring you a reason to get sober. Recently, I got one of those sentimental emails about life. It was call *I've learned*. It had passages about things that appear to be universally true. One of the passages was: *When there is nothing else you can do for someone, you can pray.* It has stayed with me for two weeks, and at my age that's a record. I know you are laughing at this corny joke, because I can see your face clearly in my mind, and I know that laughter comes easily to you as it has to me.

So I will pray; not for your recovery from alcoholism as I once did, but for you somehow to remember somewhere deep inside that your life has had purpose and meaning to all of those who have loved and been loved by you. How lucky we have been.

Love,
Mom

Greg's Last Birthdays

13 April 2003, Sunday 2:00 pm

Dear Greg,

Happy Birthdays. I can see you rolling your eyes. I'm sharing it with DeAnna, Mike, Gary, Darlene, and Harry since they have shared so much of their lives with you. I'm reading it to you because you don't read everything I send to you; and this is important stuff.

Today we are celebrating your birthdays, both of them: 13 April 1964 (when you arrived on a beautiful spring day as a baby, new to the Earthschool); and 26 December 2001 (when you arrived in a blizzard in Hageman Village, New York, to start again to learn how to live).

Your original birth brought me great joy; you were a present to my father on his forty-fourth birthday. More importantly, you were physical proof to me that something bigger than both of us was at work here. Your rebirth brought me great joy as well, because I knew without a doubt that divine intervention had brought you to bitter cold New York; and the harsh experiences ahead would bring you new life. You raged against everyone at first, but your body began to get stronger; you faced multiple illnesses with courage, and you began to grow toward wholeness. Your heart began to soften and you rediscovered Love; you touched many lives, and you were no longer alone. In my heart, I can still hear you ending our phone conversations by saying, *Love Ya Mom.*

This afternoon in your honor, we will have a pizza and cake party, and share stories about you, and wish you Happy Birthdays. But this year you have given us the gifts: Uncle Pilate got your guitar; Aunt Erma got your Aloe lotion, DeAnna got Grandpa's old desk and some of your music, Michael got your Electric Dart Board, Matt and Tom got your cars and marbles (not to mention your handmade rubber band ball). Beth got your dresser, Jessica got your Cymbal clock, Gary got your old musical albums as you instructed. Shaunda got your wolf posters and rug, Uncle Virgil got your Ford hat (we had to make him take it). Leigh Anne took your picture. Darlene got Ted E Bear, also known as Theodore Elvie; and Karly got your

"Greg's number one on the planet" clock. Dave took your vacuum cleaner; I'll bet that ticks you off. All of us took something to ease the pains in our hearts. We love and miss you; you made us laugh.

As for me, I've kept you; you and I have been together on this spiritual journey for thirty-nine years. Someone, whose opinion I respect, once said to me that I thought I knew how the Universe works, but I didn't and he didn't; he said no one does. I believed him. There is a visible order we can see in nature, but we cannot know what each life's purpose is to be; we can only trust and accept that *the Universe is unfolding as it should*[5]. The purpose of each life rests within each soul for each person to discover in his own time and in her own way. We can't know how many lifetimes that can take.

I am grateful to the Universal force that brought your life to mine. We shared joy and sorrow. We shared tears and laughter. We shared anger and forgiveness. I learned most of what I know about tolerance and compassion from the experiences we shared. I do not believe our souls are together by accident; there is much more to learn, and I trust that our souls will meet again. Until then – *C-Ya*!

Happy Birthdays
Love,
Mom

---

5   Excerpt from Desiderata, author unknown

A Life Remembered

He came to us small, thin, and wrinkled—slightly blue. He left us small, thin, and wrinkled—slightly green. What came in between was life—his, mine, and those he touched. He made us laugh, he made us cry, he gave us hope, and he filled us with despair. Five years have passed and I see his face clearly in all its moods: angry, scared, loving, joyful, and laughing. His eyes twinkled and his mouth spread wide to show large teeth stained from his habits in life. His heart ached for love and he sometimes grasp to keep it as I too have done. I see him as a small child full of wonder at the sunset. I see him as a young boy burdened by the weight of too many large newspapers as he began his paper route, and a young boy buoyed by the accomplishment of his deliveries at the end of his route. I see him as a teenager wishing for more height so that he could play basketball professionally; practicing for hours on our driveway court. I see him as a young man with charm and a sense of humor that made him love sales at an auto parts store. He was critical of people who didn't live up to his expectations, which may have reflected his disappointment in his capacity to live up to his own. At his depth, he was love; and he touched each person he met in a way he/she would not forget. I saw him as an alcoholic too drunk to stand. I saw him as a recovering addict too sick to continue to live in his body. I heard his expression of love found too late to continue life on Earth, but early enough for him to feel blessed by it. He brought joy and learning to me especially and for his physical life, I will forever be grateful—just as it was. His essence lives within many and is a reflection of his authentic capacity to love. Today I miss him, but most days I can still hear him laugh and feel his Presence.

In The Beginning, We Ran

It was a beautiful spring day when he arrived at my door. He was dressed in running shorts and seemed eager to share my time. As he entered the door of my apartment, I noticed that his hands were shaking. I thought he was nervous, but later found out it was much more than that. But that is a different story.

He had come because he had entered us into a race that day; our first date. He had entered us without my permission for he was not someone I would have chosen to date at that time. His persistence had worn my resistance down and now here I was! At the race, we ran; he swiftly with strength; me not so swiftly with persistence. After the race, he introduced me to his friend and his friend was much more appealing to me than he was.

The race was held in Crystal City, Virginia, and sponsored by one of the hotels there. A band had been hired for dancing in the street after the race. It played loudly, but no one was dancing so I suggested that we break the ice and dance. He under the influence of a few too many beers said, "Yes." It was fun and the announcer gave me an envelope as we danced. In the envelope was a gift certificate that was good for one year and could be redeemed for "dinner for two." I remember thinking, "Now, I'm stuck with another date." At that point, I had decided one date with this Marine was enough. I danced with his friend and asked him if my date had a drinking problem, and if I should get a different way home. He said, "No." The day continued into evening as we danced and laughed and he began to sober up for the ride home. I began to notice that behind his loud exterior was a shy and fearful boy; it was appealing even then.

At one point in the day, there was a moment when time stood still for me. I was sitting on the ground and it was clear he started to and wanted to kiss me, but then decided against it. It was a beautiful moment when I felt our hearts connect; and without my full awareness, my life changed forever. I fell in love with an untrustworthy charming con artist, and the drama of exciting moments and excruciating pain became our way of life. It began with a choice to run together. His choice was to enter us in the race, and my choice was to agree.

Today it has been 21 years since that memory of sweet stillness, of that kiss that didn't happen. Our life together has ended because his way of life was to keep running in fear. He chose to live a duplicitous life always searching for some unknown something; I chose to no longer accept his choices as mine. I'll never be sure if he ever felt deep love for me, but my feeling is that we both will remember some precious moments when we stood in total stillness, which our authentic connection co-created. As the song goes, *some people wait a lifetime for a moment like this*, and we shared many—or so it seemed to me.

A Room; A Transformation; A Symbol

It is not just a room! It is the place of betrayal that has been transformed into a place of healing. It is my creation. It is where we made love, it is where we fought, and it is where we worked side-by-side and apart. It is the place where he played solitaire for hours. It is a place where I wrote from my heart. It is a place where our children and friends slept when they visited. It is the place he brought someone else to hold, and as her card to him said, "to share the moon." After my discovery of his unfaithfulness, it is where I brought my pain.

At first I came into the room so that I would not forget what he had done, so that I could find the strength to look at my life exactly at it was and to accept responsibility for what I had helped to create. In the room were all the signs of betrayal that I had not seen before; sometimes we only see what we want to see. As I sat on the mattress that lay upon the floor without a frame, my eyes were dry and my heart was still. It was as if I too was a damaged remnant of another time and place. As my tired spirit observed more closely, I saw red wine stains upon the rug, walls scared with bits of metal where pictures had once hung, black marks where he had piled his papers, new stains upon the comforter and sheets, a coaster on both sides of the bed, a book he had carried into the room to share with someone else. As I asked myself why our life together had ended as it had, I noticed a lifeless fly had suddenly filled a far corner of the room. It seemed enormous. It held my gaze and would not let go. As I moved to pick it up, I knew I would not die there surrounded with sadness. With the choice to remove that death from my surroundings, I began to restructure not only the room, but also my thinking and my life. Eventually the room evolved into a visual symbol of my rebirth.

The transformation has taken months, but the room is now complete. It is not a perfect symbol of beauty and balance, but it is filled to the brim with my essence and my love of life. In the place of a mattress left unadorned upon the floor is a new delicate antique pewter bed. Its old covering—found deep and forgotten in a closet—is edged with ivy, and its top is a patchwork of soft purple and pale yellow flowers. I curl up on it and watch my tiny TV, eat from a tray, read my book, or just sit in peaceful quiet. An afghan made by my sister keeps me warm. At times I cry, but not as often as before.

When the tears flow softly down my cheeks, I am grateful for their cleansing. It clears my vision and I see the wise old owl—newly framed—that was given to me by one of my favorite aunts as a graduation present. It hangs above an old oak desk I bought as a gift for my husband over twenty-five years ago. I see myself in a small mirror that has traveled to many places with many people. I see an abstract boat poster from a museum in Greece and I recall a loving moment that quickens my heart. And I chuckle as my eyes fall to rest upon a cartoon poster of a man and a woman in a balloon among the clouds. Tied to the bottom of their basket is a rainbow. The caption says *Take a Rainbow With You*. It reminds me how often I have shared this symbol of love. As I plug in my old nightlight, the shape of a rainbow appears out of the darkness upon the soothing blue wall over my new bed. My heart is alive and my eyes have regained their twinkle. My step has recovered its bounce. I know deep in my being that the healing process I have begun will continue.

Now I come into this room to remember, to rest, to learn, to write, to plan my future, and I am transformed by my own power of healing. The room is only my symbol, and I love it!

My Unkindness Revisited To An Old Friend

Dear Harry,

Although I have not changed my mind about your behavior, I have looked deeply at my own. You will never be "dead to me" because of my basic belief that we are all One; it would be like declaring a part of me as dead. In my moment of rage at the world not being as I would like, I forgot that. This week I cut my finger and as I placed the bandage on it, I thought about whether or not I would ever cut it off completely if I had the opportunity to support its healing. The answer of course was that I would not! My personality has chosen to suffer much with your personality's ups and downs. But each time, my soul slowly remembers that at the level of essence, we are all in this together. The fear within my personality cannot understand why your fear-based behaviors are as they are or why you would choose over and over again a life of uncontrolled drama that is the natural result of dishonesty in any form. I look out my window at the peacefulness of the mountain and understand only that my own peace is my work and purpose—it is the natural return to my original essence before this incarnation ends. I am far away from that essence on some days and quite able to touch it on others. Clearly, I am unable to abandon you. I feel deeply that my soul's love for me, and the part of me within you, will be enough to sustain us as we live apart.

Long ago, we shared a song that said, *if I fall behind, wait for me; if you fall behind, I'll wait for you.* People heal at different rates and for some of us it takes more than one lifetime. You have chosen a separate Path that no longer seems to support mine during this incarnation. We are in the twilight of this physical life and you seem to continue to accumulate toxic karma that will eventually require balancing. Also the fear of my personality that wants you to hurt is in need of healing. I am doing so many amazing things that I have wanted to do; my book is almost complete. I'm beginning the Virginia Naturalist Program next month. I'm taking part in improv theatre, I'm teaching what I believe is supportive of others in my own community in my own way, I'm studying human behavior, I'm dancing and working out doing yoga and other sports. I'm living in the moment as best I can. I love my role as Mother, Grandmother, and friend.

I once imagined that you would be sharing all this with me, but I realize that like the cut injured finger on my left hand, you need more time to heal yourself. I don't know how to supply the bandage for that; that is beyond anyone's power but yours to create. Loving all that I am in this moment is the first requirement for loving others well; that much I've learned.

I want to want you to heal even if it is with another that you love well; I'm not quite there yet and it hurts, but that is my own Path for healing. More than that I want you to deeply learn that each of us is enough; no lying is necessary. That too must be your work if you choose. My wish for us both is that whatever arises serves an awakening of compassion for all beings even when we just do not understand each other. I miss you and would appreciate it if you would from time to time let me know where you are and if you're doing okay. My connection to you has been and is one of the deepest parts of who I am in this incarnation; I do not want to completely lose touch. I never tired of being together with you as I do with others. I am choosing life; what are you choosing?

Namaste (the light in me honors the light in you; it always has and will)

Love
Phyllis

"Sometimes People Leave You Half Way Through the Woods...."

There is a stage play made up of a consolidation of fairy tales. It is called *Lost in the Woods*. In this play there is a song that goes, "sometimes people leave you halfway through the woods."

For many years and numerous times without conscious awareness, I have had a fearful part of my personality that has felt left halfway through the woods. It is really an old old story, but this time I'm sharing it with new awareness, and it feels healing. Those who left me, so my fearful part's story goes were: my brother, my Father, my Mother, my former husband, my son, and most recently my designated (by me) partner for life, and then that same partner again and again. Apparently he didn't understand my plan for him.

When I came into the Authentic Power Program at the Seat of the Soul Institute, I felt broken, sad, and tearful with self-pity; I felt totally lost in the woods of my life with no way out. The sadness was so dense that even the anger couldn't get through. With the support of those in the program along with Gary Zukav and Linda Francis, I began the healing of the fearful parts of my personality and grew closer to my soul. But as I began to resist the deeper healing needed, my fearful part felt they too had brought me only so far and then had abandoned me in the woods. I fell back into the fearful part of me that had supported and kept me safe during my travels through the dangers of previously unfriendly forests. The problem with this strong and dependable fearful part is that it encourages me to find my way alone and numbed out. As the years have gone by, it has become a heavier and heavier bag of external courage that creates many obstacles to my spiritual growth, but it also has created the barrier that protects me from feeling the pain of powerlessness.

I have judged others as unfair to me and blamed them for leaving me behind and not supporting my growth through added responsibility for newer people coming into the program. When I chose to participate in the Program for another year, one of my spiritual partners welcomed me. My fearful reaction to him was to say; "the rest of you will need someone to create lessons for you." That reaction was so painful, I doubled over in rage at what my world was like in that moment—indulging my anger to avoid again the pain of powerlessness in a dense woods of fearful parts run amok.

I have been with the shame of that reaction and have challenged it during the days since. It is clear that there is a different way to cross the other half of the woods. I've witnessed others doing just that. They have had the courage to look for the support of loving faces on their journey and to share their deepest pain while I have resisted. At times one of those supportive faces was mine and my fearful part took pride in that fact.

My grandson has inherited the family fearful part that sees the world as unfair and blames others; he is nine today. If I am to support him in healing, I must first find the courage to heal myself. It is my deepest intention to learn how better to support him, others, and myself. The courage to look at, to feel deeply, and to challenge the fearful part that feels so powerless to do that, must be found no matter what. Einstein said that, *a problem cannot be solved with the same consciousness that created it* so I'm going to need to ask for the support of others even in the darkness of the woods. My fearful part that does not trust must be challenged. That requires an opening of my heart to what "is" in each moment, and the fearful part doubts my ability to do that. My body is filled with pain as I write this with the awareness that no one has truly left me in the woods; I've given my fearful parts the power they needed to choose to stay behind. It is my deepest intention to withdraw my permission for them to continue to block my way. It is too painful within me now to resist turning to see all parts of me—the fearful and the loving. It is time once again to choose deep and lasting change. It is why I'm here in this place, at this time, in this physical body, with all those who journey with me.

Authentic Power Update

Dear Gary and Linda,

It has been six months since leaving the Authentic Power Program. My life lesson for this period has been to look at what has been most difficult about creating authentic power without the active support of an organized group. For me, it has taken a conscious effort every day to remember my intention to continue to grow spiritually. It is easy within the comfortable life I have created to forget the fearful parts that do not get dramatically triggered on a day-to-day basis.

The realization that my spiritual growth is my responsibility alone was a good beginning. The coaching sessions supported that learning, and those recordings of those sessions gave me a tool I could return too when I felt the fear of overwhelm and aloneness. When I created the opportunity and then made the final decision to leave the Authentic Power Program, your choice to not respond to my decision email triggered my fearful part that needs attention to feel safe and to know I'm cared about. I used that painful experience to look at other places in my life where I felt someone else should have behaved differently. That led me to examine the fearful part of me that takes my sense of belonging to a group from not only what I contribute, but from how that contribution has been visibly appreciated by others. Even in my comfortable life, there were many; some involved family relationships and others just casual acquaintances and friends. I have challenged that in each moment by just feeling the disappointment in my chest and knowing it is more about me than the others with whom I'm interacting. A few times I reached out to others for support indirectly, and when they didn't respond as I expected, my fearful part blamed them instead of acknowledging that I did not ask for their support directly. Another lesson that keeps repeating.

In early summer, I had an "ah ha" moment when I saw what life would be like without an image. I took that moment and turned it into a small discussion focus for the spiritual group that has been created by a few of the women here in my community. It was an amazing experience for me to openly share with them my reliance on images and hear their experiences.

One of the women had a very active fearful part during the discussion, and I was able to just be present with her energy as I felt she was not open to seeing her images differently. Although I had some discomfort in my solar plexus, I was able to keep an open heart and be grateful that she was in the group; I could see that her skepticism was a gift to the others and to me especially. I could see in her a previous familiar fearful image of my own; my compassion for her allowed me to see the changes that have occurred in me.

Also, I have agreed to lead a meditation hour in my community, and that choice has brought up a lot of fear about whether or not I'm capable of doing this with a loving intention rather than the fearful part that wants to be seen as "the leader." I've reminded myself how much meditation has enhanced my life and how perhaps it could support others. My deepest intention is to support others and not let the fearful part that doubts my goodness to interfere. As you've said often, intention is the source of all creation.

An old friend and I have spent a lot of time together the last few months. His life is much more complicated than mine at the moment and I have supported him as best I can. I am aware that I have a fearful part that wants him to mean more to me than he does, and a healthy part that knows he is not the right person for me. On New Year's Day I shared what I was feeling with him. Although it was difficult to do, I feel my authentic sharing with him has strengthened our long and deep friendship. Surprisingly, it has also supported me to know I can make a healthy choice even when a fearful part is active.

I'm sending you energetic support for the coming year, and I appreciate all the opportunities for learning you have brought to my spiritual growth. I am studying with Tara Brach through online presentations. She is a Buddhist teacher from the Washington DC area. Her teachings are much in line with the authentic power program. I continue to create weekly life lessons for myself using my experiences and writing about them each Sunday. As always, I continue to write daily; I feel it is my gift. I'm sharing my writings with more people with less fear of disapproval.

I am using my workshop CD's and my old life lessons to remind me not to let comfort set in and to remind me that enjoying life is a healthy intention.

There is nothing to earn, nothing to prove, and no image to maintain. I've experienced much Grace that has supported me through the many challenges of the past year.

I'm sending this life lesson to you with the intention of updating you on how I'm doing as I promised, and to ask you directly for your energetic support as I continue to create authentic power in each moment.

With love and gratitude,
Namaste
Phyllis

My Grandmother's Favorite Place, And Mine

It was 54 years ago, but I remember it clearly. The large feather bed in my Grandma Ferguson's house became my refuge from harm. My parents had given me permission to stay two weeks with my Grandma and Aunt Rosa in Lexington, Kentucky. When Dad and Mother drove away, I was overcome with the anxiety of being without them. Now looking back, I know my Grandma sensed my fear.

My love for her was real, but that day her soft skin and deep wrinkles seemed unfamiliar and foreboding to a small child. She said, "Let me show you my favorite place, you must be so tired." And, there it was. I climbed up and up into what seemed like a cloud, all white and engulfing. As I lay down the welcoming bed snuggled against me, cool at first and then deliciously warm. Grandma completed my cocooning by pulling the colorful quilts up to my ears and by telling me she made them herself when my Dad was just my size. It was hard for me to imagine him ever having been just my size, but the story added more comfort and warmth. Grandma brought me the cookies we had made together that afternoon and sat delicately at the edge of that incredible bed.

The secure feeling of that grand old feather bed has stayed with me forever as a living memory from my childhood. My grandmother's favorite place became my favorite place for two entire weeks. Even now when an overwhelming fear dares to venture into my life, I seek refuge under my covers, hold them close, and remember a similar bed so long ago. When I do, I grow in courage and can soon rise to face my fears. I can still hear my Grandma Ferguson s chuckle, and I feel protected by her memory.

The Power of Winter Solstice

This year my Winter Solstice celebration was as it always is and yet entirely new. I'll begin in the middle and come back to the beginning and ending. There I sat in a beautiful Zen-Garden created by David, the beloved; it is his home. The night is overcast and very still with only the sounds of the crackling fire and the waterfalls close by. I can hear my own breathing and sometimes David's. My heart is steeped in gratitude for a year of learning how to accept love without attachment or expectation. I place a small stick from my bouquet of sticks into the fire David has built. I voice that what I learned is that it is essential to love myself in order to receive the love of others; that giving and receiving love requires the same energy. For me, that has meant learning to trust and live with an open heart. It has not been easy all the time. I am so full of gratitude for this year of love that I find it difficult to speak so I just open myself to the experience without filters.

I've brought a rock of quartz and granite to use in this annual celebration. I will use it as a talking stick and then pass it to David. It is black with a large white stripe through its center. It is infused with all the love of the past year. I share that it represents yen and yang, dark and light, difficult and pleasant, despair and joy, death and life, winter and summer. It is my gift to David's garden should he choose to return it to the earth. As I pass it to him, I ask him to consider infusing it with his energy and then to see if it feels right for him to add it to his garden. I'm a bit surprised that I am not attached to what he chooses.

David reaches out for the warm rock; there is stillness. He takes his time and then rises to place his stick from my bouquet into the fire; there is stillness. Just as I feel he will remain silent, he speaks of his first experience of celebrating Winter Solstice, his daughter, his garden, the talking rock, and his plan to add it to his garden. He expresses that the rock fits into his hand perfectly, and that he has a knowing it is meant for his garden. He feels so present and gentle to me. He does not speak of love, but I can feel his loving essence blending with my own. There is stillness.

I have recorded *The Sun at Midwinter: A Meditation,*[6] and I turn it on and it begins out of the stillness, and we listen. I have used this meditation each year, but hearing it in the night air spoken in my own voice is new. As it ends, we return to stillness and I feel the coldness of the night entering my body. It feels like a reminder of the work needed ahead to maintain a warm and open heart. I light a candle from the central fire and pass it to David. He receives it in silence and lights the larger protected candle that will burn until morning. Its brightness will remind the sun to return as the ancients did so long ago.

As planned, David and I write upon a paper star something from the past year that we want to create *less of* in the coming year. I write, *selfishness*. I place it on the fire, the energy of the fire pushes it toward the edge of the fire, and it doesn't burn. David writes on his, throws it into the fire, and it dissolves in the heat. David asks if he should push my star into the fire; I tell him no. It looks as if it may be difficult for me to keep this intention to heal. Then I write something that I feel is within me that I want the energy of the fire to take into the Universe. I write *Love*. I stand and place it on the fire; the edge of it catches and the star flips over and consumes my *selfishness* star. David says, *that was needed!* I am touched with deep compassion for the clarity of this message from the Universe: loving acceptance will be needed as I heal my selfishness. David takes his turn and his star ignites and dissolves. His face is soft in the glow of the fire.

The time has come for David, if he chooses, and me to set an intention for healing for the coming year—something that we want to create *more of* in our life between now and the next Winter Solstice. David seems excited and pleased to participate; his face is amber in the firelight and his eyes are moist with tenderness. I explain that the plan is to write the intention down on a star and either give it to the fire to expand into the Universe or hold it close to remind us of what is intended throughout the year. I choose to write on two stars; *compassion* and then *acceptance*. I place *compassion* in the fire, which transforms my request into energy immediately, and then I place *acceptance* in my pocket knowing that I will need a reminder for that difficult growth. I close my eyes and choose not to observe David's choice. My work has begun. There is stillness.

---

6   A meditation from *The Winter Solstice, The Sacred Traditions of Christmas*, by John Matthews

As planned, again I turn on the recorder. Again I hear my voice, but not quite my voice, begin to read an excerpt from *365 TAO, Daily Meditations*[7] entitled *Night*. It is beautiful, it feels just right, and then there is stillness, and then the coldness of the night has moved into my feet. It is time to go inside.

I give David his first singing bowl, we sip champagne, we share dinner, we share about our lives, and we dance quietly to the lullabies of Shaina Noll.

Now for the beginning I promised—David and I met in October, and our hearts joined in a way that allowed us to support each other and enjoy this amazing intimate Winter Solstice experience. I make really good Sausage and Spinach soup and he makes wonderful smoothies and waffles. We are dating and sharing, but our relationship needs no label. We simply find joy in being together in the present moment and are content to allow the future to unfold, as it will. We are very different and we are very similar—we want to know each other, which is very different from knowing about each other. Many times during the last few months, we have touched the stillness of a beautiful Winter Solstice night each in our own way. I carry that stillness born of trust when we are apart.

---

7   *365 TAO, Daily Meditations* is written by Deng Ming-Dao

Sacred Moments: Thoughts and Feelings

A small picture of delicate beauty; it was so beautiful that we all just stopped and stared at it in awe; that something so little could be strong enough to withstand the blizzards of last winter. It was tucked under a rock right in the middle of the Appalachian Trail in the Blue Ridge Mountains. Hundreds of people must have walked right over it, but the Universe provided it the shelter it needed. Nature is awesome.

If I Were Dying

Henry Thoreau wrote:

The only way to tell the truth is to speak with kindness.
Only the words of a loving man can be heard.

I read this quote early this week with a deeper understanding. My father use to say that kindness was something you could give away continually; it didn't cost any thing, and it always came back. If I were dying, I would want to allow the kind and compassionate part of my personality to have more freedom and expression. The fearful part of me that protects this tender side has had a long reign.

I have journeyed toward death with a number of people, and I have found that they were not much different facing death than they had been in facing life. Most of the things I find valuable, I believe would still be important to me if I were facing death: quiet places in nature, contemplation about what was happening, introspection about what I had co-created while living, spending time in quiet conversation with others—one on one—about what is important to us both, etc.

Last week during my daughter's visit, I did not cancel all the things I love to do as I have in the past. Instead I invited her along. She seemed to love seeing more of my life than I usually share with her. We talked, laughed, and shared in a way that was easy and natural compared to other visits. My intention is to reveal more of myself to her than I have in the past. I want her to know me and feel she can let herself be fully known if she chooses.

As I get older and closer to death, I marvel at how many opportunities to really live are presented to me or co-created by my actions. I do not want to miss them because I fear disapproval or failure or not being good enough or a disappointment to someone. In many areas of my life, I have taken risks and I love adventure. I want to explore my emotional landscape with that same curiosity and that same sense of adventure. I don't intend to wait until I know when I'm dying. My fear around coming to the end of my life is more about giving up physical existence and attachments to those I love than fear of the unknown on the other side of death.

Each person I've loved that has left the Earthschool before me has left a void that grows smaller with time, but cannot be filled by other things or people. Slowly, I have begun to remember with gratitude how much they brought to my life. I sometimes fear that my death may leave that same void in those who love me. Also I sometimes fear that others may see my life as worthless to them and not miss me at all unless I conform to what they believe should be important to me. I'm challenging that each day by quieting my mind, asking for guidance, making a choice, and experimenting with the results.

We are all dying all the time; it is the natural order of things.

Learning About "An Equal Music"

In my small mountain community, July is dedicated to the Performing Arts Festival each year, and the entire community participates to make it happen. This year it began for me as our book club chose to read *An Equal Music* by Vikram Seth; and then we invited one of the newly formed Academy student quartets to play for us and contribute to the discussion of the book. *An Equal Music* is the love story of a gifted violinist and pianist and the interactions of the different personalities necessary to create a chamber music quartet. In the story, the pianist eventually becomes deaf, but continues to play as a soloist from her memory of sound and creates what the author calls *an equal music*. To the surprise of the audience, she plays a flawless performance.

Later in the week, I attended and ushered at an orchestra presentation led by an amazing conductor, Christopher Zimmerman, with a featured world-renowned Spanish pianist, Gustavo Diaz-Jerez. They played Beethoven's Piano Concerto No. 5 in E-flat Major. As the music rose and fell, blasted and whispered, I was in awe of the unison and balance of the music they co-created. I could see clearly the importance of the support of every musician as one after the other, and often collectively, they supported the play of the pianist. When they finished, the members of the audience were on their feet. Their faces bright, their appreciation loud and visible, their hearts seemed open and totally present to this inspired performance. I was one of them, and I saw all of us as souls contributing to the experience of the others. It was a different kind of equal music.

It is Spanish week at our Performing Arts Festival in Wintergreen, Virginia. So the very next morning, the Spanish Composer, Anton Garcia Abril, wrote the featured music. He was present for the morning concert along with the Ambassador of Spain, who volunteered to be his interpreter because the composer wanted to speak directly to the audience. As a special surprise tribute to the composer, a young boy, perhaps 12 years old, was introduced to play one of the composer's creations on the violin. His mother was to accompany him on the piano, and their page-turner needed no introduction, for he was Gustavo Diaz-Jerez, the world-renowned pianist from the previous evening, and the boy's father. The talent and skill of this young boy was inspiring, but what touched me most was seeing the composer kiss the child with tears of gratitude streaming down both their faces, and the quiet attention the father had paid to his task of turning the musical pages. They each had a responsibility to the performance, and they understood the importance of their part in it. Without the composer, there would have been no music, without the famous pianist there would have been no page-turner, without the young boy and his mother there would have been no performance of the music, and without the audience there would have been no one to receive their gifts. The experience was a powerful demonstration of an equal music created by their authentic power.

Each of these experiences was deeply moving and reminded me of what can be co-created by completing each task in each moment for the pure joy of knowing that the experience will be different if someone does not do his/her part. Living in this awareness, I want my life to become an equal music.

An Evening Well Spent

It was a rainy, cold, Friday night so I was surprised at the size of the crowd when I entered Lecture Hall I at George Mason University in Fairfax, Virginia. It was a half-hour before Toni Morrison was to begin her reading, and yet, there were approximately 100-150 people milling around.

As they waited for the program to start, the people were varied in their appearance and conversations. They were black, white, young, old, male, female, ordinary, offbeat, quiet, and talkative. They appeared to be there for different reasons as well. They came in groups socially. They came singly with pen and paper in hand; probably they were students. Some came in quietly and sat alone to enjoy what was to come.

Toni Morrison arrived on time to find her audience tired at week's end sitting in an extremely warm, uncomfortable auditorium with only a bare stage, a podium, and a cup of hot coffee to aide her; and of course, her "work in progress." The president of the writer's club introduced her in glowing terms. We all shifted in our seats to get a better look and applauded out of habit. Perhaps just pleased that she was punctual.

Toni Morrison was black. She wore a black simple dress with a heavy ornamental necklace. Her hair was gray and still eschew from a bout with the wind and rain outside. Her face was not beautiful in conventional terms, and she was overweight. She had a casual manner that indicated she was relaxed and comfortable in what she was about to do. Even before she spoke, she was a commanding presence in the room. She began to speak and the sincerity of her words and the soft mesmerizing quality of her voice soon transformed our mixed group into an intimate unit interested in only one thing. That one thing was to hear her every utterance. She told us she was writing the "absolute best thing in the world," and we believed it because she did. She told us the work she was about to read depicted a small-town family in Ohio in the mid-19th century. The "work in progress" from which she was about to read was called *Beloved*.

She took a long, slow sip of coffee and told us how good it tasted and then she began to read. The words and characters of *Beloved* compelled us to listen intently and breathe slowly. The room was very warm and sleep would have been easy; and yet, we dared not let our heavy eyelids close. If we did, we might miss a hidden clue as to the identity of the mysterious character, Beloved. So we gazed at this woman and were captured as much by her presence as her wonderfully curious story. When we were totally enraptured, a character from the book, called Seth asked, "How could Beloved know these things which she had not been told?" We all wanted to know too, but Toni Morrison stopped the reading.

For an instant the room was suspended in silence, waiting; and then the audience was on its feet in spontaneous applause. We no longer applauded from mere habit, but from admiration. She had come to us with only her talent and had succeeded in making the words of her story a lasting memory in our minds.

She ended the session with a short question and answer period. Some of the questions were about her characters, but most people seemed to be seeking a magic formula for creating great books. They wanted to know how she went about the writing. She showed a slight impatience with these types of personal questions. When she spoke of her writing talents and published works, she was warm and funny, and you could picture her sitting down in an old robe and spinning yarns about the world around her.

I cannot speak for all who were present, but for my husband and me, we loved her performance; and why not? She had read the "absolute best thing in the world" with great feeling.

Her Name is Sara

Interesting lines creased her youthful face with years of time. The gray hair on her head seemed like a halo of magic. It was short, perky, tidy, but not at all perfect. The sound of her cultured voice spoke of another era when women were always, always ladies above all else. She held me spellbound with stories of her past, and drew me nearer with the inflections of her almost haughty tones. She was a stranger. We had spent only seven hours together, and yet, we were truly friends. She said, "My dear, you don't make friends, you simply recognize them!" It is a quote that may not have been created by her, but when it flowed toward me from her, it became her own.

Her movements were slower than mine of course for she was 81; nevertheless, there was spring in her step and timelessness in her soul. She came from a wealthy heritage probably, but I believed she was no longer rich in the common sense; "just comfortable," she said. Some time ago she had joined the wage earners of the world in body, but never in mind or spirit. She talked of her future as if she had no plans of ever dying. That was amazing since during the previous few weeks she had been sick enough to be hospitalized. She mentioned death, and I asked if she was afraid. Easily she said, "No, mostly I am curious." She showed me a photograph of a portrait that was done of her many years before. Her nose was slightly upturned and her haughtiness was plainly visible. She was hauntingly beautiful then as now for undoubtedly, her magnetic beauty had always come from within.

Her eyes glowed; she laughed heartily; she missed nothing. In her I had found something I wanted to emulate. There was about her an aura of ageless wisdom. Whether or not we would see each other again made no difference for we had connected and will remain.

Her name was and is "Sara."

The World Is Not How I Planned; It's Better

Sometime ago I took a trip to Ashland, Oregon, to attend a workshop. My specific intention for the workshop was to cultivate kindness. Within an hour after it began, I was filled with judgments that triggered the fearful part of me that guards against being victimized and anger erupted inside me and splattered on others I love. That was not what I planned. As I was fuming in my room, I began to look at how many times I had victimized someone else, and just as importantly, myself. As I felt the pain of being victimized and being the one to victimize another, my heart began to soften. I set a new intention, to support with kindness everyone at the event in anyway that I could even though my heart raced and my solar plexus cried out, "foul!" Everyone seemed different from this perspective.

The focus of the event was to look at the fear of dying from the perspective of a multi-sensory human. Something about the topic had triggered a lot of fear in me. I felt facing death would be okay, but leaving behind the ones I love wasn't. I felt I'd just rather not look at that. Like it or not, one of the exercises was to imagine what I would do if I had only a week to live. At first I was feeling open and tender. I felt I would be more loving. I felt I would want to go to everyone who had shared my experiences—the difficult and the joyful—and tell them that their being in my life had made a difference in it. Then my protective thoughts took over. I heard myself say, "Whom are you kidding? If you had a week before you died, you would use it to find a way to keep living." In that second, I saw a snapshot of how I live. If the world is not the way I want it to be, I try to fix it so it will be. I resist what is happening when it doesn't fit my plan for my life. I feel entitled to have my life be exactly as I want it to be. It isn't of course, and so I suffer needlessly. I rail against things in my mind not for just a moment, but sometimes for years. I understood it was important for me to see this truth at this time in my life. It wasn't what I planned.

I began to look at all the things I resist and one in particular came to mind. I resist letting others know me. I have a part of me that fears if others know the unwise actions I've taken in the past, they will reject me totally. I decided to challenge that fear and shared with the participants of this workshop my most shameful past action. I had kept it from them for many years. As I was sharing and the pain was overwhelming, I noticed their faces. They were filled with love for me and compassion for my pain. I knew that not sharing at this deep level with those I love had kept me separate from them. Marcel Proust once wrote, *The real voyage of discovery consists not in seeking new landscapes, but in seeing with new eyes.* As I looked at those who love me with new eyes, I knew that the love and compassion I was seeing in them was a reflection of the love and compassion I am capable of feeling for others and myself. I felt free in that moment to be all that I could without guarding against dangers, imagined and real. It wasn't what I planned.

The next morning I had an early meeting and was scheduled to fly home on an overnight flight through Seattle, Washington, to the East coast. Having that early meeting was not what I had expected when I made the reservation. I was exhausted from all of the deep soul work and I felt I was catching a cold, but I had a reservation so I trusted all would work out. I napped on the sofa in the hotel as I waited for my airport shuttle. When I arrived at the airport, all the flights to the East coast had been cancelled because of weather. I could choose to rail against what was happening or embrace it. I took my flight to Seattle and spent the night with friends I love. I rested for eight full hours and took them to breakfast. They showed me their home and parts of Tacoma, Washington. They were a wonderful port in both my storms; the one provided by the weather and the emotional one I had created. I loved the time I spent with them. They dropped me at their airport in the brightest part of the day. I felt light and I knew something important had occurred. The Universe had supported my need to rest, and I was buoyed by the experiences I had not planned.

On the flight home, I met a young man, Kevin. He was on his way to Salvador. He was bright and handsome and filled with the excitement of being twenty-three and beginning an adventure. We shared some of our most important feelings about life. If I never see him again, I know that our lives touched and both of us learned something about ourselves that we might not have if they hadn't. It was not in my plan to be on the seat next to him; I was supposed to have flown home the day before, but there I was. It filled me with joy that he asked for my email address with the intention of adding me to his contact list. He planned to share his stories and adventure through emails with his family. I felt honored. As we landed, he turned and said he hoped he found a Mother like me everywhere he went. I could see his fear of the unknown emerge, and I wanted to reassure him. Instead I challenged my need to Mother him, and said, "Have a great adventure; see everything." His smile spread and filled all who saw him, especially me.

It was late when I arrived at my home destination. Nothing had gone as I planned. It was 1:00 am, and I was tired. As I lay down to sleep, I realized that because I did not resist my experiences, my reality had been better than my plan. The last thing I remember feeling was a deep and abiding gratitude for what is! That's huge.

One Point of View

Arising at 4:15 am, I grope in the darkness as I prepare for my Inauguration Day adventure. My friend sleeps peacefully, and I am filled with the energy of expectation of whether we can catch the train, will there be a parking spot for the car, where will we find a spot to stand on the Mall, will we be able to hear, did we bring enough food. All thought vanishes as I feel the warm cleansing water from the shower, and I am joyful to have this day whatever it brings. I am filled with the excitement of the moment. I dress quickly and warmly, wake my friend, gather our food, close the door, and head for the train station. It is almost empty, but those who gather in the cold are open and friendly; their faces glow with anticipation of something of which none of us seems sure. Some have tickets for the parade; some have tickets for the Capital grounds. Some like us have a loose plan to be part of history however that occurs for us. The voices are filled with soft conversation, sleepy sounds, and gentle giggles. A young black girl is heading for her office that overlooks Pennsylvania Avenue. An inaugural party is being held all day and into the evening with her fellow workers. As we get seated on the train, we take off layers to find comfort in the warm train car. There is a parade of people entering the car with us. They are young and old, black and white, laughing and serious, hopeful and grumpy, alert and sleepy. They have one common goal and that goal is to be a part of the Inauguration of Barack Obama, soon to be our forth-fourth President. He is half white and half black, but he is often called the first United States, African American President, and he is the symbol of the change we believe is happening throughout our country and the world. He represents acceptance and equality for millions who have rarely experienced either.

As we arrive in Washington DC, it is clothed in the stillness of darkness although there are thousands of people all around. The Capitol Building glows and seems the only light. As always when I enter this beautiful city, I feel my heart overflow with tenderness and gratitude for the freedom it symbolizes for me. We shuffle our feet like Penguins in winter and begin our march toward the Mall. Some with tickets are directed right and the rest of us are directed left. Hundreds of young people with red hats are stationed here and there to encourage us to keep moving and to direct our next turn toward an entry point. We stop to take pictures of laughing faces and dark shadows. I love being here and know inside what a privilege it is to have been able to come. My friend's face is solemn and he looks cold. I wonder if he would have chosen to come if I had not wanted to come, and I feel grateful for his friendship and all the adventures and loving gifts we have shared.

As dawn breaks over the Capitol, we find ourselves clustered with people of all sizes, shapes, ages, and ethnicity. Their faces are beaming, and I am reminded of my intention to see beyond personalities to the souls of those who surround me. They are from far and near, rich and poor, dressed in warm coats and not so warm coats. They have carried food and are attempting to buy it. They have brought blankets on which to rest. They stand on one foot and then the other. We will be here for about six hours, each person occupying about a 1.5 feet by 1.5 feet space. We twist and turn and chat about nothing and everything. We say our feet are really cold. Our eyes turn to the large screen above us at every sound. No one wants to miss anything. After about two hours, a replay of the celebration at the Lincoln Memorial from the previous day begins. We hear President-elect Obama say, "It is what is between (the stones). It is you!" The crowd stands in silence and seemingly in meditation as to what that will mean for our future. Some have tears, some have bright smiles, some are expressionless, and all seem entirely present. The energy of "being totally present" is awesome.

As the Inaugural events begin, senators, House of Representative members, Cabinet members, celebrities, dignitaries, former Presidents, Obama's friends and family, etc. create a parade of visual external success. At one point, a well-dressed woman looking somewhat stiff appears on the screen from the Capitol steps. A young black man standing behind me says in a comedic tone, "Born to be rich!" I could feel his resentment covered with humor, and wondered if our vision that "we are all one" will actually ever be possible. Most of those on the swearing-in platform are white skinned. As quickly as the fear comes, it is gone and the good humor around me returns. For most of us on this day our intention seems to be to support this young man, who is willing to take on the seemingly unsolvable problems that hang above us.

As the comings and goings on the screen continue, there are moments of stillness and moments of jubilation depending on who appears before us.

Then President-elect, Barack Obama, appears, entering from the back of the platform. Eyes turn upward toward him, hearts lift with joy, voices call out his name, and American flags wave. To a casual observer the world seems to be as it should be in this moment. To those with a deeper sensitivity and those who take a longer look, it is clear a "Savior" is being sought and the "hope" of redemption is at hand. A violin begins to play and there is a beautiful moment of Grace when I can see what a loving world could feel like.

President Barack Obama is sworn-in and as he approaches the platform to speak, there is stillness like the moment before a storm. I feel I am in the presence of a soul that is fulfilling his destiny and the world waits. He does not disappoint. His speech is eloquent, forceful, sincere, and gentle; he speaks of the support that will be required by all to meet the challenges that are before us. The tears that flow throughout the crowd begin to dry and the reality of personal responsibility seems to settle upon us. When he finishes, applauds are loud and the crowd waves their flags, and the energy has suddenly changed.

As we head for the train, spirits are high and conversations are of what happens next. One young girl is collecting flags; she needs forty-four she says. People hand them over, some eagerly some with reluctance. I am beginning to really feel the cold wind blowing around me. As I turn toward twelfth street and the ride home, I look back to see an army of young people with plastic bags cleaning the litter from the Mall. One says, "We're doing what we can to help the park service." My eyes fill with tears of tenderness as I see inspiration transformed into action—at least, for this one moment.

There are almost 2 million people on the Mall for the Inauguration of President Barack Obama and many have had a different experience than mine. Mine is one point-of-view, and I am open to hearing the views of others so I have a more complete and comprehensive picture of this blessed, sunshine filled, cold and crowded, winter day. In the end, isn't that the intended message of this day of Grace?

Flight, Fright, and Fantasy

Getting up early gives you more time to contemplate the day's adventure. You've decided that a lifelong fantasy's time has come. Today you're going skydiving! You look at yourself in the mirror and there are signs of morning: lines on the face, bags under the sleepy eyes, hair flat on one side and rumpled on the other. Today, if you look closely, there is something else. There is tension around the mouth, but you tell yourself you're handling it well. You do all the usual things, like sing in the shower, put on your jewelry, dry your hair. Then the phone rings and you jump two feet off the floor. Your friend is here to pick you up. His voice says, "Are you ready?" You reply with false bravado, "Sure!" Silently you tell yourself that you really didn't want him to back out. You grab your bag and head for the elevator. While there, you hope no one will notice that your hand is shaking a bit as you press the elevator button.

There's the car to take you to your fate. You get in and buckle up. You laugh about the risk of driving forty miles versus skydiving and agree that driving is far more dangerous. The queasy feeling in your stomach tells you that you are lying to yourself. There is idle chatter, but your mind is not retaining much of what is being said. That's great, just when you're about to go into the training designed to save your life you suffer brain stagnation.

You arrive at the airfield anxious (and I do mean anxious) to get in the air. The class starts late. The flight might get scrubbed because of low clouds. It rains a little. You sign a waiver saying the only person to blame for your "death or bodily injury" is you. Your brain yells tear it up; get out of here while you can! You swallow hard and try to ignore the voice. Everyone else seems to be having a great time. They say the sky is clearing. The tension around the mouth from the morning is now sheer panic at the back of the throat.

Training is over. You know everything now; you're prepared for your first jump. You really are getting into that plane. Is it too small to get off the ground? You lean forward over the jumpmaster to put more weight toward the front of the plane. You breathe deeply as you clear the trees at the end of the short runway. Open your eyes! You are no longer in panic within your throat; it has grabbed your entire body. You try to smile, but your mouth is frozen and very dry.

You're up there. The first man, your friend, jumps and disappears. The second man jumps and disappears; then the third, and the fourth. If you weren't scared stiff, you would be shaking all over. The airplane circles the field. The jumpmaster calls your name. You move like a robot. The parachute is very heavy, so are your legs. Your mouth does not function very well; you lips are stuck to your teeth. You're in jumping position. You whisper to the jumpmaster, "I'm a little scared." He says gently, "I know." Then, he barks to you the first command, "Put your feet on the step!" His compassion is short lived. Oops! Not a good thought. The wind is so strong, you are so little, but somehow you make yourself put your knees and hands out that door. The second command comes abruptly, "Hang from the strut!" You do not hesitate, but you see your feet on the step as you stand up, and the ground below seems so distant.

The fear seems to dissipate as you realize the decision is made and you will jump. Your mouth is still too dry to swallow comfortably. You're out there. You are hanging like a flag under the wing of that noisy plane and you think, almost calmly, "I'm risking my life for fun." At that second, what you think may be the last word you'll hear is shouted above the wind as the jumpmaster yells, "Go!" Incredulously, you inwardly shrug and think, "Oh well." You release your death grip on the strut. Did I really think death grip? Then, so very fast, you are falling away from the noisy plane.

What a glorious feeling of fright and flight. Hurled through space for six seconds, you call out the numbers you were sure earlier you would forget to say. You look up as the canopy is opening, and you watch (though slightly dazed) as it continues to open. You are surrounded by silence. The only sound is your heartbeat racing. The parachute becomes a perfect canopy; you're not going to die. The brilliant blues in the canopy against the white and light-blue sky will forever be a photograph of captured time. Your fantasy is fulfilled and it is just as grand as you imagined. You float down to the earth right on target, and your moment ends, sort of. Your legs are totally weak, your mouth still just as dry, your stomach more queasy, but your chest is filled with an exhilaration you will never forget, and some will never experience.

Suddenly, your body cascades backwards, you are suffering motion sickness and definitely falling hard. You are hidden completely in a mountain of silky parachute. A photographer snaps a picture for his paper. For better or worse, your fright, flight, and fantasy moment is forever captured for the local news! You knew you could do it! Right?

Early Kayaking

It is funny how easily I can get up for doing something new and adventurous. Yesterday it took the form of kayaking on a canal in Maryland. I rolled out of bed with jubilant morning energy at 5:30 am. The sun was just peeking out to greet me. I was excited by the thoughts of what I could experience. As always, I needed food. So quickly I ate cereal and juice in the kitchen and then off to my favorite morning sunspot to sip my coffee. No matter how early I get up, I want this time of quiet to contemplate the day and think about whatever arises. Today I can't really remember what was on my mind yesterday morning; cleansing is a daily ritual for me.

Staying on my chosen subject seems difficult for me sometimes; like today. But as the story unfolds perhaps I can focus more on it and keep this from turning into a book about my "meditations of the mornings." However, that could be a good future book title.

I had packed my lunch the night before and packed a change of clothes. I wore my purple bathing suit, a white cap sleeve shirt with tiny colored strips, and purple shorts. I took my purple hat. I was as colorful as the morning. The sun was glorious. I picked up Janet and Tammy, and they seemed eager for the day. Both of them wore black, mainly because they look great in black and wear it most of the time. We took George Mason Drive to Route 495, and it was a leisurely talkative trip. Since we have Jim in common (Janet's husband, Tammy's father, my boss), we began conversations about him to break the ice. We soon tired of that and decided to leave all Jim stories at home with the dog. The dog is really Tammy's but Jim has developed a great fondness for him. More about this cute little dog could make a story in itself. Oops, back to my kayaking tale!

We arrived exactly on time and Violette's Locks was buzzing with activity as the group readied for the trip. There were twelve women of various ages and interests joining together for a morning of adventure, and we were high on energy and low on organization. That didn't seem to matter at first. The mood was get your gear and get into the water. Some of us did that more successfully than others, but we all got it done. Janet and I tried to wear our sun hats under our helmets, but my brim was so wide that the helmet pushed it into a "u" shape that reminded us of old fashion sunbonnets, and I could see and hear nothing. The guide said that my red helmet and purple hat would have made a great picture for the Washington Women's Outsiders Group, but we were not organized enough at that point to be taking pictures. I gave up the "hat under the helmet" idea quickly.

The canal was muddy but quite clean with a slight smell of fish or perhaps "female fear." We got ourselves into a huddle in the middle of the canal and introduced ourselves. We discovered we were lawyers, executive assistants, teachers, computer associated persons, mothers, grandmothers, students, old, middle-aged, young, not so young, etc. Then we played a game to get use to our boats. A strip of tape was hung from each end of each boat and the person that could capture the most strips of tape won. It was difficult to maneuver since all of us were novices, but we tried. One woman got five. I got two. We played again and the outcome was the same. It was more luck than skill to be able to be in a position to grab a piece of tape. Some of the women were very passive and only took the tape that presented itself, but others of us whooped and hollered as we tried to get positioned to capture the tape. The outcome mattered not, we were having a great time, each in our own way.

The teaching of the strokes was very low-key, and the ability to do the strokes was non-existent at first. So we all crisscrossed across the canal from side to side trying to keep our boats in a straight line and moving forward. It seemed impossible, but we all struggled to get it right (unnecessary struggling doesn't help rowing, but is necessary for learning that fact). The shadows from the trees protected us from the brilliant sun. Some of the women progressed faster than others, and we were shown different strokes, which we also could not accomplish. For the first time in recent adult memory, I was not frustrated by not getting it right away. I felt comfortable with the trying and happy to be out and doing on this beautiful day on the canal. When it came time to put on our kayaking shirts and do our wet escape from the kayak, I was feeling fearful. The instructor said turn the boat upside down, pull the skirt, push the boat away from our butt, and stand up. Sounds simple, but the decision to actually turn the boat over all strapped in like that made my mind reject the whole idea. So from past experience, I decided to put my mind away and just do it. It was not the most pleasant of my experiences of the day, but I had done it by putting the fear away for just an instant. If we could do that with all of life's events, we would probably experience transcendence and happiness much more often. Janet and Tammy followed suite and did a great job of overcoming their fear of being trapped upside down. We were elated and the paddling now seemed a bit easier. We went up and down the canal shouting encouragement and turtle sightings to each other. It was turning into a great day.

Then the instructors split the group: five going to the river (this included Tammy) and four staying in the canal (this included Janet and me). Janet and I made great progress with the paddling although going straight in boats that are designed to go in circles and turn easily was a challenge to the end. We learned to paddle backwards, two forward strokes, how to turn the boat quickly; and then with great bravery, Janet and I did the hillside slide into the water. We trudged with our boats up a very straight twelve-foot embankment with our boats. Our feet were sliding in the mud and we were grabbing handfuls of grass, but with the instructors help we made it to the top. Then in heroic fashion we plummeted down the slope to the canal water, and for one exciting moment seemed free of time and space as we entered the water like a submarine and came up rejoicing in our ability to overcome fear. I wondered why overcoming fear always seems so rich an accomplishment. Janet had gone first without hesitation. She is a lovely woman. She too is fifty-eight with white silky hair. She is very creative, a bit quiet, but insightful, and seemingly honest with herself. Maybe all women of fifty-eight have reached the point in their lives that allows them to be self-accepting and nurturing as they have been with others all along. We know the how, but sometimes have difficulty finding the direction to self-nurturing. Later Janet and I discussed how lucky we felt to be able to take part in the day's adventures. We also congratulated ourselves in working and staying fit to allow ourselves such freedom. On the way back, we played a game of shark and minnow. Janet was the last minnow and the instructor and I tracked her down and helped her to become a shark like the rest. She had gotten much better at paddling, and we had a hard time trapping her, but we were persistent. Persistency seems to be the greatest skill needed for kayaking.

As Janet and I sat at the water's edge discussing the philosophy of growing old gracefully and having the ability to be free enough to try new stuff, Tammy arrived. She was wet from head to toe, mud in her hair and hate for all outdoors in her heart. The river had proved a trying experience of limited success (in her opinion) and a lot of hard physical work just to survive for a first-time novice kayaker. She approached carrying the stress of the experience in her face and body; and Janet asked her if she had fun. She said: "Look at me Mother, do I look like I enjoyed this. I've just returned from hell; can we just go home now?" Janet and I stood silent as we let Tammy have her moment of physical release. We were all very tired and hungry, but I had not noticed my hunger until Tammy came back unhappy. This seems like more evidence of seeing the world as we are instead of how it truly is. That evidence has come to me more and more of late. That day it made me smile, but not so Tammy could witness it; she was in no mood to be comforted by humor.

We returned our equipment to the trailer and headed for the car for lunch. Food and relaxed laughter about the good and bad of the experiences helped us all recover our good mood of the morning. Even Tammy began to see the humor in her experience. We headed home after lunch full of chatter and hope for another adventure on another day. Because of who we have been, who we are, and who we will become, I have faith that the adventures will be plentiful and rich with wonder. Maybe sea-kayaking next, flatter bottomed boats I've heard! That could help!

Midsummer Night's Musing

It is a curious mix of ages, personalities, appearances, skills, and insecurities. It is backstage opening night; there is fear, excitement, giggling, cockiness, and patience. These people are here with egos that allow them to believe at some level they can bring a character they've never met to life successfully. And yet, there seems to be in these actors a need to be reassured that they can indeed accomplish this task. Many have shared that they are shy without their roles. A small newspaper article about the performance adorns the wall. It seems like early applause; the actors huddle around to drink it in.

"Fifteen minutes," comes the call from the Director. The energy lifts. Some are pacing, some reciting their lines under their breathes, some are reading, some are dancing, and some are sitting in utter and controlled silence. All of them are preparing for "the show" to go on and munching whatever they see that feeds their creative spirit. Each of them at this moment seems separate, but each is aware that he or she needs the other as the play progresses. Words of encouragement and admiration are plentiful.

"Five minutes," comes the call from the Director; the House is open. She alone seems sure of what is to come next. Around the room energy stirs as costumes are adjusted, lines are mimed, nervous jokes are launched, and back pats are exchanged. Being open to this energy brings a heighten awareness of the creativity swirling through the air. One actor talks of his past experiences, another actor speaks of the length of time its been since being on the stage, another actor laughs loudly out of nervousness, or jumps up and down to calm herself. Fairies dance on tiptoes. The children actors are playful and noisy. The adult actors, just as noisy in their own way, attempt to quiet the children. The actors no longer seem separate; they seem equal in a way that seems to brighten them all; faces are radiant all around. The feeling of being supported grows as each small group for each scene begins to gravitate toward one another.

"Places," comes the Director's call. The time has come' *A Play there is...*; *Midsummer Night's Dream* is about to come to life at the Hamner Theatre, and it is a sold-out crowd. Behind each stage entrance, the actors are silently jumping, dancing, shaking their arms, and revving up their energy. This first-scene's energy will set the tone for all that is to come. The actors whisper to each other, "big energy" and giggle softly. And then suddenly, they advance through the curtain to find their audience. The faces in the crowd are as varied as the actors' and expectation and curiosity fill the black box stage.

One scene follows the other; actors come off stage pleased, disappointed, elated, fearful depending on their own judgment of their own performance. Not one word is exchanged that would be critical of another actor; there is only supportive energy to be found. Enthusiasm mounts as the final scene of the Play approaches; they have almost done it! They have collectively brought the words of Shakespeare to life in a way that has never happened before. The audience is laughing and actors are smiling and moving freely about with relief and fatigue. The Director reappears with "congratulations."

Curtain call is at hand; all the hard work and creative energy pours out to a receptive and adoring audience. The Director seems pleased; the Actors grateful! Afterwards it is quieter backstage as actors gather their belongings and head for the lobby and the anticipated appreciation that inspires their performances and feeds their souls. And oh yes, discussions have already begun on how to make tomorrow's performance even better. Directors' and actors' creativity demand the next challenge, the next scene, the next play, the next part, and the next audience.... For them, there is never a final applause! As Shakespeare explains:

> *Ever shall in safety rest*
> *Trip away; make no stay;*
> *Meet me all by break of day.*

The Reunion

It had been a long eight-hour drive, a quick change of clothing with no shower, and a hurried search for the country club—that had changed its name—where the reunion was being held. Not what I had planned or how I had expected to arrive at my 50th High School Reunion, but that was my reality of the moment. The room was filled with senior citizen's I didn't recognize at first glance, but at the registration table a man and woman I would have known anywhere greeted me. Their smiles held warmth and their hands held a goody bag along with a book created with our pictures, past and present. I felt at home. I arrived late and when we were called to sit down, I was left to choose the last table where only one other person was sitting. I knew and loved that person, but I wanted to visit with everyone. I felt my heart react with disappointment that seemed like fatigue. Then the organizer of the reunion, an old and dear close companion during my school years, teased me and said our sitting there would never do. People rearranged their tables so that we could join them. I felt the old relaxation of being home return.

The food arrived as we laughed, talked, teased, and remembered things differently. It tasted so good. A few gifts were exchanged and we laughed and ate some more. As the old 60s music began, we roamed around the room, checking in and reconnecting with those we had known well and those we had only known from a distance. It was remarkable how those "unknown senior citizens" when I entered the room were transformed into the seventeen-year olds I had known so well. It was magical; time vanished and personalities emerged that were familiar and startling at the same time. Each of us had faced challenges, responded to those challenges, and created full and interesting lives. We shared them all and laughed and cried through some. It made me remember how close we had been in that small country school.

As that part of the reunion came to an end, we made plans for the next day. Some of us were going to attend an outing to a historical museum and others were playing golf. I as usual wanted to do both, but had chosen the museum. Having been away for so long, I didn't know where the museum was so one of my classmates offered me a ride. We laughed and remembered that when we both started our first jobs at Wright-Patterson Air Force Base 50 years ago, I had given her one. When I arrived back at my sister's home, I was too excited to sleep so we talked and reviewed my yearbook until 1:00 am—more laughter and more memories. Fun!

The historical museum was interesting, and I learned more than I had ever known about Springfield, Ohio; but more importantly, I learned more about my classmates than I had ever known. We went out for pizza and promised to see each other at the Alumni Banquet later that evening. We were the honored class and planned to give a $1300 scholarship to a young woman; she was planning her studies in deaf education. That afternoon I felt so tired, I fell asleep on the sofa during the short time I had planned to spend with my sisters. They looked at my memory book while I slept; I felt even more at home.

At the Alumni Banquet, I reconnected with students from other classes I had known and not known. At the table we discussed who had changed and who had not. We shared our perceptions of each other then and now. It was surprising for me to hear how differently some saw me and how differently that had been from how I saw and still see myself. I now understand that I was arrogant, beautiful, popular, quiet, serious, playful, funny, smart, athletic, graceful, mean, stubborn, and elegant all at the same time back then. Now, it seems that they see me as relaxed, fun, and still beautiful. What more could a girl want from old friends? What I learned about myself in those conversations is that I am all of those things and none of those things depending on who is looking. I also learned that even in unawareness, I am having an impact on others with my actions and responses to theirs. I also learned how much more comfortable I am in my own skin than I have ever been. The courage to know myself supports my experiences—the fearful ones and the loving ones. Reunions trigger both. The evening ended with hugs intended to send some classmates off on a cruise and hugs for others who were having breakfast together at another of our classmate's homes the next morning.

Arriving late to breakfast, I was greeted with the cheers and warmth of the small group remaining there. My classmate is a fabulous cook; it is her gift. Again as we shared, I learned more about them and more about me. I shared that I was meeting my old boyfriend for dinner, if he chose to show up and that I wasn't sure if he would. We shared our memories of him. I was so excited about reconnecting with him and curious about the fact that he seemed hesitant to commit to the meeting.

As I hugged my classmates for the hundredth time, I could see not only their old personalities but also their beautiful youthful faces surrounded by their current ones. It touched me in a way that felt as if my heart was opening and expanding just a bit more to include this new experience of them and me. I was grateful I had come home for this.

I called my old boyfriend to see if he was coming to dinner. He answered the phone and had been wondering why I had not returned his call. He had left a message on the wrong number and had tried to reach my brother to find me. He sounded nervous. I was grateful that I had followed my instinct to give him one last call. We met for dinner and for me the years of disconnection vanished, and we laughed and laughed and laughed and remembered, and remembered and remembered. He said I was still beautiful and I said he was still funny; I feel both of us were telling our truth for it seemed in that moment we were back to a time when life was still before us and life itself was beautiful and funny. I remembered things he had forgotten and he remembered things I had forgotten. In sharing, we now both have recaptured them. He laughs loud with his whole body just as I remembered him so many years before. He remembered the exact days when we started dating and when we went our separate ways. Life for both of us has held many fearful challenges and loving moments. I feel our retouching helped us to know the benefit and growth that came from all those moments.

I ended my weekend with two of my sisters, one brother-in-law, and one niece. It was Monday morning and yet they made time to share breakfast. One of my sisters and I danced in the parking lot to a song about knowing each other as we truly are, and I felt that we did. I stopped by where my niece works and bought coffee for my trip home. On the street as I was leaving, a young woman in tears approached me and wanted to know if I was going toward Fairborn. I said I wasn't, but could I help? Her car had broken down and she had no money to call someone to meet her children, and she was worried they would arrive home from school to an empty house. She asked for fifty cents to call her neighbor. I gave it to her, sent her in to see my niece to use their phone, and then I did something I would have never done before. I held her quietly until she stopped crying. I felt at home and I could feel her take energy for her journey to hers.

As I drove toward my amazing life in the mountains that I now call home, I knew that the feeling of home is available to me anytime I allow my heart to be open and to be present in the moment. Perhaps that is what reunions bring, a chance to reconnect with what is important within ourselves or at least in this case, me. In reality fifty years is but the blink of an eye.

"Deep Security"

I read a book entitled, *The Age of the Unthinkable*, written by Joshua Cooper Ramo. The book has a political/military bent, which would not normally draw my attention, but since "unthinkable" seemed to call to me and a friend recommended it, I chose to read the book. In the book, Ramo discusses the successes of people who have been able to see what is possible by looking more closely at what actually exists in a way different from what others might be able to see. He talks about seeing beyond the obvious large image in a picture to see what change in the environment might be coming. He talks about a strategy of "deep security" that comes from building an "environmental immune system" that can adapt to the unexpected and unknown much as healthy physical bodies can do. I was intrigued by his discussion of "mash-ups." He describes a musical mash-up as two very different rhythms being combined to make a new and innovative sound. He gave many examples of people who have been able to create innovation in this way—not just in music.

At the same time, I was reading the Shriver Report, *A Woman's Nation*. On the surface, these two writings had little in common. *A Woman's Nation* is a discussion of the history, the present, and the future of women in the workplace, community, faith-based organizations, and at home. It discusses how far women have advanced in the business world and what it has taken to do that. The report compares the needs of our society now, based on this change, with the reality of how the Nation as a whole is currently operating. It seems to conclude that there is a disconnect and that in order to create a more user-friendly world, we need to do the "unthinkable." We need to look beyond the status quo and really see how as a society, we can initiate new models of operation that will help all in our changing society to contribute in whatever way their talents and skills allow.

Combining the essence of these two discussions seemed like an obvious "mash-up" that I could explore further; since both of these ideas seemed to say that when all is connected, whatever the individual parts create, it affects the whole.

During my own self-study with Gary Zukav and Linda Frances during the past eight years, I've come to understand that all living things have a divine connection that is invisible, but that can be accessed. For discussion purposes, I will call it spirit. Getting in touch with this unseen but not unfelt part of myself has enabled me to create "authentic power"[8] or in Ramo's words create a feeling of "deep security." By learning to access my most loving parts even when circumstances outside of myself are difficult, I have created a different kind of "spirit-based immune system" that permits me to "act" within any experience rather than "react" unconsciously to what is happening. It has changed me, and it has changed how I view the world. It has allowed me to see that the world is constantly changing, and those in it are co-creating what we perceive as good and bad experiences. It also allows me to see that the difficult experiences make the most noise, but it also allows me to look beyond the noise. Looking beyond, I can see that the "deep security" I feel within me is quietly invading the writings of the most prominent leaders of our society: politically, militarily, socially, etc. It assures me deep within my own being that the world of my grandchildren will be more harmonious and supportive to all people than the world of my grandparents. To contribute to this transformation, my intention must be to create authentic power rather than to look outside myself for external material power and safety.

It did not surprise me to see that in the *Epilogue* of *A Woman's Nation*, Gary Zukav is quoted as follows:

> *When we align our thoughts, emotions, and actions with the highest part of ourselves, we are filled with enthusiasm, purpose, and meaning,* writes Gary Zukav in his best-selling book The Seat of the Soul. *"When the personality comes fully to serve the energy of its soul, that is authentic empowerment.*

Zukav was a visionary in 1989, and he could see beyond what "was" to what "could be" if we created a "deep security" within our own being. He had begun to see possibility where others had seen difficult experiences and

---

8 Gary Zukav defines "authentic power" in his book, *Seat of the Soul*: "…a power that loves life in every form that it appears, a power that does not judge what it encounters, a power that perceives meaningfulness and purpose in the smallest details upon the Earth."

the dysfunction of our current systems. Now others are not only seeing beyond what is, but are finding the courage to discuss it more openly. I believe that is progress.

In Ramo's book, he quoted the sociologist Immanuel Wallerstein, who has said: *...What we do to others, we do to ourselves.* Ramo adds: *This is as true for good as it is for ill.* Ramo also quotes the American philosopher John David Garcia, who once said *that we should reject the notion that increasing human happiness is the most important goal for society. Far better, he said, to increase human creativity. Happiness will follow.*

Through my own experiences, I have discovered that I am the creator of my own life as well as all actions I choose to take as a response to and with others. What I do individually matters and brings the opportunity to change to others as well as to me. When I am creating authentic power, a power that comes from the divine source within me, I am creating a feeling of wellbeing that cannot be taken from me. The essence of who I am will continue long beyond physical survival in this incarnation. That knowing builds my "spirit-based immune system" and gives me my sense of "deep security." It quiets my fearful thoughts about victimization.

At the end of his book, Ramo asks this question: *This age, what does it demand of me?* The question inspires me to look beyond what is obvious, to see all that is in front of me, and to look deeper and deeper within for my answer, and to trust that it is there!

Gray Thinking: Shifting Perspective After Fifty Five

After attending an Authentic Power Workshop in Ashland, Oregon, I got into a cab with a gentleman over fifty-five. It was 4:30 am and I just wanted to sit quietly and rest. It was the day after the presidential election and the cab driver was eager to talk. He said he was really scared about losing his health benefits, his first amendment rights, having to accept gay marriages, and many other things he saw as his freedom of choice. I asked him if it was possible to be open to seeing a new administration as bringing supportive changes. That really triggered his fear and he shared that all politicians were the same, corrupt, self-serving, and untruthful. I decided to just listen and see what I could learn about me from his sharing. The longer he spoke the more agitated he became. His expression of fear felt much greater than just an impersonal commenting on the state of the country. At one point he said, "Laws are laws, rules are rules, and black and white does not leave room for gray." Again I shared gently that I was beginning to see even in a black and white picture some shades of gray. He bristled again and began to tell me a personal story.

Earlier he had run for mayor of his small town, and he felt he had lost because his opponent and the news media told and printed lies about him and his integrity. I asked him if he could see from his own personal experience that some politicians, namely him, were not dishonest and that perhaps his belief that they were all dishonest could be coming from a fearful place within him. He paused and took a deep breath and then began again to talk and label groups and people from a very judgmental place. He didn't seem open, so I decided to change the subject and said how beautiful Ashland was and how much I loved coming. His demeanor changed and he agreed and shared how much he enjoyed living in Ashland. Then he added a "but." He said, "The people here are nice, but the 'rednecks' that drive trucks and follow too closely behind him really scare him." He was off again into his fearful perspective of the world being an unsafe place with both hidden and obvious dangers.

Later on the plane home I sat by a fifty-five+ woman. I was reading an article by Geoff Olson in which he wrote: *Albert Einstein once said the*

most important question a human being can ask is, 'is the Universe friendly?'
I was considering how I would have answered it when I was younger
and how I would answer Einstein's question now. It was clear that the
woman next to me was in a mood to chat so I chose to listen. She shared
she had been visiting an uncle who was dying from cancer. She said he
was very brave and gave her comfort about the loss of her daughter about
seven years earlier. She went on to say that three daughters and a "dud"
husband survived her daughter. She had fought long and hard to "rescue"
her granddaughters through the courts. She had been successful and now
her granddaughters were what she got up for each morning. She described
how at eight her oldest granddaughter had planned her Mother's funeral.
As they stood by the gravesite, the granddaughter asked, "What now
Granny?" She said she knew in that instance she could not take time to
grieve for her daughter, because her granddaughters would take their cue
from her. She went on to say that she still carried the pain of loss and had
gained a lot of weight, had broken her ankle and hip in a fall; and although
her granddaughters didn't know it, she felt the unfairness of having lost
her daughter too early. She was a hospice caregiver and said she saw the
unfairness of life all the time.

Although I spoke to this woman about how differently I had learned to see
death during the past few years, she seemed unwilling to open to any idea
other than it was her duty to suffer this unfairness and fill her own life with
serving others. The world was unfair and she could not change it.

As I left the plane, I began to consider the sharings of these two people and
to think back on how hard it had been for me to change my perspective
about the difficult experiences of my own life. I began to examine why
and how I had taken a black and white view of the events and when I had
begun to see shades of gray in my thinking. Just accepting that my belief
of how things "had to be or were" could be inaccurate and using that small
glimpse to create a window to see and transform my beliefs had ultimately
changed my life into a more joyful one.

During the last seven years, I have learned through my own experiences
that I have the power to create my life and change my perspective no matter
how old I am. During that examination of my thoughts and the feelings
within my body, I saw myself as a victim of an unfriendly Universe. Little
by little I began to question whether or not my difficult experiences were

what had created the sadness I felt. What I learned was that it was during those difficult experiences that I had grown and changed and had begun to shift my perspective. I began to see that without all those experiences, I would not have arrived at this more joyful place late in my life. I would not have learned that I do not have to live up to someone else's expectations or lock myself into the guilt and failures of not living up to my own. I began to see that the Universe has supported me with the most perfect of experiences based on the choices I have made so far. Now I set my intention to create differently from a place of love instead of fear, to live in the moment and know that things are happening as they should. I am open to seeing each moment and experience differently. I cannot change what I have already created, but now I have an opportunity to add to a collective energy of change that has the potential to change the environment of my grandchildren.

I am over fifty-five and I have an intention to open to all possibilities. I judge what I am experiencing less; I take responsibility for what I feel and think and do. I am choosing to embrace what I call "Gray Thinking." I have a knowing that the Universe is friendly. I want to support others especially those who are over fifty-five to see the possibilities of what they can contribute and create just by shifting their perspectives. I can think of no better way to support my children and grandchildren than to add my joy to the collective energy that surrounds us all. In each moment, it is up to me to decide whether I believe the Universe is friendly or not. That basic choice will create how I see my life and the experiences I co-create.

Fear Is A Choice

Today has many elements that I could choose to fear. Within me there are feelings of betrayal, abandonment, not being valued, and loneliness. My heart is heavy, my stomach feels cramped, my footsteps are slow, and my head wants to bow. Also within me are feelings of understanding, excitement that comes with newness, hope for a new world order, and an unmistakable spark of joy. I sit with a sense of wonder and gratitude that I am a part of a Universe that has comforted and guided me throughout my life even when I lived in unawareness. My choices have not always brought feelings of happiness, but they have always brought learning.

Today as I welcome all the fears that this day has the potential to bring, I will acknowledge them, and then choose to put my attention on the things that bring me joy. I will not allow the shadow of another person's choices to define my day. My life is expanding in many ways, and I want the colors of this new life to be built on a foundation of love and wellbeing that cannot be altered by outside events.

The people that I am drawing to my life are changing. Because my heart is opening and my choices are brighter, I see that spirit reflected all around me even when my personality is not quite in alignment with my soul. I am beginning to see beyond the personalities of those I encounter, and recognize that they too are healing souls. Some are content and some are splintered. Some are troubled and filled with fear. Some have something intangible that sends me a message of something greater than is explainable. I want to have the courage to let my soul make my choices. My fear is well developed, but the love I am discovering within me is a deep well of courage that will help me make choices that produce a meaningful and creative life.

It is a difficult day; my fears are strong. I have a growing pain across my back that brings tears of release to my eyes. They are not tears intended to alter someone else's behavior; they are cleansing tears that lessen my pain and help me to see this glorious winter day before me more clearly. Today I will create a sacred space just for me and allow all my fearful parts to come into my awareness with the intention of complete healing. I do not know what my life experiences are going to be later today or tomorrow, but I have this moment. With the help of the nonphysical guides that come to me through my writing, I will choose to live life without being controlled by my fears.

A Moment's Thought

Let me tell you about an imaginary place I discovered. There is a place I see in my mind. It is warmed with a ray of sunshine; yet cool to the skin like a spring brook. This wonderful enchanted haven is filled with all the shapes, textures, and sensations of our world. One only needs to imagine a feeling and that feeling will become a part of the environment for you. Imagine, for example, a spring rain on a warm summer day, a cold winter breeze filled with moisture, or the wetness of a snowflake as it melts upon your tongue. There are no buttons to push, no money to spend; the only requirement is a moment's thought. Imagine one thought and you can be in a lush green garden with a weeping willow fanning your face and the smell of fresh rain beads upon the grass. Blink your eyes, and you can experience first hand the rough surface of a western mountain range as you look down on clouds that mask the summit and your sorrow. You cautiously reach out your hand and the cloud caresses you with the promise of tomorrow. Perhaps you need only, just for a moment, the comfort of an old familiar room; believe it with your heart and it is with you.

Imagine through your memories a cashmere sweater your Mother once wore, and you are touched with its gentleness and her essence. You suddenly smell a woodworking shop that reminds you of a special contentment during your youth. It is filled with the smoothness of the small wood shavings that cling between your toes and warm your soul. Who could resist the feel of silk passing across your body? That feeling could be yours with only a whim. This loving magical world can ring you with happiness, because the hug of a friend will surround you just because it is desired. Loneliness will be replaced with the musical laughter of children, the bold yipping of puppies, the whistles of trains, or the sweet cooing of a new borne baby. Whisper a wish and the tender sighs and burning passions of lovemaking exists here in my mine's eye for everyone. Anyone, in this extraordinary place can create a unique utopia or some will call it heaven. Can your mind dare to imagine such a place?

Being A Child

The feeling of rain on a warm summer day is sometimes a way for making the heart laugh. Rain like life is always viewed with the mood and feelings we bring to it. With laughter, the gray sky fills with the colors of the flowers on the ground, the flash of brightness from passing cars, and the green of the earth. When we face that same gray sky with a heavy heart of sadness, the heaviness of it presses down upon us like lead.

How strange and miraculous is the working of the human mind. The powerfulness of our thoughts can paint a world of both darkness and clarity.

It had been a long time since my days had been filled with the laughter and squeals of children. Then I saw and heard her there at the store's piano, so very tiny. She was creating uneven tones of a piano concert with small hands eager to try something new. She didn't seem to mind the rain outside the window. She reminded me of the promise of a future ahead if the courage could be found to not stand-in-place or become lost in unsupportive thoughts too long. In other words, find the courage to live with the wonder and acceptance of a child!

There can be no growth without the willingness to step-off-the-rock; take a risk; make music only our hearts can appreciate! But, once that courage is ours so is the experience of a full and productive existence. I had forgotten the magic of being a child and of creating such sweet sounds of music on a rainy day.

Defining Harmony

I am finally ready to write about creating harmony. As I do, I speak of myself in the third person because in so many instances that's how I see myself. There is a part of me that wants harmony and love in my life, and another part of me that wants others (and myself) to behave in a way that fulfills my expectations, and a third part that is the observer of all my parts. So I felt that I could not write about harmony when I was so out of harmony within myself. So I postponed writing and continued to focus on defining internal harmony. The goal at first seemed to be to eliminate my unwanted conflicts of behavior. Over time the goal became to accept the disharmony. Finally, it has been the discovery that harmony is not going to be found in my head.

Here I am writing about harmony without a clear vision of what I will write. The harmony I need within me is acceptance of the personality that my soul has chosen, a vision of what I have come in this Earthsuit to heal, and an intention to acknowledge that all the experiences within this existence are designed for my learning and healing. During the last few days, I have realized that for the last five years I have been attempting to heal by eliminating all the parts of myself that do not seem worthy of existence. Many times I have intellectually stated this intention without really understanding from my soul that I was attempting to eliminate a fearful part of me that my soul had earlier chosen in order to support my healing and existence.

This morning as I sat in meditation and looked at harmony in a different way, I felt such peace as I surrendered to the fact that my personality was and is a part of this Earthsuit, and my soul is the love that must take charge of my choices. One of those choices is to understand that healing does not mean that I will never be in conflict or that I will never be angry, or sad, or joyful, or excited, or goal focused, or repentant, or self-absorbed, separate, jealous, or judgmental. I will continue to some degree to have all of these parts. Also I know that I have great love and gratitude for the opportunities my personality has brought into my life. More and more each day, I understand my power to create my life; as that understanding grows and becomes responsible choice, my creation is more and more filled with love and less and less filled with fear. Harmony no longer means the absence of conflict within others or myself; harmony now means that I stay within my soul's truth as I create my life. If I am angry, I will feel it; if I am joyful, I will feel it; if I am judgmental, I will acknowledge it; if I feel loving, I will trust it. When these emotional states are present, I will make a responsible choice to act differently than I've reacted before. If I can't do this in every moment, I will be grateful for the opportunity to learn that I cannot. My intention remains to heal completely; I do not have to set a deadline to race against. This intention for complete healing is a part of my being, as well as my intellect. It's been a "good" morning.

Non-Physical Guides and Teachers

I want to express my thoughts about my non-physical guides and teachers. They do not take on any sort of physical form even in my mind, their messages come in a sudden knowing that there is some action I need to take or avoid. This knowing comes from deep inside me unannounced and without doubt of its correctness. It comes through the voice of a trusted friend's advice or an interaction with someone that I do or do not admire. The messages come when my mind becomes very still as I face a decision in my life. The knowing is rarely as dramatic as others describe theirs, although a few times in my life I have created the voice and image of a past loved one to assist me. Whether or not these appearances in my mind were real or created by my longing for them doesn't seem to matter. Their voices brought with them the wisdom for responsible choice.

Today as I heard others' questions about connecting to non-physical guides and teachers, I felt a knowing that I must listen closely to the answers that came from them. So I did and in that listening, I heard that it doesn't matter where or how we gain our guidance, the answer is to be open to it and trust that within ourselves we have the answers for our lives. On the difficult days as I struggle with my decisions and make the best choices that I can, the voices may be very soft and my need for stillness even greater in order to gain the strength I need to make a responsible choice. Some days I am more capable of listening than others, but the knowing that comes with attention to my deepest self is always there waiting for me when I am ready to hear. During the last week, my guides have had the sounds of the collective voices of those I love; I am filled with gratitude for this opportunity to share and revere our perceived weaknesses and strengths; so often they seem the same.

The Healing of Jealousy

If philosophers are right and opportunities for healing are created in order to facilitate that healing, I must come to recognize the behavior pattern that is associated with any feeling that propels me into an unhealthy, unloving behavior. Once the unhealthy behavior in need of healing is known by me, I must change how I behave when that feeling arises. Until I can step back from an unwanted behavior, declare that it is unwanted, and discover its origin, the same opportunity to heal will be created over and over. Once I recognize, challenge, and then respond in a more loving way, I will begin to change the unhealthy behavior and heal. With healing comes peace and diminished experiences of the painful consequences of the behavior.

An unhealthy emotional behavior that needed healing in my life was jealousy. I knew it was unwanted, I had told myself many times it was unwanted, and I could go for long periods of time without it being apparent; then boom, there it was back. When I got comfortable with the idea that there had been some healing, I fell back into my familiar old pattern. My emotional dysfunction and my soul's purpose seemed to be in conflict. I wondered if my soul's purpose could grow stronger over time? If it could, would I ever declare victory and be permanently healed and move on in wisdom instead of pain? It seemed like an exploration of what had first triggered my jealousy could support my healing.

As a small child, I adored my brother and followed him everywhere. He had been sickly early in life and my father had been away in World War II. My Mother's time was consumed by the needs of her children, with my brother's illness seemingly the greatest need. As a child, I believed that my mother loved him more; it was not a good feeling. My brother could do all the things that I found most interesting better than I could; I loved him and tried to emulate him. I was two-years younger than he and most of the tests I presented to myself were physical accomplishments, so I had little chance of success. Without recognizing it as such at the time, I felt pride in him and jealousy of him simultaneously. When we went off to school, things changed because I was a better student. We shared a classroom for years where comparisons were made. All of a sudden, the teachers openly favored me. My love of learning and my ability to achieve seemed to give me favored status with my Dad as well. Oh what a great feeling that was as a child of five or six. Although, I felt badly for my brother, favored status was nice and I grew to like it. I believe being favored became one of my very early life's intentions. The stage was set for experiences that could support spiritual growth if I chose, or I could choose to react inwardly to the pain of perceived injustices. I have done both.

I have known that I could accomplish what I set out to accomplish if I was willing to work toward it. It was a stabilizing and good quality. I do not believe that my efforts were for favored status only, but often favored status was the result. Over the years, my self-worth rose and fell with perceived favored status. I could not be second best; so when someone else achieved favored status, jealousy reared its ugly head. The more deeply I cared for another person, the more deeply I felt the pain of jealousy. I successfully pushed it away and did not act on it often, but there were times when the feeling of being "less than first" was overwhelming. When it was, I became angry, hurtful, confrontational, and sometimes an emotional outburst would leave me shaken. When it did, I felt shame; picked up the pieces and again resolved to do better. But deep inside, I wanted the person involved to declare me special, more special than any other. Jealousy was self defeating and irrational, and I did not want it to be a controlling emotion in my life. There was a part of me that wanted it resolved permanently and another part of me that knew it was an old, familiar, and practiced personality pattern designed to get what I wanted—favored status. It also brought with it a great deal of emotional pain and separation from others.

I have worked long and hard to know all the fearful parts of my personality, to develop emotional awareness, to make informed conscious choices, and to change what I create in my life. Anis Nin said, *There came a time when the risk to remain tight in the bud was more painful than the risk it took to blossom.* When the pain of staying becomes greater than the fear of the unknown, change occurs.

Because I could no longer remain in the pain of jealousy and create a joyful life, I chose to change. I have come to know through experience that my sense of worth can only come from within me, and who I am is enough. I understand that jealousy came with me into the Earthschool and its healing is part of my journey toward wholeness. I have made great progress, and now I can authentically cheer the accomplishments of others. Yeah me!

My First Home Alone

Many years ago, my first home alone was a small apartment that I rented. I will never forget my first entrance into the hall after the apartment manager gave me the key. It was so still as I turned the key in the lock, and the hinges squeaked and groaned to announce their displeasure at being bothered. The door did, however, yield to my push. I stepped inside, into an empty entry hall. The walls had been newly painted and I reached out to touch them. They were dry, cold, and smooth against my hand. I remember that I was so exhausted. The pain of the two weeks before had taken my energies. As I walked toward the empty living room, my drooping shoulders seemed to lighten, and I knew I brought only me into this small packet of emptiness. Moving through my small place, I felt free of many of the stresses that had haunted me during the last few years. A new start would begin in this empty place, and I could feel it coming. The floor was newly waxed, but old and uneven, and I tried to imagine how my furniture would look. I arranged and rearranged my thoughts. It occurred to me then, as it sometimes does now, freedom can be so quiet and yes sometimes daunting.

The trees outside my French door, above my miniature balcony waved and called to me to step outside. It was March, but there was a hint of warmth in the breeze that touched my skin. It seemed to promise me so much, but I didn't know what avenue was promised. Happiness and laughter filled that apartment at first, followed with weeks of loneliness and fear. The growth and knowledge of the experience to enter and then the experience to leave that small place stays with me. My new apartment, very much like the first, but filled with reality instead of only dreams is a more balanced and stable place. The closeness of the walls reminds me of the need to expand my inner awareness instead of my material belongs. The lessons have opened my life. The lessons have taught me to take risks and to reach out to life, to give myself room to fail, to pick myself up, and to reach out again and again to find the best in every day.

Moving Thoughts

Slowly my mind becomes aware of morning. I open my eyes to a room that has become more than familiar; yes a part of my very being. For it was here inside these walls that I learned to laugh and cry; in fact, feel for myself. This small, quiet place is where I grew up. The sounds here are unique. The people noises are muffled, but distinct and recognizable. They come from people who are steeped in routine so that their daily movements are predictable. They add to my longings sometimes, but mostly they comfort me as I snuggle down cocooned under my layer of blue down.

Music, low and far away, comes to me first from a radio topped by a stuffed bear that was given to me with love from a special friend. Each morning I am touched by the memory of receiving it and holding it close. It filled that morning with laughter, and I named it Giggles. Memory laced with intermittent music floats over my head as I resist waking. I have never been a morning person.

Slowly I become aware of my surroundings. A sign over my closet reminds me to "hang loose." So I try as I stretch and my hands brush the smooth pine of my big cannonball poster bed. My husband and I saved for months so I could have a bed that reminded me of my grandmother's. Like Grandma's, mine is high off the ground, but mine is not a feather bed. I think of her and the love she shared with me. She is a part of me as surely as I am a part of my children.

At the foot of the bed is the soft blue and white blur from the afghan that my sister spent hours making. It came to me at work and filled that day with a special kind of sweetness. It reminds me of a more troubled time when we held each other close for support. She doesn't know how important her love is to me, but I do.

And then as if by magic, he enters my mind before I am quite awake, and the thought warms my body for he too has become a part of this private place. His gifts are everywhere, a card, a duffle bag, a teddy bear, a piece of jewelry, a small shell. They all claim their space. His place is stillness deep inside me, and I treasure him there as I plot my life from day to night. I'm glad for his love, but I'm able to stand-alone probably for the first time.

My eyes are open now, and the urge to move comes slowly. I hear the birds outside my window and know I will soon miss their music. The air conditioner hisses and announces its power to cool, the thud of the paper being delivered resounds from the front door, a car engine turns over as someone leaves for work, doors open and close often as the inhabitants of this place go out into their world.

My deep sleep has left me woozy as it always does, but renewed. I'm fully awake. My love poem captured forever by a loving friend in cross-stitch hangs above my head. Yes, that's my jewelry box, my jeans hanging on the door, my cobweb in the corner, my pillow covers I made myself years ago, my needlepoint pillow, my children's picture on the dresser, my handmade shell box designed by my daughter, and a soccer ball candle given to me by my son. Sadness comes to me as I thank of my losses born of my need to explore a different life. I love this small, quiet place. How can I leave? It represents my newfound self-contained security and freedom. Thoughts invade uncontrolled, and jump from memory to memory. Everything in this room holds a piece of my soul. Be it good or bad, I want to hold on to all these pieces.

Suddenly, I smile and a new idea makes its way into my brain as my feet touch the carpet that we installed together. Now I laugh out loud for none of the things that I use to support me are really a part of these four walls. They actually reside inside me, and I will carry them with me no matter where I go. The walls will change. I will change and continue to grow. My memories are unchanging and they are mine forever. I guess I'm ready to move; the wonder of a new day has touched me quietly.

Ageless Athlete

If you are a female and was borne in the 1940's, you'll understand me when I tell you women of that era rarely became athletes, great or otherwise. You'll also recognize the phrase, "I'm just not coordinated enough to play sports." You remember that being a sports nut was not the feminine thing to do. And, if you did go against what was expected of the "weaker sex," you probably played volleyball, slow pitch softball, or six-member team basketball. At times, your gender may have been questioned openly. That's a different story. Let's get back to six-member-team basketball. That was an experience that would make today's young female athletes gag in revulsion. The area of the floor was divided into two halves with three forwards on one end and three guards on the other for each team. No one crossed that centerline! Each player was allowed three dribbles and then they were forced to stop immediately and either pass or shoot. Do you have any idea how far out you still were from the basket? The modern day "lay-up" was not in the realm of possibilities. Running end-to-end of the floor like the "guys" would have been much too strenuous for our "weaker" sex. We wouldn't have had the stamina, and we might have injured our dancing feet.

Those of us from the 40's who dared to chase our older brothers around were known as the "tomboys" of the neighborhood. Our friends and families whispered when we came near about us "growing out of this phase." It has come as quite a shock to some that at 42, I am still going strong in a phase I hope will last forever. It hasn't always been easy though.

A few years ago I decided as an ageless athlete of 35 to take up one of Northern Virginia's booming sports, Soccer. I phoned the local league representative to find out what I had to do to get on a team. She said, "How long have you played?" I said, "I never have." I heard the young woman suck in her breath and suppress a giggle. I guess being 35 and starting a new sport seemed a little unusual to someone who had used a soccer ball for a pillow seat since birth, but I was determined. She said, "You'll have to start in the white, beginner's division and the new team forming needs an organizer." You guessed it. Me! I wanted to play, so I felt I had no choice but to agree.

I'll never forget that first practice. It was raining, but we were undaunted. We showed up at the park not knowing what to expect; all ages and sizes, but no skills. One of the women brought her husband along as the coach. He threw the balls out on the grass and for the next hour we all worked diligently to bring our foot back then forward and make contact with the ball in front of us. It was required for us to breath during this process, and most of us were so out of shape that breathing became gasping for air; back to the kicking of the ball. This was not an easy task. Other people's feet and ankles seemed to bounce around and get in the way. If you can imagine an ostrich kicking a pumpkin while standing perfectly erect, you can picture how most of us looked that day trying to kick a soccer ball. We hardly heard the coach say, "You'll get better. The only way from here is up." We couldn't hear because our ears were experiencing ringing sensations. If we had heard him clearly, we would not have been as sure as he that improvement was going to be possible. Bruised shins hurt!

We were even less sure of our capacity to improve the following morning when we tried, unsuccessfully in some cases to get our aching bodies out of bed. No one warned us that the back of your neck could get sore from kicking a soccer ball. The pain in the neck might have come from standing bent over at the waist looking at our feet as we swung and missed, swung and missed. If you think that isn't possible, try it.

Seasons have passed and we've all moved on to other teams. Some because we've improved remarkably to the point where we needed to play with more skilled players for challenge. Some because we will never get any better, but we just can't admit it and so we have moved from team to team to keep our self-delusion in tact.

As an ageless athlete, borne in the 40's, I find it uncanny that I can now do all the things those adults said I couldn't do as a kid. I have this overwhelming desire to take out an ad in the local school paper which reads: *Wanted: Freedom to run as far and as fast as I want. Woman who was restricted from running the length of a basketball court as a child can successfully run six miles as an ageless athlete of 42, and she demands an explanation!* The kids wouldn't understand my outrage, but a few old decrepit gym teachers just might.

If you are one of those women who has been standing on the sidelines of sporting events watching husbands, friends, and children playing, and then lamenting, "I'd love to play, but I'm uncoordinated," S T O P, SAY THAT NO MORE! Pick up the closest ball, buy a pair of running shoes, climb a hill. You'll be surprised how easy it is and how great you'll feel doing it instead of making excuses. You'll start to get fit. Your friends will look and ask about how you've changed. You might even get a whistle now and then. Would that be bad? Most surprisingly of all, you'll like yourself better than you ever thought you could. In a matter of months, you will transform from an "aging woman" into an "ageless athlete."

Dreams and Reality

When I was a young girl, I dreamed of traveling to the wonderful places I read about. The visions were so real that I just knew they would become the realities of my adult life if I just believed.

One flight into fantasy took me on board a romantic cruise ship. My plan was to be 27 years old and take this amazing cruise all over the world. The trip would last a complete year. It would be filled with romantic adventures one after the other. The man of my dreams would emerge, and dancing under the stars, surrounded by the waves of the ocean, overcome by the music of Beethoven, we would kiss. He would be beautiful, embodying all the virtues of the perfect man: good looking, but not to pretty; glowing with warmth but not too flashy; obviously gentle, but never feminine. He would hold me as if I were fragile, but knowing because of my need to be independent that he could not hold me too tightly. Of course, in my fantasy, we would marry on board ship. Flowers from around the world would decorate our marriage alter. They would be of every color and hue. My "perfect stranger" would see them and compare their color to my brightness and for him the flowers would pale in comparison. We would travel the world together always in complete agreement as to what would hold importance for the two of us. A child's fantasy, yes. But when I was thirteen, it seemed possible. I still dream of travel.

After The Storm

The air is hot and heavy so I choose to walk instead of run to dispel the sadness that has overtaken me since I heard he is leaving. He is going again. The daisy I picked says he loves me and I try to believe, but this emptiness seems overwhelming. His comings are like a storm; the quiet anticipation followed with anxiety and stillness. There are many clouds left hanging, but will they bring the fury of another storm or pass over and be harmless?

The darkness gathers, thunder rolls, and he like the storm comes unannounced into my life. Like the storm lifting me and other things in his path. The height of his storminess is unexplainable. I soar with him among the clouds and touch the sky knowing it is not reality, but a dream carried on the wind. But, I forget in the midst of the dream and want to cling to him in flight forever. Inevitably the rain begins soft and slow and then hurls itself among the treetops, and the wind that he creates leaves me destined for a fall back to the earth.

At first, I catch a rainbow and hang on, but like the storm the rainbow fades away and I am left with no place to go, seemingly unable to fly without the wind from the storm. On my way back to earth, I slow my descent with a wayward branch, a spark of light, a leafy treetop, so my crash is never fatal. There I am bruised, but safely back on the ground, surrounded by the litter of the storm. A twig scampers, a leaf winds its way to the grass, which is dewy with raindrops. It is very still, but cooler. Except for an occasional rustle in the trees, it is as if the storm has never come.

A residue of sadness remains after the excitement of each storm.

Fear After 9/11

Fear can be a source of great energy that calls us to act or a source of paralyzing energy that makes us hide. It can create an adrenaline rush that alters our world forever regardless of how we use it. The tragedies of the last few weeks have disrupted our illusion of control over the events of our lives. Each of us is fearful and sometimes it is difficult to know with certainty what will trigger the feeling. Some are afraid of what we know; some are afraid of what we don't know. We fear for our safety, we fear being alone, we fear large crowds, we fear darkness. I believe the basic fear residing in all of us is fear of "losing control." The ultimate lose of control is death of our physical bodies.

Why do we need such control? Why do some of us need control so much more than others? Have we lost touch with our faith in the "natural order of things?" Do we see ourselves as separate and apart from a universal purpose? Are we afraid that the universal force most of us call God is not capable of supporting us in achieving the ultimate knowledge living is to bring? How can we use this fear to promote learning for us individually and collectively? These are rhetorical questions to help generate thoughts and feelings; I do not have answers. What I do have is a growing faith that the events that bring us fear also bring us our greatest learning. Each of us must use the energy generated out of our fear to reflect, to discover, and then begin to learn our intended lesson. Fear is not the absence of courage; it is the energy source that has the potential to produce courageous acts.

A courageous act could be a father of four deciding to leave a job he hates. A courageous act could be a woman accepting that her marriage will not get better and moving on. A courageous act could be to tell someone you need him or her. A courageous act could be going into a burning building to attempt to save a stranger or friend's life. A courageous act could be to unlock our doors and have faith that our children will be safe in our own backyards. A courageous act could be to champion a friend even though it will make us unpopular. A courageous act could be to tell your boss you disagree with his treatment of others. The list is endless and happens every day somewhere in the world. When we face our fears somehow they lose their power over us. It is not easy; if it were, we would not need courage.

I believe that every living thing has a purpose and a place; that all events ultimately achieve a universal good. I have seen that a sunflower cannot easily thrive in the shade for that is not its purpose; and a weeping willow must have room to spread its roots so that it can provide shade for that is its purpose. The decisions we make to act or not may make it harder or easier to achieve our purpose, but in the end our deepest intention will be served. If we could overcome our fear and the need to control our very existence, to listen quietly and calmly to our inner voice, and to trust that it is our hearts not our minds that tells us our truth, if we could believe that the things we perceive as bad may bring us a better understanding of who we are to become, we might naturally create an environment that would nurture us to live happier more fulfilling lives.

When we are harmed, we must become more alert to the danger, but we must not hide from the experience. We must become more open to the experience so that we can learn. As all of us find strength to go on with our lives, maybe we need a new bumper sticker that defines the acronym FEAR. Maybe it should be Free, Eager, Aware, and Resolute. It will not give us control, but it may inspire us to courageous acts and enrich the quality if not the length of this life.

Intuitive Thought Creates Access

As I am meditating this morning, I have what seems like an inspired thought about the intuitive intellect of the human species. I recognize it, because when I'm in the groove and close my eyes, I see purple surrounded by light. I decided to entertain the possibility that through our intuitive thought the human species—with the help of divine intervention—has created a model of our spiritual universal connection within the physical realm. I am speaking about the modern technology all around us that seems to work without any visible connection, but allows us to connect with others all over the country, earth, and Universe. This information system is dependent on the energy currents that swarm around us all the time. I'm talking about the wireless telephone.

I am reminded of the energy currents that flow in and out of the body all the time. We can't see them. Sometimes we don't even know they are there; we often don't know how to tune in; and so we stay separated from the wholeness of our soul. Much like the wireless phone is the connecting instrument within our wireless information system, the heart is the wireless spiritual universal connection. The ability to connect is within and around us on the existing energy currents, but if we don't understand the operating system, we remain isolated and seemingly alone. We know the wireless phone exists; we know the heart exists; we don't always know how to access the energy currents that feed them. If it's the use of the wireless phone we need, we ask for instruction, read the manual, and practice connecting. If it's the heart, emotional awareness must become the instruction. We can ask for guidance from other sources—physical and nonphysical—but ultimately access comes only through knowledge and practice of using our own specific unique emotional system.

After we learn how to access our emotions, we come to a more difficult part. Do we choose to tune in and connect, or do we hit the OFF button when the energy currents are disruptive to the status quo? Do we access a strong current in an inappropriate way or at an inappropriate time, or do we control our buttons from within to create harmony, sharing, cooperation, and reverence for life? Conscious choices of how to use our intuitive thought as well as our technical information systems help us to create the desired experiences of our lives. It connects us to the present moment without fear and gives us authentic power.

Large Block Letters

A few days ago a friend, "Melissa from Connecticut," gave me a small book; she said to help me dream. I had forgotten that I had asked her to do that. Today as I flew back home, I finally really received "Melissa's small gift." Earlier I had opened and then closed the small book quickly because "JESUS CHRIST" was in large block letters on one of the first few pages. I grimaced because I had run away from my family for years because of just those words. The same old fear of limitations clutched at my chest—could I never be free of them? A day later, I picked the small book up again and read a short passage that sat quietly under JESUS CHRIST; it was from another book, *The Garden of Good and Evil*. It said: *When you play songs, you can bring back people's memories of when they fell in love. That is where the power lies.* I loved that. So I thought I might read the little book after all, but later.

Later came today as I waited for my flight. So engrossed was I in the words from the *Bible* that I missed the call for my plane. Then the public address system shouted, "Would Gardner P please report to the gate for boarding." I jumped up and bolted the 15 feet to the gate; the small book in my hand.

As the stewardess spoke with unusual humor about the boredom of what she had to repeat day after day, I went back into the small book. The words quoted from the *Bible* were ones I had never heard, and I found them beautiful and compelling. They spoke of a Mother's love, and pieces of the human personality were described as pieces of a quilt. There were also other quotes that I have loved for a long time scattered among the *Bible* verses. Marcus Aurelius wrote, *The soul is dyed the color of thoughts.* There was a verse about prayer (from Ephesians 6:18) that echoed my own thoughts about to whom a person should pray: *Don't worry about finding the perfect words for your final prayer tonight. Fall asleep remembering to pray in the Spirit on all occasions with all kinds of prayers and requests.* And then another: *What has God saved you from? What does he still need to save you from?* (Exodus 15:15). And the words of John Bunyan started Chapter 2: *The best prayers have often more groans than words.*

So grateful was I for this small book of light. I closed my eyes to feel the wonder of the moment. I thought about how fearful I had been of the vengeful God of my youth, and how that fear had kept part of the messages and the wisdom within the Bible from reaching me. Suddenly some intuitive thought told me to open my eyes. As I did, I saw an Alaskan Airline plane framed in my small oval window. On its tailfin was a painting of a man with horns; it looked like the "devil" of my youth. So startled was I that I continued to stare; it was not horns at all; it was white fur inside of dark fur surrounding the face of a broadly smiling Eskimo. How could I have not seen such a beautiful smile? The lines in the tailfin of the plane divided the white fur from the black and made it appear pointed and horn-like to the scared child within me. Immediately I truly knew that there is no "devil without," it is the "devil of fear within" that threatens a joyful life. But I am not JUST that FEAR! As "Melissa from Connecticut" stated in her wonderfully written new child's book, *I AM SOOOOO MUCH MORE THAN THAT! I am a worthy human soul.* Now I must set an intention to look long enough at my "devil of fear within" to give recognition to my song and my memory of self-love.

I still do not accept that Jesus Christ is the only Path to God, but I can certainly hear a biblical song and take comfort from the inspired wisdom that his life co-created upon the Earth.

Thank you for your small gift of dream light "Melissa from Connecticut."

Sixty-Six Reasons For Gratitude

In a book called *A Whole New Mind*, the author, Daniel Pink, suggested that on each birthday, it was supportive of happiness to make a gratitude list of the same number of things as years lived. This resonated with me, and I began the process of selecting the items for my gratitude list because my 66th birthday was right around the corner.

It seemed like an easy and joyful exercise as I began: Daughter, son, two grandchildren, son-in-law, three sisters, brother, Mother, Father, old friends, new friends, etc. As the list grew, I began to judge my gratitude and debate within me if I really felt gratitude or if I was just adding them to the list because it seemed appropriate. I asked myself—if the list was just for me and what I felt grateful for, why would I censor and/or judge the list? This gave me my "Ah Ha moment" of the week: I was judging my capacity to appreciate the beauty that has been and is my life, and at the same time, ranking the people and experiences of my life as to their worthiness of my gratitude.

I also realized that I had a secret that a fearful part of my personality attempts to hide from my soul and others, which keeps me separate from my wholeness. During an authentic power workshop, many people seemed to have "secrets" they wanted to share. Each time they did, I felt pain in my heart and solar plexus, but didn't understand what that pain in me represented. Each time someone shared, my thoughts went to Greg, my deceased son. Each time I asked for clarity and nothing came. The last meeting of the workshop, I remembered an experience I had with Matt, my grandson. I had persuaded him at the age of four to go out with me to play in the rain. He didn't want to go, but as I urged him to put out just a toe, then a foot, then both arms, he eventually eagerly jumped wholeheartedly into the rain shower. His eyes shined, we danced in circles, he splashed his feet in puddles, and he fell in love with the experience of the rain. He wanted to climb a tree, but it was time to go back inside—he didn't want to go, but it was getting cold and I wanted too. When we arrived inside, Matt's mom and dad met us at the door with towels and laughter. They had been watching us play through the window. As they rubbed Matt dry, a big tear appeared in each of his eyes. He said, "I wanted to stay in the rain and climb the tree, but Grams said no." Mike, my son-in-law, explained that there was a time to enjoy the rain and a time to get dry. One of the giant tears in Matt's eye spilled over on to his cheek and he said, "But Dad, I really, really, really wanted to play in the rain."

As I remembered my experience with Matt, I asked what that had to do with my reaction to others sharing their secrets at the workshop. I felt the tear in the corner of my eye, and I remembered something I had really, really, really wanted, but did not get. Greg's birth and death felt very much the same to me, and I felt grateful for the experiences his life had brought to mine. I wrote about them, I repeated them; I resisted the need to question why things had turned out as they did, and I went on with life. A woman, whose son had died, was just a part of who I was. When others spoke of their sons, I turned a deaf ear and consoled myself with other thoughts. I sometimes felt pain, but mostly justified in my mind the disconnection I created from others' joy.

Lately, many experiences have triggered my sense of loss of Greg's physical life, and it has become harder and harder to resist the pain I have felt deep inside of me. The answer to my question about the shared secrets came from my memory of Matt's disappointment. The secret I resisted hearing from me, was that I wanted Greg to live a long physical life, but he did not; but I really, really, really wanted him too!

As I began my gratitude list, I felt that I had uncovered yet another secret that brought with it the pain of deep shame and unworthiness. I realized that a small fearful part of me really had not wanted him to live ill. I had supported him emotionally, physically, and economically for a long time, and I was very tired. I was unsure if I had the strength to continue to support his intention to heal. When the nurse at the hospital told me she had opened the window of Greg's room so his spirit could fly, what I felt more than anything else was relief. Intellectually I can justify this relief; but in my heart, it feels small and self-serving for a Mother to feel relief at the death of her child. How on this soon to be 66th birthday, could I find gratitude for that experience?

Then I read a quote this morning, and I also heard it clearly. It sounded like what I imagine the voice of compassion would sound like if I could hear it. It was the gentle wise voice of a woman expressed with the tender unfiltered caring of a child. The answer to my question came through this quote from Tenzin Gyatso: *If you wish to experience peace, provide peace for another.*

I plan to continue my *Sixty-Six Reasons for Gratitude* list until my birthday. I intend to include without judgment or analysis everything for which I feel the slightest amount of gratitude. Prominent on that list is my gratitude for my human experience of having a personality that will continue to contribute to what I really, really, really intend for my life: to do my best to appreciate all the experiences I co-create—large and small, painful and joyful—and to align my personality with the needs of my soul.[9]

The first thing on my *Sixty-Six Reasons for Gratitude* list is rain, the second is butterflies.

May all people find peace in our gratitude this Thanksgiving.

---

9   Gary Zukav suggests in his book, *Seat of the Soul*, that the authentic needs of the soul are "harmony, cooperation, sharing, and reverence for life."

Feelings About Valentine's Day

Today is a declared holiday. It is a time when romantic love takes center stage. Those "in love" give flowers and candy and declare undying affection to their current Valentines. It is a time when those who are "not in a romantic relationship" can choose to feel alone and abandoned. I have been both on numerous occasions.

This Valentine's Day brings new awareness to me. Instead of pretending this is just another unnecessary commercial holiday, which sooths the fear within me, I have decided to look at all the different types of love that illuminate my life: old friends, new friends, family, experiences in nature, wisdom from a divine source, precious books, imagination, living in the country, favorite old shirts, souvenirs of past experiences, memories, writing, reading poetry, amazing health, appreciation of this day, dreams of tomorrow, and on and on. The list is endless.

What feels most important is appreciation of this day. More and more the wisdom of living in this moment becomes clear to me. It sustains me to remember that difficulty is hidden in moments of ecstasy, and learning and future joy hides in the shadows of dark moments. How could a physical life, focused on existence, be otherwise? Death of the body awaits us all. So many experiences in life come suddenly without warning and my purpose is to respond to them from the healthiest part within me. As I gaze backward into my patterns of pain, I see clearly that it was my responses that kept me in suffering. As I gaze backward into the magical happy experiences of my life, I see clearly that wanting them to be permanent has kept me in suffering.

Today the sun is out after weeks of snowy weather. The birds and animals outside my window go from here to there and back. The clouds flow above with the lightness of feathers. The trees cast their shadows. The wind sings a song through my chimes. My house fills with the sweet smells of food cooking. My mind feels still and patient. My heart feels open and receptive to whatever this day brings. I've sent my love of many colors out into the world. In the silence of this moment, it returns to me a hundred fold, and I am filled with gratitude for this life—on this day—in this moment.

May all beings know a deep and enduring peace, may all beings awaken and be free.

Meditation Dialogue

I have been reading *Tomorrow's God* by Donald Neale Walsch, and perhaps that is why my meditation experience is full of questions for my own Divine Presence. As I struggle to quiet my mind and come into the present moment again and again the question, "What is my purpose?" passes through. I acknowledge it and let it go only to have it return after a few moments. I let it go again. It returns again. I begin to have a dialogue with myself that does not feel very loving. "What is wrong with you today; why can't you just be here; why can't you let go of the mental chatter; why, why, why?"

As I give up and start to end my meditation, the question alters and becomes, "What is the purpose of that?" I surrendered to this question—if I end this session of meditation, I will avoid the original question that is returning and returning, because I feel I have asked it so many times and that no answer has ever come. Usually the question brings just a vague feeling within me about writing and that I should be writing. I love to write and do often, but I am often unsure as to what significance my writing has in my life. I question if what I write can possibly serve others. I've attempted to write books; I've attempted to get published. That is not why I write. I've continued to write about what I see, only because I see it."

With that thought the original question surfaces yet again, "What is my purpose?" I just let it be here: repeating, repeating, and repeating. I do not seek an answer nor resist the question being here. I just sit, and sit, and sit. Then from what can only be described as my own voice with a more tender note, I hear: "Record what I see in this moment!"

"Record what I see in this moment?" That is what I've been doing within my writing for my whole life—how is this helpful?" I ask. Then again my own tender voice whispers, **"Record what I see in this moment—in this present moment; that has been what has supported life over and over again."**

In this moment, I see frustration, restlessness, dissatisfaction, sadness, aloneness, but it occurs to me that all of these are just thoughts and judgments I see through my mind. I go to my computer to record what I see in this present moment:

"Record what I see with my heart?" "That is really what I write about."

"What purpose does that serve?"

"It connects me with something bigger than me; with more clarity than I actually have."

"Does it enrich my life?"

"Yes, very much. I feel it is a gift I've been given."

"Sounds like enriching my own life is a very clear purpose."

"Yes, but how does this serve others?"

"Do I share my gift with those I love? Does it enrich their lives?"

"Yes, I believe it does; my writings seem relevant to ordinary human life and experiences."

"Do I share my gift with everyone?"

"No, my writings seem too personal, and I feel vulnerable, and not good enough. They might misunderstand why and what I share." They might judge me in some way.

"Do I have the courage to serve others even though I feel vulnerable?"

"Maybe. Sometimes. Yes."

"Do that now without attachment to the outcome. Write and share what I see with my heart just in case it could serve others."

"Could that be my purpose?"

"The answer to that will come through my writings."

"My answer is no answer?"

"I'm the creator of my own purpose."

"I get it!"

POEMS OF REMEMBRANCE

Winter Walk

Snowflakes rest among the trees
Peace rests within the heart
Feet fall gently upon the Earth
Silent whispers of belonging

Moving Inspiration

The bird on the wing
Is a beautiful thing
It doesn't worry
It sings.

A butterfly flutters
And lights on a tree
It never wonders
Oh my, am I free?

Me, on my bike
In love with the speed
My heart seems to whisper
I'm all that I see.

And I pray for the courage to live
And to be!

The Shell

By DeAnna Colglazier

The shell is in the ocean
The ocean is in the shell
Am I the ocean or the shell?

Life on the Beach

A Memory, A Grain of Sand

It is a memory, a grain of sand
Time passes
Other grains collect
It becomes a mountain of rock

No amount of rage satisfies
When tears are needed
A flood overtakes
It becomes a river of regret

No amount of regret satisfies
When forgiveness is needed
Compassion is lost
It becomes a valley of isolation

It is a memory, a grain of sand
Time passes
Other grains collect
It becomes a hillside of joy

Emotions like grains of sand
They come and go
Life is restored
What remains is a pillar of love

Laughter: The Gift

Laughter was the gift I gave
First to me and then to all
The more I gave
The more I found
It filled the heart without a sound

My childish heart leaped out to hear
As often as it came
I 'Elfed' myself
And danced around
It filled the heart without a sound

St Nick was seen on a motorbike
He waved and I waved back
His helmet slipped
His smile abound
It filled the heart without a sound

The stream it bubbled ov'r the rocks
A quiet place to sit
The children came
Their laughter crowned
It filled the heart without a sound

Peppermint cookies a special treat
Pumpkin bread was shared
Love went out
By air and ground
It filled the heart without a sound

Laughter was the gift I gave
First to me and then to all
The more I gave
The more I found

My child was freed without a sound

A Box For Sharing

Winter is a time for sharing
A time for giving and for caring
Sometimes together, sometimes apart
But always connected within the heart.

Here is a box just given for fun
To one special daughter, an old and new son.
Now open this box to see what you find
Do it together—children should mind.

The presents inside each have a name
Just as the recipients, none is the same.
May the sharing of presents fill your sweet home
And your hearts be with mine wherever
you roam.

A November Stroll

Leaves crunching under foot
Voices low and hushed ahead
Trees casting long narrow shadows
Moss colored water in the reservoir

Fallen trees creating barricades
Sunshine sparkling upon the ripples
Laughter coming in shared waves
Leaves danced upon the autumn breeze

The sky shining a Colorado blue
Stringy clouds misting it snowy white
Rocks of quartz littering the soil
A Poet's genius remembered with awe

See feet moving
See eyes smiling
See hearts singing
Pure white quartz rock said, "take me home"

Remembered
A November stroll!

Windy Morning

From this place of doubt and fear,
The wind howls and shoves the trees roughly about.
The branches dart franticly to and fro.
The house cringes and creeks in reply
And the sun is hidden from view.
I curl into my blanket.
Thoughts are of what to do if a tree should fall upon me.

From this place of love and joy,
The wind sings in the treetops and the trees dance in rhythm.
The branches sway with grace and beauty.
The house applauds as the chimes ring out
And the clouds softly cover the sun.
I snuggle into my blanket.
Thoughts are that tomorrow the air will be so amazingly clear.

Authentic Power

What is this pain of not belonging
That seems so much a part of me?
Could it be true and only hidden
That I'm no different than the tree?

The winter comes I seek the quiet
Of nature in the frozen earth.
It helps me understand this suffering
It has been so from death to birth.

I whisper to the sky and it responds
With gusts of wind so strong, appealing.
It shouts right back without a pause
To each life comes this time of healing.

The earth is but a place to learn
Its powerful wisdom calls out to me
With its own balance of joy and pain
Perhaps no different than the tree.

When in the spring the tree turns green
And buds burst forth toward summer light.
The earth, the tree, and the authentic me
We'll open our hearts and again take flight.

What is this feeling of deep belonging
That brings authentic power to me?
A gift from myself that fills me with joy
That I'm no different than the tree.

Surrender

Sitting here surrounded by lake
Loving the ripples the water makes.
A dragonfly soars gently down
Its landing happens without a sound.

My heart becomes so quiet and vast
No question comes oh will it last.
My feet are planted within this space
And trust rests simply upon my face.

Thoughts of Life invade my mind
A voice, a whisper of love confined
Two eyes that tell of sadness past
A soul so longing to hold on fast.

My heart feels a forgotten tug
A long ago memory of a warming hug.
Promises come so strong and tender
To trust this means I must surrender.

Nature brings me back in shock
A bird has landed upon this dock.
A moment that will not come again
I must not miss it—I surrender.

My Heart Opens

An old year brings a full blue moon
The earth is white with snow.
Memories chase within my mind
My heart opens.

Shadows dance around the yard
The clouds are soft and still.
Memories chase within my mind
My heart opens.

Family sends their gifts so sweet
The paper is bright with color.
Memories chase within my mind
My heart opens.

The mountains pale within the night
The trees are bare and gray.
Memories chase within my mind
My heart opens.

A new year comes with morning light
The future is all unknown.
New memories will invade my mind
My heart opens.

The Beauty of Mother's Day

For DeAnna

Walk on the rocky mountain trails
Bloodroot, wood betany, columbine, trilliums
Landscape is alive with miniature glory
Each step disturbs yet nurtures the soul.

Sun and shade show their strength
Nature responds with golden alexander and violets
A Mourning Cloak butterfly flutters its wings
And a Christmas fern completes its cycle.

Resting time after a long mountain hike
Deck ablaze with sunshine, pollen, and shadow
A cool drink wets the growing appetite
Flowers of my garden call for attention.

Mother's Day bouquet takes rapid form
Camera clicks the beauty of the moment
Azaleas, irises, sunflowers, sassafras tree
Mountain laurel, rhododendron, and cherry bush.

The variety of this simple landscape
Shouts its beauty for all who see
A rare gift of nature to share with my child
Whose beauty is beyond what was ever imagined.

The Need For Compassion

Together at a time of loss
Searching for just the right words.
What can possibly be said?
No need to fix a loved one's tears.

Together we witness injustice
Mourning for what we see.
What can possibly be done?
No need to console or justify.

Together we feel separate
Longing for a deep connection.
What can possibly be expressed?
No need to flail and rave.

Together lost in a fearful past
Stuck in repetitive thoughts.
What can possibly be changed?
No need to vanquish pain.

Together with love and compassion
No fear to block our souls.
What can possibly be supportive?
Ask for guidance and just stay.

Making Rainbows

Car needs washing
The message came
But denial followed
And denied the claim.

It's way too hot
The sun is brutal
Car can wait
Replied my noodle.

Responsible choice-oh there it is
Car so needy is a daunting test .
Out I went with soap and brush
Told denying thought to take a rest.

Soapy water sloshed up and down
More on me and then on the ground.
Then in awe I stood back to see
A million rainbows had come around.

The more I washed
The more they came
And cleaning my car
Will never be the same.

Beloved

Beloved, a beautiful word
It fills the heart with wonder
It fills the mind with possibilities
It calms the spirit.

Beloved, a beautiful word
Its sound is of music
Its meaning is clear
It calms the spirit.

Beloved, a beautiful word
It speaks of equality
It contains no pressure
It calms the spirit.

Beloved, a beautiful word
It knows no limits
It holds no strings
It calms the spirit.

Beloved, a beautiful word
It brings a smile to my face
It brings energy to my dance
But mostly, it calms my spirit!

Nature's Magic

Magic in nature comes as a surprise
Tired, sick, unmotivated you venture out
Driven by some unexplainable need to succeed
And then you soar, lighter than air.

The trees whisper in a faint breeze
Autumn is everywhere calling your name.
A red bird flutters his wings for you alone
The dry leaves rustle quietly on your path.

Whatever the need that brought you
Your are blessed with this spirit of life
This day reaches out and surrounds you
Granting snatches of unforgettable happiness.

Your feet no longer touch the ground
The breeze at your back sings and laughs.
Two old familiar faces remind you of time passing
The magic makes you smile and call hello.

Thankful for the drives that brought you here
Moments so noisy and filled with the hush of fall
You are transported by magic into weightlessness
So lucky, you too are a creature of nature.

The Mountain

Time stands at attention as the wind billows in space
Yet hearing the wind we create stillness within.
Wonderment crowds out mundane thought of life's burdens
Awe comes to us on the wings of a bird in flight.

Voices whisper from behind a tree as an unwelcome intrusion
The majesty of the mountain again overtakes us.
A small white flower so strong withstands the wind upon the rock
Artistic creation floods our vision and hearts.

One so young is captivated by the newness of life
One not so young is reminded of the richness of each day.
They linger to learn from each other the secrets of the mountain
They will not meet again, but they will remember.

Fate

A smile, a touch
A moment of quiet
A song, a giggle
A softly spoken word.

Yesterdays are gone
Tomorrows may not be
But, for today
My heart sings.

Love's Cycle

Candles glow, a fire flickers
Silence screams from empty corners.
Memories crowd the raging mind
Waiting seems to deepen the hurt.

Dogs bark, birds sing
Laughter echoes from the past.
Thoughts of other days appear
Tears of happiness are finally found.

Footsteps are heard on empty stairs
Loneliness seeps into the heart.
Winds of change blow mixed feelings
Fantasy and reality become confused.

Ringing phones, dancing feet
Voices of the present fill the room.
Old emotions are put away
A smile of hope covers the face.

Music plays, a touch is felt
The warmth of caring overwhelms.
New memories are being made
And love's cycle begins again.

Symbols

Rain followed by bright sunshine
Makes nature's rainbows;
A symbol of storms ending.

Tears followed by friend's touching
Makes visions of rainbows;
A symbol of souls healing.

Darkness

Eerie lights play upon the ceiling
Windows turn gray with twilight
Rooms roar with deathly silence
And faces contort with grief.

Time slips into endlessness
Furniture becomes shapely shadows
Pillows become lumps of sodden clay
And darkened faces disappear in grief.

Slumber comes with haunting visions
Dreams are born of daytime fears
Bedcovers make heaps of colorless sand
And breathing is shallow with grief.

Eerie lights play upon the ceiling
Windows turn yellow with morning dew
Birds chant forlorn melodies of love
Yesterday is stolen by grief.

Reality

There is a dark side no one can enter
There is a light within no one will see
There is a quiet ending no one will notice
Morning will bring sunshine and someone will rise to meet it.

Harmonious Motion

Motion in harmony with nature
Feet rising and falling upon wet grass.
A balmy spring like breeze
Rustles the crisp, dry leaves of fall.

Motion in harmony with nature
Soft like the touching of moist lips.
A gentle caress upon the face
Stirs the passions of the body.

Motion in harmony with nature
Making the ordinary extraordinary .
A fluffy cloud passes across the sky
And the moon is hidden from view.

Motion in harmony with nature
A single leaf falls upon the earth.
Music is heard in the treetops
And a man and a woman become one.

Recognition

The sun is but a ray of light
That hides the darkness fears of night.
Life must touch this dark of night
To feel the need of sun this bright.

Before Me

There it is before me
Gentle like raindrops on flower petals
Strong like waves crashing against the shore
Sometimes there is trembling.

It has come unexpectedly
Finding me not ready but I do not run.
I am not afraid though I should be
The timing is not right.

Its presence is unsettling
For it is not perfect even from this distance.
Reaching out there is no need for holding
It stands in quietness.

The surroundings are filled with emotion
The forces of gentleness and strength are joined.
Trembling becomes a soothing touch
There it is before me.

Sharing Warmth

The air is empty but for the loneliness
There is a persistent need for shared warmth.
What is this need for human connection?
Is there no way to feel complete alone?

The activity level has been high
The feeling of fatigue overwhelming.
There is comfort in knowing one's own worth
But still the room is wrapped in silence.

Closing the swinging doors of the mind
A smile radiates toward me from memory.
Arms extend and enfold me with tenderness
An imaginary presence fills me with desire.

This love cannot be pretense—can it?
Though distance separates us we are together.
Somehow love reaches through space and time
The room fills with sunshine warming me for sleep.

Time Captured

The room hung heavy with the gloom of smoke
The lights played frantically around the walls.
The vibration of the music entered the mind.
The surrounded bodies moved in riotous fashion.

The contrasting dark and light pulled them close.
Their muscles entwined as their emotions rocketed upward.
They were caught like fugitive slaves within the elements.
And then, the music stopped!

"Zoe" Speaks

You are not alone
I am your divine essence.
You are a physical being
I am your spiritual presence.

You must listen with your heart
I will whisper what you need to know.
You must trust the voice from within
And always your Path I will show.

You must see all others within yourself
It will guide your heart toward wholeness.
You must heal the fearfulness within
And change your thoughts to soulfulness.

Your Path is filled with chosen small steps
And I will lead the way.
The result will be huge changes in life
Experience is your teacher each day.

Each new experience is a treasure for you
It brings opportunities to share.
Learn not by the experience, but the action you take
With intention to love deeply and care.

You have a purpose that is bigger than you
To connect with all others and explore.
Your purpose is just to co-create love on Earth
For "Zoe" means "Life"; nothing more.

A Soul Story of Joy

And, at that sacred moment, a butterfly in the garden left its cocoon and landed near, but not too near the earth.

A Lifetime of Joy Happened
in a Day: A Soul Story

Forward

Once upon a long, short time ago and in a very near, very far place, a not so young, very young woman found a year of lost joy and embraced it with com-passion and con-fusion. The time was yesterday in a small, not so small town in the good ole, not so good, young USA.

It started early as she looked out her window at a strange new site she had seen a million times before. It was a small structured garden filled with a multitude of plants: trees of many colors, flowers of different varieties and sizes, ground cover of different shapes. In the middle of this bright and quiet garden stood a magnificent blue spruce tree, its tall trunk straight and its limbs in perfect symmetry. She loved it—it was her favorite tree and she knew it well—so well in fact that it seemed to draw her in. As she started to go, her eyes noticed the delicate-looking green ivy that grew below her balcony as the background for the roses and other bushes. The roses were pink and yellow and there was a single bush whose buds had not yet opened. She imagined its color as purple. As she imagined, she wondered why the bushes were at different stages of development. Could it have something to do with the angle of the morning sunrise? Since she really had no idea what roses need to grow perfectly, she sought refuge from her pondering in the beauty of the majestic blue spruce.

The Garden

Out came her camera and she began to take her pictures, but for some reason the ivy kept calling her, "What about me?" The ivy was growing beyond its boundaries and was threatening to destroy the structured, if not formal, garden. Her focused, not so focused mind judged that "not good." She sighed and raised the camera, for her goal was to photograph all the parts of the garden so that she could share its contents with someone she loved. Although he wouldn't see it all, she thought she could capture its essence. Alas, as she continued, she knew she could not depict the entire garden by taking pictures of separate plants. There was a particular,

206

expressive essence surrounding each plant, but the garden's essence grew out of the combination of all of the plants in unison. So she aimed her camera toward the roof and snapped a picture of the sun rising behind it into the garden. She felt a flutter in her heart that she believed was joy.

She was near this small garden because she was attending a self-awareness conference, and a day of learning called to her. She wanted to learn; so much so that her legs felt weak beneath her. Her image of the majestic blue spruce called to her, "get it together girl; you made this commitment so get crackin." She rubbed her head, because suddenly the vivid yellow rose from within her said, "at least stop and see the elegant lavender dress, and you'll be better prepared for the day." The dress hung tall, proud, and purple like the blue spruce in the late mist of a spring rain. The fragile fringe on the scarf around the neck and the subtle ruffle at the bottom of the dress were the perfect touches. A dress shop named "Red's Threads" had created this hotel window display. She had been stopping each morning for the last few days. She was in the middle of reading a book entitled, *A Red Thread: A Love Story*. How weird was that? Using her new learning about self-awareness, she took this as a "sign" that she should honor her growing strength by going to town to buy the dress. She loved that she could feel her joy even though earlier she had been a space cadet, forgetting routine stuff all weekend.

The Choices

From somewhere deep in her chest, a voice reminded her of her intention to learn all that she could about this new process. It was insistent as it nagged at her, "keep your commitment, don't screw this up, and don't disappoint yourself." Her vision of the Japanese maple from the garden appeared within her and cast its shadow upon her lovely inner yellow rose. Some of the vividness of each was lost. Her inner majestic blue spruce shouted, "Do things right or you'll ruin my garden." The misty joy she had felt on the balcony above the garden started fading away. She headed for the conference room that she knew was filled with opportunities for learning as a growing sensation of pain held her chest in its grip. Then a small, not so small voice said, "Be gentle with yourself and remember the experiment we planned." The sudden surge of joy overwhelmed the woman as the pain lessened. She breathed in the clear air and her lungs expanded. She gave herself permission to have fun today no matter what. She would not disappoint her inner yellow rose. She smiled and remembered that the night before she had received "a sign" from the universe that joy was now supposed to fill her life. With uneasiness she entered the room.

The experiences of the morning were full of choices, and she made them one at a time. She tried to tell a few of the women about a country and western song that made fun of people because they failed to see the obvious. She couldn't remember the name of the artist, she couldn't remember the name of the song, and she couldn't really remember many of the words. The pain grew. The joy lessened. The jest of the story was that sometimes in life you wish you had "a sign" that said "stupid" that you could hold out to all those people who seemed to miss the obvious. She was trying to say that she knew she should by joyful for all that was in her life, but that she had missed it until last night when her angel sign had been "joy." Air expanded her lungs; the joy returned; she laughed; she cried, she screwed up, she began again, she apologized, she took responsibility, she swore inwardly, she challenged, she retreated, she vacated, she scanned, and she knew joy again. It felt light, it felt good, and she felt she had the right to be joyful—more pain was suddenly in her chest. "What was that about?" asked her Japanese maple. She breathed deeply and relaxed. The conference ended and her yellow rose smiled.

The Dress

It was time to go and buy the purple dress. The majestic spruce nagged in her ear, "In spite of yourself you saved the garden;" the yellow rose rejoiced and sang; the Japanese maple allowed the sun to fill her life without comment. Its leaves glowed above the shadow it cast on the ground around it and her. Her joy was blessed—the garden could be damned! She suddenly remembered the lonely, empty park bench in the park. With courage her inner park bench of safety said, "Apologize to me later; I sit alone today; go be free!" So she went to buy the dress for the majestic blue spruce. How pleased it would be! What fun! What Joy! What anxiety! What con-fusion.

The woman from the garden, we'll call her Cynthia, almost missed the bus (pain), she made it (hope), she found the store (perfect), the first dress was the right color and style, but it had no ruffle and no fringe (pain), the second dress was "the" dress (joy). She tried on the dress and it looked a bit big (disappointment, pain, con-fusion). She approached the clerk (suspicion, pain). The clerk said that Cynthia needed to tie the small pull-string bow to create small gathers in the back (hope). As she did so, the dress transformed and held the beauty of the majestic blue spruce (joy). She fidgeted in front of the mirror of happiness. Another woman's yellow rose appeared in the store and said, "That color is perfect on you (doubt and pain)." She smiled at Cynthia and said, "It's a beautiful dress. The ruffle and fringe add just the right touch of softness." Joy returned to Cynthia. The majestic blue spruce said, "For God 's sake, just buy the blooming dress—I want it (pain, con-fusion)." She bought the dress. As the clerk folded the dress it became a very small bundle, but the ruffle and fringe kept slipping out of the tissue paper. She loved the way the fringe and ruffle twisted and turned inside the bundle. She loved the dress (joy). She was not so sure that she was feeling every decision she made deep in her energy system as planned.

She rushed out to meet a new woman friend, but she was presented with two of her other friends instead. For some reason, she felt nervous and reassured herself of her intention to accept whatever came after each choice—conscious or unconscious—at least for this day. She sipped the cool cream of the frappachino, but she was restless and her stomach fluttered and her forehead began to hurt. She chatted for a while and then asked the women to forgive her, but she intended to head for the park instead of continuing on with them to shop. She hoped they understood. She stood and walked away. She gazed into the sun and apologized to the Universe for being in a world where she sometimes just had to choose to be a stranger to herself and others. She was surprised that the choices she made today with difficulty were humorous after the fact. So unusual was this feeling of joy that she felt slightly disoriented. A small gentle voice said, "Take a few minutes alone; you've earned them."

The Park

She practically ran for the town park to continue to photograph the bits and pieces of what she encountered in each moment. She heard herself laugh out loud. The first photo she took was of a sign at the entrance of the park; it said, "Meet Here." It reminded her of two other signs she had once photographed, "Wrong Way, and One Way." They were appropriate then, but this was now. She danced her feet around the ground for she was so excited to be here.

Each park piece came to her through the camera lens as she walked and she snapped away—recording, recording. The freedom she gave herself to take photos at random was like music and her heart hummed and the voices around her and within her came into focus with the objects. She had a preponderance of evidence that she was part of the Universe, and she wanted to hold onto it; but alas, she had made commitments. She could keep her commitments to others made earlier in the day or continue to hold on to these precious moments of freedom—the first in a very long, not so long time. Cynthia knew that back in the garden the Japanese maple was spreading its shadow on yet another rose and perhaps the purple bud had bloomed. She could see the colors of each fading. She raised her head this time and her internal rose quietly bowed to commitment and headed to find a pay phone. As she looked around, her internal Japanese maple clouded her thoughts with failure, because she had left her cell phone back in her room. Her pale yellow rose smiled and sang a tune and turned to take one more photograph. She got a cramp in her calf, and she knew she had failed to drink enough water to sustain her through the warmth of the day. Her yellow rose groaned and she searched for shade as the cramp moved down toward her foot. She said, "Damn cramp" out loud, took off her shoes, and rubbed her foot. As the pain lessened, she picked up her camera to take another picture of her favorite part of the park—the bubbling rapids of the high-water creek. The translucent creek seemed to reflect the energy currents in her body today, raging one moment, almost silent the next. Alas, the camera had no power. She had ignored the warning light that morning in order to stay in the garden. In an instant, the groan of her yellow rose turned to roaring laughter and she floated off the ground. She threw kisses to the small purple flowers that seemed to be dancing everywhere she looked, dancing just for her. She ached from the joy within her and around her. The softness of her tears felt like the petals of the flowers that had been nurturing her all day.

The Couple

She headed out of the park to find the phone booth—didn't see one, hardly cared. But there in the square was an information booth. She floated to it, and there she found an elderly couple. They smiled and exchanged hellos.

They were from Cynthia's home state—knew it well and now had retired to this magic place. She gathered the brochures they gave her and noted the time. Her Japanese maple warned her that she had to hurry. She asked where the nearest phone booth was and with a glimmer in their twinkling eyes the couple said in unison—there! They pointed through the opening at the back of their booth. It was there through the window at the back of the information booth directly behind them. She heard her child's voice ringing with laughter. It said, "Here's your sign." She too began to laugh, the man and woman laughed with her—no one needed an explanation. She had been so concerned about finding the booth that she failed to see the obvious and the Universe laughed with com-passion.

She made her call and touched one of the persons she loved most and told him about her magnificent day—the ups, the downs, the laughter, the tears. She told him she had only four minutes because she had no more change. His voice was gentle when he said, "You sound happy." The phone clicked—times up and he was gone as he said something she couldn't hear. She thought: "He's okay, but what she meant was I'm okay." She felt giddy with anticipation of what would come next. She needed to find a bathroom. Some routine things could not be ignored this day. She went back to the information booth to get directions. She said to the couple, "If the bathroom is as obvious as the phone booth, send me to the one across town." They laughed again and said that it wasn't quite that far, but it wasn't too far. The old man began to give her directions and the old woman interrupted with, "Send her across the bridge—it's nicer." He said back to her—with a patience that comes from acceptance—that of course he would. He pointed to a very small, not so short alley through the shops that led to a small, not so flat bridge in the open, not so open-air market. At the near end of the bridge, a young woman played softly on her guitar and sang. Cynthia's yellow rose wanted to stop, but some things can't wait. Her impatient Japanese maple pushed her over the bridge and promised she could stop on the way back; she had goofed around enough for one day. Her majestic blue spruce pumped her limbs in the gentle breeze; was she waving? Her tree folded her arms with patience and caring, but not too much patience and not too gentle caring. Cynthia knew this appeasement would not last long if she didn't continue to maintain the balance of the garden.

The Musician

A few minutes later, Cynthia crossed back over the bridge and again heard the gentle voice of a musician. It sang, "You don't have to be strong; you aren't in this world to be all alone." She froze, transfixed before the young musician and within that moment the space between them closed and they were one. Within each was all the sorrow of all women. Time disappeared and they felt the strength and wisdom of a loving Universe. An old, but yet new "sense of belonging" watered the yellow rose and she imagined a new bud opening—it was definitely purple. The music stopped and she placed money in the jar as the young musician put down her guitar and greeted her. Cynthia knew exactly what to say. She told the musician, "Today you are my gift; your song was just the message I needed today." The musician's eyes moistened and she said, "It is a very old song; I hardly ever play music from that old CD anymore." Cynthia asked her if she had a copy of the CD. The musician looked down at the table of CDs between them and picked it up. She had only one, and its cover contained a picture of cuttings of tiny purple flowers and loving phrases of comfort about finding one's self. The musician mentioned it was mostly her own songs, and it was the only CD cover she had designed and created herself. It was just a collage made from newspaper and magazine clippings. The yellow shape at the top was a piece of paper she had picked up off the floor that was sort of heart shaped, but not a perfect heart, wrong color and all. It seemed perfect to Cynthia. She told the young musician that it seemed like a soft velvety yellow rose petal as she stood in the shade of her Japanese maple tree. With trembling hands the not so young, young woman from the garden bought the CD. The musician again sat down to play. Each knew they had been a part of a sacred moment that would never come again. It was as obvious as the table of CDs should have been. Again that gentle voice whispered, "Mom, here's your sign!" A light giggle filled with love was heard throughout her inner garden.

Cynthia asked the musician if she could stay through another song and the musician paused, put her hand to her head, and said she was frightened that she would be unable to think of anything else that would be good enough. The woman from the garden assured her it didn't matter what she chose, it would be perfect. The musician sang, "Why Wyoming, Why Wyoming. Why would I come to this cold place and call it home? It couldn't be understood with a rational mind."

Cynthia's yellow rose said, "Be gentle with yourself—the Universe is unfolding as it should." With tears of love, the woman from the garden recalled her last conversation with her son, "Mom, this place is covered with snow, it's cold as hell, sometimes I hate it, but it's my home now. My new apartment is awesome." She had hid her tears from him and said she knew. He said, "Love ya Mom" with a lilt in his voice, and she had held that sound in her heart as she went about her day—that long ago day was filled with heavy sorrow for what could have been and what she was certain was near at hand.

But on this day in the sun, the memory filled her heart with his energy, and she shook with joy as she headed to find her friends for dinner. She had to tell them about this day so she would be sure it was real. She wasn't sure they would believe her. She was sure if someone told her she wouldn't. She found them, showed them the CD. The woman from the garden explained all the symbols of joy she had been given. How could they be real? How could the joy to fill a lifetime happen in just one day? The inner yellow roses of her friends said, "Of course they were real." They had no doubt. One asked to be taken to the musician to buy a CD for herself. For a moment, they couldn't find the tiny alley (pain), then they did (joy); then the musician was closing down (pain). She didn't have another CD like it (pain). Then the musician remembered she had an unwrapped one in her case that she could sell (joy). They all talked at once, they were giddy, and what once sounded to the woman from the garden like idle chatter sounded like love.

As they went back through the alley to the street, the young musician ran after them and called, "Cynthia, Cynthia." Her voice was high with excitement. They turned and the musician told the woman from the garden she had to tell her just one more thing. She said she was not supposed to have played in the park that day; she had been riding her bike and another musician had not shown up; she was just filling in. Another sacred moment passed between them (joy). The young, but not too young musician's voice, filled with the beauty that comes with hope, said, "Please give my website address to anyone you meet today—I believe in serendipity." Cynthia's inner yellow rose agreed and no other trees were heard. Truth can be obvious too.

The Dinner

All the women headed back down the street toward the restaurant they had chosen, but it was closed (pain). They found another (joy). Another woman joined them and now they were five. They chose to sit outside where the bubbles of the creek echoed around them. Their energy matched it splash for splash. First excited, then serious, then quiet and the cycle would begin again. They shared their fears for the future, their longings from the past, and they asked the woman from the garden to share her dress with them. At about that time, two more of the new friends came unexpectedly into the restaurant. Cynthia's Japanese maple said, "Saved, I won't have to show them. It is only a dress. You've made such a big deal about it they will be disappointed." But what she meant was that she would be disappointed if they didn't like it because that might dampen the joy she found buying the dress. The two women joined the table by pulling another table up to touch. They all laughed as they shared their experiences at the theatre. Every one ordered their food, each taking a turn to chatter with love for themselves and the others. For the woman from the garden, it was a new experience to be this comfortable in this situation (joy).

Suddenly out of nowhere, one of the women said, "Cynthia was just about to share her dress." It always seemed that these situations required more sharing than the woman from the garden wanted to do (pain). She made excuses about it being bundled for the airplane trip, but the others insisted. She pulled it out of the bag explaining all the while that it was just a dress and that the only really special thing about it was the tiny ruffle around the bottom and the fringe on the scarf. Then of course it was purple and she loved purple. The other women loved the dress. They agreed the fabric was beautiful, the color was perfect, the essence so soft, and they also agreed that it was the ruffle and fringe that gave it just the right touch of femininity (joy). They all sang, "I feel pretty" out loud as the woman from the garden wrapped the scarf around her neck. The ruffle and fringe reminded her of the ivy that was overflowing its boundaries in the garden that morning. It had still been moist from the dew. It had been so many shades of green, each leaf a different size.

In an instant came the old familiar voice of the Japanese maple, "You should have paid more attention to the ivy this morning." Cynthia bowed her head with sadness for she could not even remember whether or not she had taken a picture of the ivy that morning in the garden (pain). But from somewhere unknown and very near her heart another voice said, "Ivy is a creative maven, it integrates most gardens, it holds fast to the earth, but it will fill every crevice whether you pay attention to it or not. You can find and photograph it almost anywhere." The woman from the garden recognized this as truth and returned to her joy that had somehow faded a bit from the shadow cast over her by the sighs of the Japanese maple.

The day had been long and eventful and it was time to return to the hotel. Some of the women headed for the shuttle, but the woman from the garden stayed behind to relay the joy she had found in the park to the two women that came late to dinner. She was late for the shuttle and one of the other women came back for her. She apologized to her for the inconvenience, but inside her heart sang. It seemed she was always apologizing to women (pain). They didn't just leave without her (joy). She knew that had the situation been reversed she might have left them (pain).

The sun was setting and it was time to return to the garden. Cynthia had walked around and around the hotel savoring all that had been a part of this day—the joy, the pain, and all the voices within her that she had named after the trees and flowers of the garden. What a very strange day. She was alive and hopeful that this day was the beginning of many more such days. Without warning, her eyes fell upon the empty park bench; the one she chose to leave alone for at least this day. Somehow it looked different. The moonlight cast an eerie veil over the garden. Perhaps that was it. Silently with a feeling of awe still moving through her, she approached and sat down upon the bench (pain). She leaned back to look at the stars that were so separate, but not so separate and filled the sky. The majestic blue spruce had taken on a gray tint that softened it and seemed to give it peace. The Japanese maple's leaves were still swaying back and forth, but it seemed tired from its day of judgments. The yellow rose was quiet and still and looked content to have almost no color. In the darkness she couldn't tell for sure what color flower the bud had become; maybe purple, maybe pink? It no longer seemed important. What really mattered was that on this day it had chosen to bloom even though part of its day was spent in shadow. It would be a hearty rose the next time the sun rose and the Universe would applaud.

Memories of other gardens and other times came into the woman's vision. As she stood to leave, something tickled her ankle. She looked down and was surprised, but not too surprised, that the ivy had crept unnoticed around the leg of the lonely empty bench. The creative maven had found a niche and had chosen not to shrink from the task of growing wherever it could. Alas, it had not ruined the garden; its unseen growth was just the right touch to add essence to the garden. The woman in the garden sat very still; could this be another "sign?" She had not discovered the essence of the garden, but she had known joy. As she rose to leave, her shadow fell upon the ivy and she shivered. A voice filled with gentleness and knowledge said, "Mom, here's your sign! As you enter the garden, your essence defines the garden, as does everyone's. With each soul the essence is changed, but not too changed. Con-fusion is okay, for all this cannot be understood with the rational mind."

Unrestrained tears of joy, like soft rain on the petals of a yellow rose, fell upon the cheeks of the woman from the garden and all pain faded. The tears were not tears of great loss, but tears of renewed hope for all that would be. All day she had missed the obvious. But now she had really listened and heard this voice that had called her Mom. Alas, out of her con-fusion came com-passion. It was not the voice of her deceased son. This soft, but not too soft voice was the healing gentle voice of a young, but not too young, woman whose music was familiar.

Together they turned and left the garden!

And, at that sacred moment, a butterfly in the garden left its cocoon and landed near, but not too near the earth. The hearty but delicate ivy hugged it close and the empty, but not too empty park bench settled into the earth for the night.

MEMOIR OF A MIDDLE CHILD

What is there about my life that will have meaning to those in my family yet to come?

As I have so many times before, I will just let the words flow from the magical place of spirit that has always assisted and surprised me when I write.

————————

The living of your own life writes the book of your most sacred truth, and offers evidence of it.

Neale Donald Walsch

Preface

When my daughter, DeAnna, called to ask me to write a history of my life for her 40th birthday present, I'm sure she meant names, dates, and places. But for me, life is so much more about the essence of living than when or where things actually happen. As I sit down to write my throat is tight and words seem to fail me. What is there about my life that will have meaning to those in my family yet to come? Do I talk about just the joys of my life, which are many; or do I share with authenticity about the great learning that has come through all my pleasant and difficult experiences?

As I have so many times before, I will just let the words flow from the magical place of spirit that has always assisted and surprised me when I write. I write for clarity in confusing times. I write to express my deepest feelings and longings. I write to those I love. I write to explore my imagination. But mostly, I write because it is when I write that I am most present with the unseen guidance of my ancestors and the compassionate assistance of a wise Universal energy force that unites me to source. So present am I within these moments of creation that they seem to exist apart from everything else but me. As I begin to write, my words take on a life of their own, and I sometimes am bowled over because what I had intended to write and what I actually write are poles apart. Later it can seem as if someone else must have been the author.

For me the question of source—what it is, why does it matter, and how can I touch it— has been the single most compelling force in the creation of my life as it exists in this incarnation. Perhaps that is the reason I must say yes to the writing of this personal memoir, and then get out of the way so the story can move through me from source. If I am able to do so, then I will give one gift and receive another on the glorious occasion of DeAnna's 41st birthday.

Choosing Life

I have no memory of nonphysical life, and yet I know it exists. For each of us, there are choices to make to assist us on our journey into a new physical body. The choices we make become part of the essence of our souls that guide our spiritual growth. So that is where I choose to begin, telling you about choosing my life, and whom I chose as my fellow travelers. For in some ways, they were unlikely choices from a five-sensory or physical perspective.

Loren David Ferguson and Emma Vergil Haney

It was December 14, 1942, on a cold and blustery night in Mad River Township, Ohio. Emma Virgil Haney Ferguson, daughter of Harlan Haney and Fanny Adams, was about to become a mother for the third time. When I arrived, I was not a surprise for she said she had seen me in a dream. She also said I looked like baby Tarzan, long bushy dark brown hair and weighing in at eleven pounds. I've always doubted this weight since I was born at home, and I can't imagine that a scale was readily available. Yet the rumor of my enormous size has followed me through life. She called me Phyllis Reed because she was reading a book and one of the characters in the book was named Phyllis. Reed she borrowed from my maternal great, great grandmother, Cynthia Reed. Not much has been said to me about this Grandmother, but her presence has existed in my mind and spirit since I was very small. I believe her essence is represented in one of my nonphysical guides, but I did not name it as such until I was much older. I have called on her spirit to support me in difficult times, and I give her credit for my creativity. Whether or not it is true doesn't really matter; she is with me because I say she is.

But let's get back to Emma Vergil, my Mother for this incarnation. She would have winced at that statement for she was a devout fundamental Christian, and she would have scoffed at my belief in reincarnation. But I believe we had a contract to help each other grow and grow we did. It was sometimes a calamitous ride for we were often on separate sides of an idea or discussion, both needing to be right. Some of this was born out of my fear of not being noticed and some out of her feelings of being overwhelmed while my Father served in the Navy in World War II. But, that is another story for another page. Emma was five feet, seven inches of stately willowy beauty. Her face was large with a square chin and it had softness about it with pores that were totally invisible. Her body was strong and muscular from working in the tobacco fields of Caney, Kentucky, as a girl. The evenness of her skin and the clarity of her crystal blue eyes kept her looking eternally young. I cannot remember her hair when it was dark brown for in my memory, it was always turning white and it curled softly like waves of cotton tossed to the wind. She wore very little makeup, but loved the redness of lipstick on her tiny mouth—a mouth that often seemed to me too small for the rest of her. Cleanliness and good posture were characteristics she instilled in all her children. And music—she never played an instrument, but she sang me songs and hummed when she worked. She could be angry and lash out when she was frightened, and in my teenage years she cried a lot. I'm not sure why she cried, and I was never sure she loved me. Perhaps she cried for lost youth. As she aged, she grew in calmness and her friends were many. She married my Dad when she was around twenty and she brought to that marriage my older sister, Erma, age three. I'll let Erma tell that story some other time if she chooses.

My Dad was Loren David Ferguson born in Grassy Creek, Kentucky, the son of George and Mary Ferguson; he called my Mother, Vergil. He was short, five feet seven inches—same height as Emma, but he looked much shorter because his body and legs were quite short. My contract with him was also to help each other grow. He was a stern disciplinarian with a large and generous heart. Even when he spoke in harsh tones, and he did quite often, I always knew he loved me; it was in his eyes. His eyes reflected my own and were the same color, misty green. They were quiet and somehow soft even when he was stressed and tired from providing for a large and volatile family. He was uneducated in the formal sense, only attending grade school, but he was brilliant and creative in so many ways.

When I was very young before my memories began, he left for his tour of duty in World War II; he enlisted or was drafted into the Navy. I don't know much about this time in his Life for he never shared about his experiences of ships being blown up around him, or of a friend dying at the hands of what he perceived was the enemy. I did see pictures of him with his buddies and various island beauties, and he often looked a bit tipsy. The most I know about that time is that we stayed at home and waited for his return. The story that has persisted about his homecoming is that Mother was giving me a bath in a small table-sized tub. He entered the room and Mother is reported to have thrown me naked across the room in her excitement. No one has said who caught me, but I expect it was Erma.

After the war, I followed Dad everywhere he went. What I remember most is that he whistled while he worked no matter what else he was doing. He had perfect pitch, and he whistled with great tones and even greater ease. I've practiced for years, but have not been able to duplicate his accomplishment; I thought it was magical when he whistled. Now I believe it was his divine gift. He had other gifts as well. He could make anything with his hands, and he loved to work with wood. He had a garage workshop and I was allowed to help him there. He never criticized my work, but he also never complimented my work. I've come to believe that is why I need demonstration of approval from others at times, because it never ever came from him. This may have been his way of teaching acceptance, and his non-judgmental approach to my activity around him certainly gave me great freedom to try new things. It is still one of my greatest joys.

He did show displeasure at times. I remember helping plant tomatoes one spring. My job was to follow him and pull any weed that I found as he hoed them. Unfortunately to a small child, a tomato plant looks just like a weed. When he turned at the end of the row, I had carefully extracted each tomato plant that was tucked lovingly into the ground. With a heavy sigh, he said I should go indoors and help Mother until I was older. I was crushed, but never argued. I understood he was accurate; I hadn't done it right! To this day a tomato, warmed by the sun, feels like love and is one of my favorite foods. Strange, that a single moment in a young life could create such deep emotional feelings for a lifetime. Also the need to do things right has persisted.

Then there was the time I rode in a bicycle race with only moccasins on my feet. I was leading the pack and looked back to see if others were getting close. When I did, my foot slipped off and went under the spinning pedal. My ankle was very sprained and I couldn't finish the race. As Dad held me close to his chest for comfort, I could smell his tobacco and sweat; I still can when I think of him. All he said was, "never look back." There have been times in my life when I wished that I could have remembered his teaching on that day.

Dad brought Mother, Erma, and Wallace (my older brother) from Kentucky to Enon, Ohio, before I was born. Dad first worked on a farm, but later he worked for a cement company. He was the dynamite foreman. He drove a truck with a giant drill that seemed more than "just enormous" to me. One wheel was about four times my height. He let me ride in the cab. After he drilled the holes for the dynamite, he filled them with dynamite sticks and blew the rock into a million pieces just by lighting a long fuse. I thought he was the bravest man alive. Dad, Mother, Erma, Wallace, and I lived in a two-story farmhouse surrounded by about seven acres. The house was old with high ceilings and floral wallpaper downstairs. Upstairs was a bit shabby and the wallpaper had been removed on the stairwell. I remember feeling ashamed of its appearance when someone spent the night. At first I had a room alone, later shared a room with my younger sisters, and finally had a room to myself again. I loved the solitude. As I grew older both Mother and Dad continued to be my teachers and my students. I may get back to that in later chapters.

I've mentioned Erma, my sister, a couple of times for she has always been a part of my life much like a second Mother. Wallace, my brother, was two years older than I and has also always been in my life; sometimes a vital active part and sometimes a distant memory. I can't talk about them separately, for me that came together to my world and enriched it with their positive and negative influences. They both helped to mold me in those early years.

During those early years, although unaware of it, I saw myself as a victim of circumstances. My Mother already had a daughter, and it seemed to me that she favored her baby son. Erma was seven when I arrived and Wallace was about two-years old. Mother was alone much of the time in my toddler years with Dad away in the Navy. Wallace was a sickly little boy and had rheumatic fever while Dad was gone. All these circumstances helped to create my vision of my place or lack of it with my Mother. Little did I know at the time that these circumstances were intended to teach me independence and were just what I needed to create my life in this Earthsuit (my physical body).

Erma came into life as Erma Benton, and she and Mom joined my Dad when she was three years old. I called her "Erm the Worm" when I was a teenager full of ornery. She was tall with a softer face than Wallace and me. She had a gentleness of spirit and a toughness of purpose so that when she spoke, I listened. She may have been dealing with her own issues with her ever-changing relationship with our Mother and a missing biological Father she didn't know. At any rate, my memory of her is that she was a quiet, determined force, and chose her religious Path of fundamental Christianity early. That choice and others created an opportunity for her to drop out of school without finishing high school. I never understood that choice by her or by my parents, but I'm getting ahead of myself.

Before I began elementary school, she along with Wallace, created my closest world and helped to co-create my ideas of sharing, directing, and accepting or not. If Erma was my Mother figure, Wallace became my symbol of adventure. That love of adventure created many competitive games between us. One such game when I was about four or five was "Indians and Cowboys." I was always cast in the losing role, so I became the Indian. One day, a quick push from the Cowboy sent me flying into a box of broken window glass and nearly ended my young life. The scar on my left wrist reminds me still to use caution when taking risks or playing games. That caution has both served and limited my experiences.

It was through my interactions with Wallace (and Dad) that I began to believe that men's lives were exciting and women's were there to support men. I chose to believe that bigger and stronger equated to better and my feelings of inferiority and judgment grew exponentially. Other fearful parts of my personality took on the role of protector for others, especially Wallace and myself. Since victim seemed a weak feeling to have, I developed the warrior aspect of my personality early; quick to strike verbally to defend any wrong. Wallace was strong of body, tall, blond, and beautiful, but he had difficulty in school. He didn't seem to understand what was required of him, and did naughty things like tear pages out of his workbooks, tease other students, and annoy the teacher in whatever way he could imagine. Although he began school two years ahead of me, we soon became classmates in the same grade. I was a strong dependable student, and the comparisons that were made added to an already budding relationship based on fear and inequality—me feeling "less than" in some cases and "more than" in others.

I'll get back to my school years soon, but I must now back up and tell you about another tiny sister that entered my life when I was four. Betty Gertrude named after my paternal Grandmother, and I think, my Mother's deceased sister had hair that was as black as a raven's and straight beyond belief. It shone in the sun like crystals upon rich dark soil. It sticks in my memory because, except for my Dad, the rest of the family had curly or wavy hair. I loved the way her hair hung together and shimmered—envy was born in me. Mom had lost a child before Betty's birth, and when Betty came to us, she had many people that watched over her night and day to keep her safe. So much so that her smallest cry was reacted too with an intense need to fix it. These behaviors along with Betty's propensity to be fearful of noises and things she did not understand co-created a fragile and turbulent emotional world for her. One that I contributed too first, by taking care of her too often for too long and second, by demanding that she show more courage. I wanted her to develop her own power of self-assurance, but had no inkling of how that could be accomplished. As a result, I pampered her one-minute and yelled at her the next. It must have been as confusing for her as it was for me. With lots of encouragement from all members of the family, she became a very quiet and introverted child.

Two years later, Sandy joined the family; another tiny sister. She was a cherub in so many ways; strawberry blond ringlets surrounded a square face with cheeks filled with dimples like Wallace's. She was short and dimply all over; her eyes were green like mine, but they had flecks of reddish brown in them. It gave her a unique appearance—eyes and hair much the same color. She and Betty became inseparable. I took care of her sometimes when she cried, but felt that we never really got to know each other. A short time after she came into my world, my world grew wider and deeper. I began first grade four months before I became six years of age. I remember well the fear of that first day, but Wallace was there with me—he had been held back a year and was now in second grade, but shared the same classroom with me. Erma was also in the same school, but I have no memory of her at school from those early years. She was seven years older and her choices were removed from my own for the most part. School activated both excitement and fear within me. As in so many other times of fear, I called on my warrior and began my departure from the isolation and protection of family. It was time for a divergent Path.

The Good Student

As I look back on my school experience, it was the end of isolated ideas, but of course, I didn't know that at the time. In the moment, it was an opportunity to get up early, catch a big yellow bus, visit with friends, and be grown-up like Erma and Wallace. Enon Elementary and Junior High School was a small red brick building about two miles from my house. It was surrounded with lots of grass, had swings, and not very many trees. Wallace and I shared a classroom and teacher and at first that was exciting. As time passed that changed and I became the good student and he became the difficult student. In those days, comparison of skills was made with no thought as to how that would affect the children.

The teacher's name was Mrs. Long. I liked her, but Wallace gave her a great deal of trouble in the classroom. I remember one day as she walked backward down the isle between the rows of children, Wallace put out his foot and she tripped and fell. I don't believe he deliberately wanted her to fall; it was a childish un-thought-out prank that ended badly. For me it was a source of great embarrassment. He was my hero before we began school but in school, I quickly became his intellectual protector. It changed our relationship in many ways; ways, that as a young child, I did not analyze or understand. At home he was a hero; at school so very vulnerable. Most of what I remember about the first grade was the anxiety of not knowing what Wallace would do next. Mrs. Long remained my teacher in the second grade, which was my only early classroom experience without Wallace. I learned quickly and enjoyed the attention and admiration I earned by being a good student. I learned what it took to be successful and began my life of pleasing others to get what I needed or wanted. When I arrived in third grade, Wallace was in the same grade having been held back again. I feel sure that Wallace had a slight learning disability that was neither noticed nor cared about by the teachers back then.

Obscurity hides the exact dates of much that happened in my early years, but I have special moments that have stayed with me forever. Mostly the memories are about what happened between people rather than about the schoolwork. The schoolwork was easy and so required little of my attention. What was more interesting was the interaction of students with other students, teachers with students, and both with me. During that time, I met the girl that would be my best friend throughout our school experiences. She lived just down the street. We rode our bikes, we studied together, we talked about boys, and we were comfortable enough together to just be; her name was Karen. Because we were sharing common experiences, she seemed closer in those days than my sisters or parents. We told each other everything. By fourth or fifth grade, four or five of us girls had bonded and shared thoughts and activities. We were athletic at a time when organized girls' sports were not readily available, but somehow there was always a teacher that was willing to give their time to help us explore this part of our personalities. I'll pause here to share some of the memories of those early pre-high school years.

My first speech in front of the class—I loved it. My hands flew around as I spoke. After the speech, the teacher asked me to sit on my hands and begin to give the speech without them. I couldn't do it. So the challenge to me was to learn how to think and be still at the same time. The discipline to do that has served me well and the appreciation of stillness when I need to think has sustained me in difficult times.

Like water pouring over rocks, my memories are jumbled and intertwined; can't remember which happened first. I remember a teacher swatting me with a flyswatter for talking in class; funny how few names of teachers I remember. There was a small boy in fifth grade that we all teased, because he was frail and carried a large music case. Many times I was part of a group that made his life miserable. He died from his heart condition when we were in the sixth grade. After he died, I pledged to never be a part of such harmful action again, and I haven't—another difficult lesson that molded my future behavior.

I remember walking around the track with my latest "love" and being at least two or three inches taller. I remember clearly that I planned to marry a very tall man, but by the time we reached high school, the boys had grown and I had forgotten my intention.

Another time, friends and I hid in the locker room to skip class and that experience taught me the lessons of integrity and loyalty. There we were—three of us—having a great time, when I heard the door open. I quickly jumped into a bathroom stall and stood on the toilet seat. Karen and Val (I think) didn't react in time. They were caught and taken to their class with punishment promised. I stood on the toilet seat feeling guilt and loneliness—what was I going to do for an hour to entertain myself in the locker room without them? Later that day the principal came to our classroom and called Karen and Val out into the hall—the moment of reckoning for them. After they left the room, I raised my hand and told the teacher that he, Mr. Mooney, didn't know it, but I was supposed to be out in the hall with the others. The teacher must have known, because he didn't question me at all; he just said go on out. There were fearful tears in Karen and Val's eyes when they turned to see me, and I quickly confessed to being in the locker room with them.

Mr. Mooney said he appreciated me coming forth; and because I did, our punishment would not be necessary. He said he thought we had punished ourselves enough. I never found out if the teacher and the principal planned the whole scenario because they knew of my involvement, but I'm grateful for the lesson that showed me my ability to be in my integrity with courage; an experience that allowed me to trust that each would be rewarded.

Running track, high hurdles to be specific for once, was another experience in learning about life. If you jump too soon you don't make it over and if you jump too late you stumble on the hurdle—the lessons learned were: have patience, timing is everything, trust your intuition, and don't hesitate in mid-jump. Throughout my life, I've trusted my judgment and completed the tasks in front of me. Sometimes that created wonderful experiences and painful ones, but I still trust my instincts and feelings and use this process for my learning.

Mr. Stuckey was my science teacher in seventh grade. He was blond, lanky, and gaunt with big ears, but I thought he was beautiful. Our task for the class was to dissect a frog; it was the hardest thing I have been asked to do then and since. First we chloroformed the frog until he stopped breathing and/or moving. It was so painful to just watch—my first real experience with death, but not my last. The painful part was that I was taking the life from this ugly little critter in the name of learning. We stretched the frog out on a board and attached it by its feet; it looked like a small person, and I understand that a frog's organs closely resemble that of humans. Then my science partner and I dissected the frog and named and wrote about each of its parts. It seemed I had no choice. I did it with resolve—for lunch that day the cafeteria served chili; you can imagine the comments from the boys of the class. I couldn't eat at all. Later when asked to do a similar exercise, I refused. I received a reduced grade, but I had learned that reverence for life was more important to me than any learning experiment or grade, and I simply could not take another life.

In addition to all these "fun" experiences, there is a family memory that stands out. When I was in the third or fourth grade, Betty, my sister, began school. From my perspective, it was traumatic for her. She was so frightened of everything—the teacher, the bus ride, the other students, the loud noise of the bells, etc. I chose each day during her first year to accompany her to her classroom and stay with her until I had to run to make my own class. Then I would return to her class during lunchtime to make sure she was doing okay. I learned quickly to resent the time it took from my own activities, but I felt the obligation and love of sisterhood. Toward the end of her first year, we missed our regular bus so I proceeded to find a bus that went by our house. But because it was not the numbered bus we usually took, I could not convince Betty to get on board. So I gave in to her fear. That left the option of walking a busy road with cars rushing past as our only way home. I knew immediately I had made the wrong choice and it had endangered our lives. In that moment, I had a huge learning. Sometimes for a person to learn to care for herself, caretaking needs to stop so that the person can have the opportunity to overcome her own fear and create her own experiences. I could not protect Betty from life. At that moment, I took back my own life and stopped escorting her to hers. This is a lesson I have had to re-learn many times during my lifetime: sometimes I just can't make it better. Another's choices are his/her own, and my only obligation is to respect the choices.

Boys became very important when I entered junior high. They seemed to fall in and out of love only with pretty girls. I wasn't ugly, but I was not especially beautiful either. I was tall, lean, and athletic, and the other girls in junior high were beginning to have many curves where I had none. Oh the pain of it! I remember buying my first bra—a training bra it was called. It basically was a piece of cotton stretched between two pieces of elastic with a hook on the back. It was a lesson in discomfort and it made really ugly lumps under my tee shirts. I had no reason to wear it, but wear it I did.

Also in an effort to make myself appealing to the opposite sex, I felt I had to wear lipstick. In my family, lipstick along with short shorts was a sinful NO NO—two of the best traps to catch boys denied. The world was a cruel place! My need to risk sinfulness prevailed, and I was about to learn yet another lesson. Dad had said no lipstick, but I really really wanted to wear it. Did I sneak to wear it or confront the dragon and ask my father's permission if not his blessing? I will never forget this dilemma and eventual encounter. I couldn't sneak to do it—that integrity thing again. So I gathered my courage and planned my interaction with my Dad. The rest of the family was going out to church (I think), but I stayed behind with my Dad. He was sitting on the porch smoking in his white work uniform. He looked tired and not very approachable, but I felt this might be the only time to have him alone. So with trembling—and skinny I might add—legs I stood in front of him and told my story of woe. All the other girls were wearing lipstick and I wanted to too, but didn't want to sneak around to do it so I needed him to give me his okay. I will never forget the look that passed over his eyes. It was a mixture of disapproval, admiration, and amusement. Then without blinking, he said, "Go ahead, but I don't want to see any of that red stuff on your mouth." I assured him I would wear only pink. To this day I do not wear red lipstick; I tell myself it is because I look better in berry and pink shades, but a promise is a promise. Not too long after that, my Mother also began to wear lipstick. I've always wondered if my wearing it gave her the freedom to do something she had wanted to do all along. Looking pretty was very important to my Mother. Some say I inherited her vanity.

I can only guess how this solitary activity began, but my most cherished childhood memories were moments I created just for me under a big oak tree in a wooded area on the farm across from my house. I couldn't reach around its trunk and it was heavy with branches and huge leafs. It was in the center of a small grove of trees in the center of a big open field. I could see my house, but my house could not see me. There I sat with a book on my lap reading of other places and other cultures, and dreaming of the time when I would go on adventures and see all the places I dreamed were out there somewhere. It is under this tree that I began to know that my spiritual Path would be different from the Paths of my family. I learned that all people around the world did not share the rigid beliefs of my parents about God and creation. It took forty more years before I saw clearly without guilt that I had a conscious choice of how to express the wonder I felt when I touched a tree and felt it touch me back; to understand that spirituality and religion were different for me. But that is another story for another chapter.

Also during the early school years, I remember playing baseball and other games with my family. We had this big expanse of grass we called the front yard, but it was really a side yard. Dad planted a row of trees as a barrier from the busy country road. The unspoken rule was that no games were played beyond the safety of those trees. Over the years, they grew as we grew—some straight and strong, others with crooked trunks and lopsided branches. No one ever thought or suggested that they should all grow the same. The grass there was lush and green and soft upon the face and feet. Behind it was a large vegetable garden and behind that was an orchard. It was a magical place that transformed my strong and confrontational family into a laughing and loving menagerie of fun. My Mother would play, but mostly Dad watched and smoked. He was our protector not our playmate. He worked hard and had little energy left for games in the evening. I remember sitting on my foot to postpone going to the bathroom or "outhouse" in those days. I didn't want to miss anything! We actually didn't get an inside bathroom until I was about twelve. Running the fields, walking on the railroad tracks, and these family games brought me much of the pleasure of my childhood.

Being outside was peaceful; being inside was filled with anxiety, because there was always anger or a need for control lurking inside someone that could erupt at any moment. When it did, I sought refuge in my room with Betty and Sandy in tow until it had passed. I still seek a quiet space when the environment around me is unsettled and I need to re-center my own Being. Dad and Mother had great passion for each other, but often that passion was played out with yelling and crying because of their different views of how to raise children, spend money, attend church, etc. Both Dad and Mother had a huge fear-based need for safety and to control what was around them, and they passed it on to all of their children.

When I remember church in those days, I have a pain in my heart. As a child I thought religion was a source of much of the family unrest—who would go when, what was okay to do and not do, what could be said and what could not, what must be believed, what was appropriate behavior for a Christian, etc. It seemed that unlike the trees, we were expected to conform and grow exactly alike. I didn't understand that the real cause of the discontent was fear of not being good enough to be nurtured by the Universal force we then called God or Jesus Christ. Sin was a big topic and carried with it the guilt of someone having sacrificed his life for ours. It felt very heavy and created much fear in me, and I believe the rest of the family. However, what I feared was not this all-powerful God. What I feared was that I would not have the courage to decide whether or not what was being taught by my parents was true for me and whether it could or could not serve my life. I just could not see the logic behind their spoken beliefs.

When I decided that I could not be in my integrity and continue to believe the dogma of the family church, I went to my Dad and told him. I think I was twelve. He did not agree to let me off the hook completely and instead allowed me to attend a different church with Aunt Kate. That Methodist church was similar to the Baptist church I had attended before, but Aunt Kate became a source of much conversation and provided an opportunity to exchange lots of new ideas. I could talk to her about my own doubts without the harsh judgments I felt when talking with my parents. We talked about not only religious dogma, but about theatre, funny stories, our own learning and experiences, and how to create a more open life. I loved the summers I spent with her.

During this time, Imogene (my cousin who lived near Aunt Kate) became my constant weekend companion. Sometimes Karen (my closest friend) joined us. We stayed at Imogene's house more often, because she was an only child and had her own room, and because Ronnie (my first real love) lived next door. There we could sit in the back yard and hug and kiss and pretend to be grown up. I didn't notice at the time that Aunt Velma (Imogene's Mom) was old country. I loved her dogs and messy house and the freedom that comes with less control than I knew in my own house. When Dad found out that my main reason for going to Imogene's was to be with Ronnie, he stopped my visits. It wasn't the last time he reigned in my love interests. His choice was the end of my summer freedom and maybe a good thing. In Ronnie's teenage years he was arrested, served time in prison, and eventually died in an automobile accident. It was not the last time I was drawn to "bad" boy energy.

So instead of going to Imogene's, she and I began to spend our summers with Aunt Rosa and Aunt Martha in Lexington, Kentucky. We actually stayed with Aunt Rosa; she was an unmarried sister of Dad's. She taught me to play cards and shuffle the deck with a flourish. We went to the pool, wore short shorts, and went to the movies—many things that I could not have experienced at home because of religious dogma. If Dad knew what we were doing, he never confessed. Also observing Aunt Martha's life taught me that I could have a life beyond just rearing children and taking care of a husband. She lived just around the corner from Aunt Rosa and she was also a nurse and smart and filled with ideas to share. Again I was a good student. I soaked up the experiences like a man in the dessert dying of thirst. Those fun-filled days fed the part of me that longed to be unique and experience life to the fullest even though I had no idea at the time how that could happen.

I have strayed away from my early school experiences, which I had in mind when I began this chapter, but these early years were a mixture of family life and school life that I cannot divide. Sometime during these years, Sandy started school, Erma left school and got married, and Wallace just left school because it was too painful to endure. At least that is how it seemed to me. As I learned from family and school and compared the learning's, my ideas about life and my dreams for the future began to take shape. When I entered high school, there was just one thing I knew for sure—it was up to me to live my own life and to discover the Path to do that.

The Excitement of Learning

Being in high school in the 1950s was probably as carefree an experience as any teenager could hope to have during their growing and learning years. It was a time of fast cars, pretty girls and boys with ducktails, root beer floats and waitresses on roller skates, rock and roll music, sock hops and football games, drive-in movies, and big hair. Dean Martin, Andy Williams, and Frank Sinatra crooned love songs and Elvis Presley, Pat Boone, and my personal favorite—Tommy Sands joined them later. Tommy never really made it big in those days, but when he sang *Ring My Phone*, I swooned and wished he would. It was my first real love affair. Doris Day, Audrey Hepburn, Katherine Hepburn, Sophia Lorene, and Joan Crawford were the glamour queens of the day. Rock Hudson, Cary Grant, and Gregory Peck added to the Hollywood romantic mystic of the beautiful and wealthy. Everyone I knew, teenagers that is, thought love and fame could happen. For me, it was a time of pleasure and pain as with most teenagers. The memories flow in and out of my mind leaving me smiling in one moment and wincing from them in the next. I felt I had little chance of attending college. In my family, it was not customary to go on to higher education, as most had not finished high school. I had no role model to teach me how to go about it. At the time, it wasn't a crisis, because my immediate aspirations were around dating, hairstyles, and giggling about my latest crush. For whatever reason, my high school days transformed me from the skinny little kid of junior high to a svelte, athletic, and likable young woman—at least in my own mind.

My first gym teacher's name was Mrs. Bennett. We called her "boozy Bennett," because we often found liquor bottles in her wastebasket, and her breath was less than sweet when she gave us direction. She was not a perfect role model, but she cared about us and wanted those of us with a talent for athletics to develop those talents. At a time when only a certain type of girl played athletics, she taught us to retain our femininity and play sports with all our hearts anyway. So early I formed the habit of "looking good" on the field; my Mother's vanity reinforced. That habit remains today. Just because you're going to sweat doesn't mean you don't take a bath! Boozy Bennett organized women's sports across the county, between schools as well as intramural events. I loved it. We played softball (I played first base), we played basketball (three women on each end of the court;

one end played forward and shot, the other three were guards and could dribble three times and pass across to the forwards), we played volleyball (we were undefeated for four years; a record I think that still stands at Greenon High), and ran track (I was pretty fast). It was the freest feeling of my life to that point—to run, jump, squeal, and dance around in victory. Sports continue to be a time of being present with what is, absorbed in the moment. I much prefer participation to observation still.

During my junior year, Boozy Bennett was fired for reasons undisclosed, and Mr. Winters became the new athletic director. He was a wise and gifted teacher and taught many of the athletic skills we had yet to learn. He treated women's sports with the same importance as the men's sports—this was something that the girls were really concerned about when he first arrived. He taught me that self-respect and respect for others was possible, and how it served everyone involved. I am grateful for both of these teachers, because each taught me something the other could not have taught.

Academically, I was a good but stubborn student with little tolerance for rules that seemed to have no purpose except to exclude. This intolerance resulted in some difficult interactions with teachers. I was enrolled in a business program of math, English, typing, shorthand, etc. Because I was not in a college preparatory program, I was not able to take the speech class I wanted; I was furious and fought a losing battle for almost a year. That entire year, I saw myself as a victim of an unfair system, although I would not have put it in those terms then. Out came my warrior right on schedule, and I prolonged an unpleasant interaction for weeks. I railed against cleaning the publication's room when someone else made the mess; I refused to give a speech in French that was part of a final exam; well you get the picture. Because I was a good student, my behavior was tolerated and unintentionally encouraged by teachers, partly because they saw the limitations of the rules and partly because they liked me.

The teacher that most altered and influenced my life was Mrs. Dillon. She taught English and literature for four years. She taught me how to construct a sentence, to trust in the power of words, and to believe in my creative ability to use those words to convey a message. Writing has been a major part of my life since we met. I still have a hand written copy of a story I wrote years ago call, *A Date for the Prom*. It is a sentimental tale of a poor girl with no dress, no date, and no chance to go, but in the end finds a way. The grade on the paper was "A+ Excellent" written in large letters. Whether or not the story was excellent, that kind of success in Mrs. Dillon's class gave me the courage to put down my thoughts without sensor or judgment of them. Now when I write, I trust the process and just let the writing flow through me. Sometimes it needs editing, but the essence within the writing is always from a deep and wiser source than I am aware of at other times.

Mrs. Dillon taught me to seek the wisdom of other writers, one being Marcus Aurelius, a Roman soldier. His book, *Meditations,* is still one of my favorite pieces of literature. Aurelius was a stoic personality with the power and wisdom and courage to speak universal truths. From that time to this, I have been an avid reader of any subject by any author. I have found that whether or not I agree with the writing, I learn a new way of looking at an old belief with a willingness to keep an open mind toward change.

Around this period, I began my search for a spiritual path that nurtured me in a way that conventional religion had not. I read Socrates, Aristotle, William James, Emily Dickinson, Edgar Allen Poe, Ralph Waldo Emerson, Carl Jung, and Henry Thoreau. What they all seem to have in common was the ability to think for themselves, and an appreciation of the nature of physical existence with a sense that they were more than just their bodies. I adopted that way of thinking and began to describe myself as believing in the "natural order" of things. This belief continued into my fifties when the "natural order of things" began to unravel.

But during high school, that belief served me well. I had a natural athletic ability so I pursued sports, I had a bright and active mind so I studied and had academic success, I had a love of adventure and nature so I tried lots of new things. I believed that all people should have the same opportunities so I fought perceived injustice where I found it. I thought I was pretty and believed that quality attracted an array of boyfriends. I was popular so I was chosen for runner-up to Homecoming Queen and Winter Princess during my senior year. I loved drama so I was in the high school plays. I could write so I helped with the school publications. In short life was interesting, busy, and good.

Interestingly enough however, the more difficult experiences remain my most vivid memories and have brought me the most learning about myself and others. That fact reinforced that I should cherish the difficult with the pleasant experiences because of their lasting effect upon my future choices and thinking. I'll talk about just a couple. I'm not sure which year it happened, but one of my male classmates was killed during an automobile accident. He was riding on the fender of a car going fifty miles an hour around a curve after a football game; something we all did from time to time in those days. In a small town, teenagers seek adventure often in dangerous ways; his driver lost control and hit an oncoming car; my classmate was killed instantly. I remember the sobering effect this accident had on our lives, but oddly enough I can no longer remember the name of the classmate.

Four of my classmates graduated from high school already pregnant. Our class only had thirty-two girls so that was an alarmingly high percentage in those days. Some of them raised their children alone. I'll talk here a bit about my best friend. After graduation, she began dating a young man two years older than she and she conceived his child. At first she was just scared of what her parents would do or say, but a few weeks later she found she was not the only girl that was carrying her boyfriend's child. He chose to marry the other girl. My friend was devastated and I did what I could to help and support her through that time of decision to keep the baby or not. It taught me much about taking risks and living with the results. She kept the baby; it was a boy. When he was about ten, she married his father. They are still married, but she is not the light hearted, fun loving person I knew in high school. In those days, she drove with one foot on the seat, one hand on the steering wheel, and her head turned backwards to chat and laugh. Many times she drove us into a field between telephone poles as we yelled and squealed in terror and excitement. She speaks of those dangers still, but rarely speaks of the risk she took that altered her life forever. She has a beautiful son, but the price was high and the consequences long lasting. I remember as girls we talked about seeing the world, but she is still living in a small town and her eyes do not look into mine when we speak.

In high school, Rudy, Dottie, Gary, and I were inseparable. Gary was captain of the football team, Rudy was a great running back, and Dottie and I were considered two of the best catches in school by most accounts. On Christmas Eve our junior year, we went to church together and then went to Gary's house to meet his parents. We were so happy as we headed back to my home later. Mother and Dad had given me red, white, and blue angora mittens for Christmas. They gave them to me early so I could wear them on my date—it was snowy and cold. Our happiness changed to a dark, bloody, scary night when Gary hit a patch of black ice and did all the wrong things including hitting the brakes. That action propelled the car into a ditch and caused the car to roll over end-to-end and back up onto its wheels with me inside. Gary had been thrown out of the car into the ditch during the first roll over. It seems like just yesterday; the memory is so vivid.

Everything seemed in slow motion; the car turning over and over, the front door opened and torn off, the feel of wet cold grass on my hand, my head hitting the windshield, the car pitching and jumping, me falling and rolling, and my short life replaying itself in my head in a split second. When the car stopped, I was pinned on my stomach over the front seat, blood everywhere. I was wearing one of my gloves and it was matted with blood, but I was alive. I wondered where the other glove was, and then I heard Gary calling my name, almost hysterically. As he pulled me out, Dottie and Rudy arrived. They were in the car behind us. Dottie said, "Oh my God, her face is cut." Rudy said, "Put her in the car, we'll go straight to the hospital." They looked so scared, but I felt calm; I'm told shock does that to a person. I said okay, but first I needed to call home to say I was going to be late. To keep me from getting more upset, they agreed and we stopped in at the home nearby of someone Dottie knew. I dripped blood across the woman's carpet, used the phone to call, and didn't even feel a need to apologize; I was a bit woozy. I told Mother and Dad I was fine, but I needed them to meet me at the hospital. Mother said, "okay" in a worried, high-pitched tone. I hung up the phone and turned to see all those people staring at me.

I thought I remembered everything that happened after that, but the others said I blacked out and they rushed me to the hospital. I had seventeen stitches in the top left front of my head. They shaved the hair from my head, and it took two years to grow back completely. All my senior pictures look a bit funky. I had nightmares for weeks—seeing the car rolling over and over. Gary was grounded and could only come and see me by walking ten miles. He showed great caring during that time, and we dated through his first year in college and my first year of working at Wright Patterson

Air Force Base. My other glove was found matted and ruined in the field a few days later. It couldn't be salvaged and I didn't get another pair. Disappointment! Disappointment! I never knew whose carpet I stained.

I learned about betrayal during my senior year as well. At the end of the Homecoming Dance, my best friend came to me in tears. She said I had lost Homecoming Queen by one vote and that one vote had been hers. She said she was afraid if I won Homecoming Queen, I wouldn't hang out with her anymore so she voted for Dottie. I was so angry, because Dottie had won instead of me, and Gary was her escort as she was crowned. I felt as if my best friend had stolen an experience from me—I was a victim of her selfishness. I didn't forgive her, but I continued to help and support her through many things. We continued to hang out, but I held part of myself separate from her—trust no longer existed as it had before. It was the beginning of feeling angry, putting it away, and going on with life—just more guarded than before.

I graduated with honors from high school in spite of our class trip escapade. A few of the boys brought beer on the bus, got drunk, didn't go to the ballgame, and instead went to a bar in Columbus, Ohio. Because the class would not identify the guilty boys, we all were restricted in many ways including "not walking" for graduation. I believe the boys confessed in the eleventh hour because we all did eventually walk. I have little memory of the actual ceremony or the festivities afterwards. My focus was more on buying a car, getting my drivers license, starting my new job at Wright Patterson Air Force Base, and buying new and splendid working clothes. Gary was also leaving for Otterbein College that summer, and we were clinging to each other for reassurance that we would stay together forever. We actually stayed together for only one year. Dreams come and go; people grow in different directions, and lives change. Later, we understand more clearly why that needs to be so.

Working Girl and Marriage

As I mentioned, my focus when I graduated from high school was "what comes next," because I had taken an administrative support test to apply for work at Wright Patterson Air Force Base. For weeks, I thought about becoming an airlines stewardess, which seems a bit odd now since I had never been on an airplane or even a train. Dad clipped that idea in the bud—after I flew a few times later in my life, I was grateful for his wisdom about what was right for me. Now, back to the story of my post-high school work life preparations. I passed the application test and was offered a job with a starting salary of ~$4,700 a year. I only had one problem; or, maybe two! I had no car to get there and worse yet, no driver's license. I took the job anyway.

With Dad's help with the mechanical end of selection and the co-signing of my loan, I bought a kelly green, 1955 Chevy. I don't remember the price, but I loved it. Kelly green in those days was my favorite color to wear—I thought it was sophisticated and that it made my green eyes brighter. It didn't seem to matter that the top of this beauty was badly faded, and I had no money to have it painted. Denial seemed to work for me when there was no apparent logic to support my choices.

After I bought the car, Dad began to teach me to drive it. I only had three weeks, because my job started a few days after graduation. It is a wonderful memory of time spent with him. He took me to the cement quarry where he worked, and I drove all the deserted roads there over and over for hours. I'd be driving along and Dad would yell things like: stop, turn left, back-up, move to the right side! It made me crazy. Once he yelled stop, and I did stop right in the middle of the road so quickly that I threw him into the dashboard of the car. After he recovered himself, he suggested that if I intended to be a good driver, I had to make my own decisions rather than acting on someone else's reactions and behavior. I became a good driver in no time, and I practiced for a few more days and went, without any thought of failing, and passed the exam—no problem. Well maybe not a real problem, but maybe a funny story. I did great on the written exam and proceeded to the driving part of the exam. I was so full of myself—I was doing great!

Then came the parking test! I pulled up along the curb, backed in flawlessly as if I'd been parking for one-hundred years, and straightened the wheels; Done! I didn't even need to pull forward—I was truly great! The tester said, "That was perfect now pull out." I did so immediately without looking to see if other cars were approaching. He took ten points off my score for that misstep; I was ticked. I could hear in my ear Dad's warning about making my own decisions behind the wheel—I still hear him even today.

With car and driver's license in hand, I headed off to Wright-Patterson Air Force Base, Area B. I had only driven with Dad in traffic one time before. I was so nervous driving alone that I forgot to breath. By the time I arrived, I felt light-headed and dizzy to the point that I had to sit in the car without moving, close my eyes, and catch my breathe for ten minutes. That made me late, and as I rushed into the building my body shook with fright. I was seventeen and a half-years young and it must have shown, because everyone went out of their way to help me.

I spent my first paycheck on clothes. Straight skirts and long-sleeved turtlenecks were all the rage. My skirt and sweater set was, you guessed it, kelly green. It was magnificent with my car—I was living large. Did I mention it was July 1960? Air conditioning saved me from heat stroke no doubt!

I worked during the day and kissed Gary by night when he was home from school. My curfew was 11:00 pm—no excuses. If I was five minutes late, I was grounded for a week even though I was earning my own money—how unfair! Oops was that my victim energy showing up? Many nights I ran breathlessly into the house at the last moment—this constant need to be "on time or punished" further supported my growing inclination to be in control of my environment at all times. It kept me out of trouble and safe, but this same controlling behavior had a deep affect upon my relationships.

As the summer turned into fall, Gary left for school, and I began my transformation into successful administrator and cute young office girl. Soon after this time, I became the recorder for an Air Force General's meetings and the doorkeeper for the classified vault that held the plans for the SkyBolt Missile Program. It was very heady stuff for a very young, arrogant, some said, and did I mention pretty, country girl. Young officer's hung outside my door waiting for a chance to ask me out. Old generals and not so old colonels needed my help with a million things. Even my mistakes became successes.

One day, the General was hosting a meeting of several very high-ranking government officials. The meeting was to take place in the vault, and I was to record the minutes. I was now very experienced—I was eighteen and had worked for six whole months, I was wearing my skirt and sweater set, I was ready! I wanted to put pencils and pens out for each participant, so I was tugging on a desk drawer to get them out at the last minute. The door was stuck so I heaved it with all my might—I was in a hurry. As all the dignitaries entered the room, the drawer flew out of the desk; pencils, pens, paperclips, everything you can imagine sailed out of the drawer, and all over the room. I stood frozen as all those "important" people laughed and slapped each other on the back. Have you ever been eighteen years old, wearing three inch high heels and a very straight kelly-green skirt, and attempting to pick up a floor full of tiny particles as eight old men you hardly know watch with glee? That's a run-on sentence, but I think you get the picture; I wanted to skedaddle to anywhere else; but don't forget, I had to take the meeting minutes. So I did. I was concerned with what the General would have to say later. After the others had been given a send off, I looked up from my desk to find the General smiling from ear to ear. He said, "You saved the day. Before you dropped that drawer everyone was too nervous to even talk to each other, and then you made us laugh and it changed the entire atmosphere. We got a lot accomplished with your help." Like I said—it was a time of Grace, but I didn't even know what that was; I thought I was just way too cool!

1961 brought many changes. I told Gary farewell, because there were just too many social options available to me at home and at work. Either I had to choose to break-up or cheat—so I broke-up. I was offered a job supervising five older women, and I didn't take it because my boss said I wasn't ready for that kind of responsibility. He painted a dim picture of how the other women would react to working for "a kid." I was too young to understand that he was full of self-interest and wanted to keep me in my existing job to make his job easier. Several years later when I was about to be married, he apologized for giving me bad advice. It was my first experience with female and/or age discrimination. I've often wondered what turn my life would have taken if I had trusted by own intuition and made my own decision.

But I made the choice to stay and that led in the spring of 1962 to my first encounter with a bright, young, Electrical Engineer named Elvie Gardner. I met him in the hallway outside my office. He was being reassigned from down the hall to our group as the Engineering Representative to the Program Evaluation Review Team (PERT). He had this map in his hand that he was going to hang over his desk. It was a map of Europe, and he was tracking his girlfriend as she traveled with friends through Europe that spring. I thought that was the sweetest thing and offered to help him. He said, "great" and we got colored pushpins and watched Julie's progress together. We also talked about almost anything and everything; in truth I talked and he mostly listened. It turned out that I knew his girlfriend; we had gone to the same high school, but she was a few years ahead of me. That gave us even more to share. I knew things about her he didn't know. What power!

The spring went by and summer came, and Julie was still touring Europe, and Gary had been history for some time. Elvie asked me if I'd like to learn how to play tennis. I said, "okay, but that since he was seven years older than me, I would have to get permission from my Dad." I thought there was no way that would happen, but Elvie said he would come to my house and meet Dad and ask him if it would be okay. Dad and Elvie hit it off and Dad said, "yes." Surprise!! We began to play tennis, and then we began to play tennis and stop at the Frostie root beer stand; and then we began to play tennis, stop for root beer, and talk—in truth me talking, him listening, for hours. Julie had arrived back home, and things were not going so well there. I was never sure if that was because she had changed or because Elvie had become very fond of his new tennis partner, me.

Maybe both, but they broke up. Elvie and I began to spend as much time together as we could. He seemed to me worldly and wise and he found me young and enthusiastic about everything. He loved giving me new experiences and taking me everywhere I wanted to go. By August, he had fallen in love with me and I have fallen in love with love. He owned a house, and I would clean it and sing while he worked in the yard. He took me to my first live stage performance, and we shared my first Polynesian alcoholic drink. It was bright pink with a small umbrella on the side of the glass with two straws—very classy. I was tipsy and the performer later that evening at the theatre turned out to be Martha Reye. We thought it was going to be James Gardner. We laughed and laughed way too loud! We drove home with the windows down so the fresh air would sober me up before I confronted Dad. I was late! Grounded—please no?

That summer was a time of fresh flowers, soft rains, sweet kisses, and life without worry. I baked him a cake that fell in the middle, and I chopped it to ribbons because it wasn't perfect. I tried to cook him dinner and caught my hand in the electric mixer, and he had to whisk me off to the emergency room. He didn't seem to mind either event. He drove a bright red Mercury convertible, and I loved my hair blowing in the wind.

One night in late August, we went to play miniature golf. It was a cool night for August, and the stars sparkled and the moon glittered. As we sat in the parking lot, he took a box from his pocket. The glow from the box made the stars pale and the moon's glow surrounded us. He asked me to marry him, and without hesitation, I said, "yes." As we drove home so that he could ask Dad for my hand, I turned the ring over to see what a wedding band would look like on my finger. I thought it looked great; we were filled with the happiness of new romantic love. The summer breeze seemed to whisper, "forever love." In so many ways, that is exactly what it was for us both.

We spent that fall planning a winter wedding. I was born in cold weather, and I loved the snowy-cold blustery season of winter. It was perfect—the stars seemed totally aligned.

On 14 December 1962, I turned twenty years old, and on 19 January 1963, I became Mrs. Elvie W. Gardner. I quit my job to take care of him and our home. I'll pause here to tell you about how I saw Elvie then.

He was born in Kentucky to Elvie Hiezer Gardner and Clarice Johnson, and his family moved to Dearborn, Michigan, when he was a toddler. He had two sisters, one older, one younger. His family owned a large apartment house. They lived in the large second floor apartment and rented the other two. He was a graduate of Wayne State and Michigan State Universities and had come to Wright Patterson Air Force Base as an eager and ambitious electrical engineer. He eventually was transferred to the

SkyBolt Missile Program Engineering Division, where we met. He owned a three bedroom brick home in Huber Heights, a suburb of Dayton, Ohio, and he was engaged when we met. He was intense in his quest for financial success and was rewarded for that quality. He was good at what he did and other people found him a rather quiet, good listener with a good sense of humor, and an orderly disciplined mind. He was about five feet ten inches tall, with deep brown eyes, a ruddy complexion, and a mouth that seemed to be in continuous pout because of a thin upper lip and a thick bottom lip. He would eventually sport a thick and sexy mustache. He loved to play tennis and work in his yard and smoke Mixture 79 tobacco in his pipe. He actually played with his pipe more than he smoked it; busy hands seemed to help him think. After his engagement ended and even before, he was devoted to giving me new experiences. As we spent more and more time together, he treated me as if I was the most important person on planet earth. This passionate attention was great in the beginning, but as the years passed, it became a source of irritation for me.

A few days before the wedding, I was in a bridal wedding show at Wren's Department store in Springfield, Ohio. I wore a sleek Spanish wedding dress with a Spanish scarf as a headdress. It was the most dramatic look I could have imagined; I loved it. It was almost as exciting as my wedding day. I felt the pleasure of being the center of attention and the most popular bride in the show. Being the center of attention is often quite important to a middle child, and in those days it certainly was for me. That experience later motivated me to becoming a fashion model.

But in 1963, Elvie and I were enthralled with each other and anxious to begin our life together. On the 19th of January we woke to a light snowfall. I'm told that Elvie moved each item in his house one half inch before he left for the church; he wanted it to be perfect. We planned to come back to his house after the wedding and reception to dress for our honeymoon departure and have a send-off party for guests who drank alcohol.

Reverend Gray at Bethel Baptist Church in Donnelsville, Ohio, married us. The church was a small white structure with some brick as I recall, or maybe a small brick structure trimmed in white; all I remember is that it looked beautiful in the snow. The ceremony was to take place on the half hour so the hour hand would be moving up the clock for luck. Curious, I don't remember the exact time, but it was late afternoon.

For Donnelsville, it was a large wedding with two hundred guests, four bridesmaids, and four groomsmen. The bridesmaids wore bright turquoise dresses with cape sleeves and a slightly flared skirt. They were the color of my birthstone and made of satin; they sparkled and reflected the candlelight that lined the narrow aisle. At the end of each row of seats, white flowers surrounded candles. I truly wanted those flowers; they cost me a week's salary. I was able to pay for my own wedding, and Mother and Dad gave me the reception as my wedding gift from the family. I'm sure we had a rehearsal dinner, but the details of it have vanished from my mind. Elvie's four-year old niece was our flower girl, and she wore a replicate of my wedding gown; it seems a bit corny now, but at the time I thought it unique and creative. It was custom made and sleeveless. When I got it, I added cape sleeves to it so it would match the style of the bridesmaids' dresses.

My gown was a traditional wedding dress, but to me extraordinary. It cost $250—more than anyone I knew had ever invested in any dress. It was made of the softest satin I had every felt and was covered by a layer of antique silk and lace that flowed in a "V" from a point at the front waistline. The long train trailed along behind me like feathers in the wind. It was size four, taken in. Audrey Hepburn had nothing on me in the skinny category. The bodice was fitted and made of lace, sequins, and pearls. The skirt billowed out in a perfect circle with the help of a hoop undergarment—another first for me—and it filled the entire aisle of the church.

As Dad and I waited in the alcove to hear the wedding march begin, he trembled and squeezed my arm—it was his way of telling me how beautiful he thought I was, and I smiled, and we entered the church. Because of my dress filling the aisle, Dad walked slightly behind me holding my arm; he never looked more handsome or proud to me. For an instant, time froze and everything seemed surreal. I was getting married. Oh my God!

For an instant, I wondered if it was the right thing, and then I saw Elvie standing at the front of the church filled with wonder and surrounded with the smiling, laughing eyes of our families and friends. All doubt vanished as I knelt beside him for our blessing.

When we turned to leave the church, he got behind my dress and couldn't quite get beside me. Someone in the crowd yelled, "They are not even out of the church and she's leading him around already." Our guests laughed and cheered, whooped, and hollered, and swiftly Elvie jumped over my dress train to take my arm. Our photographer captured his landing. It is my favorite picture from the wedding; a moment in time when everything was at it should be and life was more than enough for us both.

Honeymoon and Early Years

The day of our wedding brought snow, as I mentioned earlier. I had chosen the perfect outfit, a soft gray jersey dress with a matching coat. After the reception at the church, Elvie's Mom and Dad threw a party at Elvie's house, soon to also be mine. Except for Erma, I can't remember my family being there, probably because alcohol was being served and my family members were tee-totallers; being Southern Baptists meant alcohol was forbidden. The day contained many highs and one major low.

I'll start with the highs. Elvie and I were so excited to be in our home together as a couple surrounded by family and friends. One of Elvie's friends had—unbeknownst to me—bet him a bottle of pink champagne that he could not get a "real" date with me. At the party, he presented us with the bottle of pink champagne. It seemed that getting married constituted a "real" date; Elvie seemed filled with pride and love that he had won the champagne and me in the same day. The air was filled with laughter and hope for a bright future. Elvie decided that we would take the champagne with us and share it when we arrived in Fort Lauderdale, Florida, our honeymoon destination. I agreed—truth be told, I had never even tasted champagne!

The low came when it was time to change into my beautiful suit for our drive to Cincinnati to begin our honeymoon. When I entered our bedroom, Kim (Elvie's niece, age three) was asleep on our bed, and Veldonna (Elvie's older sister) admonished me and said I would need to use the other bedroom to change. I told her my traveling suit was in the closet of the room where Kim slept, and I would be quiet, but I would change my clothes in "my" bedroom! Defensiveness, I'm sure was part of my reactionary tone. She immediately said, "okay, but that no one else could go in with me." I retorted that Erma was there, and she was going to help me change, and she would go in with me! This type of interaction with Veldonna was to be repeated many times during the early years of my marriage. Veldonna was use to caring for Elvie and often behaved from my perspective as if she owned his home rather than accepting that it was now mine. I was very young and didn't understand how important Veldonna and Elvie had been to each other, and I was very judgmental and unforgiving of her attachment to him and all things concerning him. That tension remained between us for my entire marriage! I feel we both acted from our fear of each other rather than from our love for Elvie.

By the time I changed, I had recovered my euphoric mood, and Elvie and I left for our honeymoon. I was disappointed that no one had decorated our car, but Elvie, being very practical, had hidden the car to prevent it. It was my first indication that we had a different view of the world, but in that moment it seemed insignificant.

We headed south and stopped at a lovely hotel in Cincinnati. We made love for the first time. It was filled with much tenderness and caring for my well-being. I remember being in the bathroom and thinking there must be more to sex than this. I was right, but that's a private story. We slept late and got up to a new snowfall. The world had been swept clean. The roads were a bit slippery so we delayed our departure to Florida for another day. At that time, I had only been to drive-in movies, so we decided to go to a movie theatre. We chose the movie, "Midnight Cowboy," not knowing its content. It was a poor choice and left us both disturbed and feeling down afterwards. It was the story of a young man who becomes a prostitute to survive in the city and meets a street person who later befriends him, and then dies at the end of the movie from alcohol abuse. It was my first exposure to and knowledge of homosexual behavior and the beginning of my awareness of a hate-filled world that I had yet to even imagine.

We were much relieved to head for Florida—it took us four lazy days, and our lovemaking took on a new excitement as we became more familiar with each other. It was four days of bliss; he loved me; I loved him. We had begun our life together! We had not yet noticed some differences that would become apparent and problematic later in our marriage.

When we arrived at Pier 66 in Fort Lauderdale, Elvie had arranged for us to be in room 119 since we had been married on January 19th. It was very romantic and that night we experienced drunkenness on pink champagne. We consumed the entire bottle, and I fell off the bed. It was an experience that brought uproarious laughter followed by quiet smiles as the story was told and retold when we returned home. We played golf, went swimming in the ocean, shopped, talked, laughed, loved, and created private memories that neither of us has ever shared with anyone else. It was a magical three weeks, because Elvie had made it special in every way that he could think of, and he was a spectacular planner. That love and devotion to making me happy never wavered in all the years we shared.

When we arrived back home and drove into the garage, we found a real mess. It looked as if the party had gotten out of hand after we left. Broken bottles were everywhere; it seemed as if the family and friends drank the contents of each bottle of alcohol and then ceremoniously threw each empty bottle into the cement floor of the garage. There they crashed and exploded all over the place. Later we learned what really happened. The left over, unopened full bottles had been safely stored in the garage when the party ended; but a record breaking cold spell descended on Ohio. The contents froze solid, and the contents expanded until the bottles couldn't hold them. Instant combustion was the result. If anyone heard the explosion, they didn't confess. The clean up together was the first official act of setting up housekeeping together. It was light hearted and fun even though we were exhausted from our long trip from Florida. The trip that had taken four days to go only took two days to return. It was time for Elvie to get back to the world of work, and for me to begin my journey as his support system.

The time flew! Elvie was active in the Jaycees, so I joined the wives' club, and we began a time in life that is hard to remember and hard to forget. The details of when and where are sketchy, but there are moments that remain in memory as if they happened today. It was a time of solidarity in our marriage, home parties, weekend outings, tennis, and just getting to know each other as we shared the duties and responsibilities of ordinary life. I quickly discovered his propensity for order and wanting his own way, and he discovered that I was very young and self-absorbed, not to mention strong willed.

One day my car was in the shop for repairs, and I took Elvie to work so that I could use his bright red Mercury convertible to go shopping. Although we had been married for a few weeks, we had really not assimilated into thinking we owned things jointly. I was so nervous driving his car. I drove very slowly and with the utmost care; he loved that car and polished it until it gleamed every weekend. I arrived downtown and was confronted with his big car in a small parking garage, but I did a great job of parking; turned off the engine, breathed a sigh of relief, and went off to buy my goodies. When I returned, I started the engine, put the car in drive instead of reverse, and quietly drove into the cement wall in front of the car. When I assessed the damage, it was not pretty—broken headlight, bent fender and fractured chrome. I stood looking at it wishing I could make it go away, but there was no solution and so like any competent wife, I just sat in the car and cried.

When I arrived home, Elvie was already there because he had gotten a ride from work with a neighbor. I entered the house, sat stiffly on the couch, confessed the accident, and waited for the screaming to begin. But there was no screaming. Elvie asked if I was hurt, hugged me and said, "Cars can always be repaired." It was the first indication of how important I was to him; as I said before—he loved that car! It appeared he loved me more. It is a moment of awareness that still brings me to tears.

Things did not always go that smoothly. One day he came home to find the kitchen rearranged, and did not find it comforting. I told him it was time for me to take over the activities of caring for our home. He tried to understand, but continued to remind me when we were out of bread. He had lived alone for a long time. My immature reaction was to keep rearranging things so he wouldn't know where the bread was kept and so couldn't notice when it was needed. We began to make allowances for the needs of the other, but we were not as open in our adjustments as I would have liked looking back. In short, we handled each other rather than confronted our differences.

Our choices created an environment of guessing how to please each other and a growing restlessness in me. I decided I had too much time on my hands and coffee clutches in the neighborhood seemed meaningless and trivial at the time. I needed more something; wasn't sure what. I called my old boss and began my plan to return to work. House care seemed important, but not very challenging. Elvie and I agreed that I would start back to work in the fall. So we began to relax into summer.

The memories of some days stay with clarity for a lifetime. We had been to Michigan all weekend visiting Elvie's parents; it had been a good visit. When we got home we were tired but happy. We curled up on our bed; one thing led to another, and we snuggled into each other's arms. It was a time of loving that seemed in the realm of the Devine, and I felt certain that I had gotten pregnant. Six weeks later, I found out I was right. I was to start back to work October first, but it is hard to work when you are retching from morning sickness. It appeared something more important was happening and work life would have to wait. We were excited and a little scared. Elvie had become extremely active in the Jaycees, and I was the new secretary of the Jaycee Wives—we were living our dream. He was busy, I was sick, but we were starting our family, and although it seemed a bit soon to me, Elvie was ecstatic.

One day, I was so sick and I was throwing up non-stop. I noticed that there was blood in the toilet bowl and I had terrific cramps. I was petrified. I called Elvie at work and he came rushing home. He called the Doctor, who reassured him I was probably fine, but if it happened again to call him. I was in tears; Elvie was pacing the floor. He went to the kitchen to get me a cracker to settle my stomach. When he came back carrying the cracker, he was smiling from ear to ear. I thought he had lost his mind. He asked me if I had eaten jello for breakfast—and was it cherry flavored? We both began to laugh and cry at the same time; our child was safe! It was jello; not blood! It is a story that has been told and retold. We have laughed and remembered, but it was also an indicator of how young and/ or unprepared we were for parenthood, especially me. I was about to have my 21st birthday.

My big concern during my pregnancy was birth defects. My sister's daughter had been born with a nerve disorder, which I was told was not inherited, but my Mother's sister had also had a mentally challenged child. In the stillness of my heart, I was worried. I pushed down the fear, hugged Elvie, reassured Elvie's family, got over the morning sickness, and began to celebrate bringing a child into our life. It was a bigger job than I had imagined.

As an impatient young woman the demands of adjusting to what I thought was an interfering mother-in-law and sister-in-law, did not sit well. Of course, expecting a baby was new for me, but I did not want their advice or their opinions; they freely gave both unsolicited or at least that's how I viewed it. I swallowed my words often, but the resentment of their actions and Elvie's perceived failure to have them leave me alone became the first sore spot between us that never truly mended. He thought harmony meant accepting their opinions and then doing what we wanted. I thought harmony was telling them directly that it was our life and they should butt out. I remember one very difficult visit when I asked in anger if Elvie ever disagreed with his family, and he dropped his head and said, "Often, but I didn't tell them." This personality characteristic of not saying what was true for him became more pronounced as the years passed. Where I was sometimes angry and confrontational, he was sometimes reticent and vengeful; these fearful characteristics, so different from each other's, created more tension in our marriage than any other thing. At the time, we couldn't see what was needed. I began to pout and withdraw in order to keep him happy rather than say what I needed to say. My anger kept me from being able to say what I needed from a loving place so I stuffed down a lot of my own needs within the relationship to keep the appearance of peace between us. I chalked up our differences to my being pregnant and unreasonable and him being busy with work and striving to gain financial success for us. That rationale kept us together for many, mostly happy years, but for me emotional intimacy always seemed to be missing. I now realize that I stopped being authentically me in order to be Mrs. Elvie Gardner, loving wife, and soon to be, adoring Mother. It was a huge price to pay, but at the time I thought Life was about compromise, and I justified the choices I made.

One of the most memorable days of my pregnancy was shopping for maternity clothes. The stores were busy and filled with the music of coming holidays. It was not the clothes I remember! What I remember as if it was yesterday was the world growing silent and empty as the word was passed from mouth-to-mouth that John F Kennedy (JFK), President of the United States, had been shot in Dallas, Texas. I rushed home in a state of shock that this could have happened to us; for that was how it seemed. JFK represented the youth and hope of a new approach to government, and his charisma and familiar face had become an integral part of the homes of the children of the 60's that believed we could change the world. The world changed without him and most of us stopped asking, "What we could do for our country?"

On the evening of my 21st birthday, I was filled with the wonders of having a loving husband, a beautiful home, a baby on the way, and of planning our first Christmas. The fairy tale seemed to be coming true. All I had to do was control how it grew—or so I thought at that early age. Elvie gave me a birthstone ring for my birthday; it was a turquoise zircon with a beautiful gold setting that glistened in the candlelight. It was the most amazing piece of jewelry I had ever seen—I love and wear it still. It is my belief that it was given with a pure love that is rare. My 21st birthday was filled with the magic of young love and the promise of a "perfect" future.

The winter passed quickly as my family got involved in helping to plan for my Dad to build Erma and her husband a new house. I was going to have my first baby. Betty had gotten married to a young man that had stood beside her during the most difficult days of her young life. Growth, change, and love were everywhere.

On April 13, 1964, 4:00 pm, Gregory Loren Gardner was born. It was my Dad's first blood grandchild, and it was also my Dad's birthday. How perfect; how scary! The evening before he was born, Elvie and I were at the building site of Erma's new home, and I was having a lot of back pain, but figured it was just from carrying the baby around for eight months. Greg wasn't due to arrive for three weeks, and I was still less than one hundred and fifty pounds. Elvie had bet me that I would weigh more than that before Greg came—it was a joke, because I had gained thirty pounds already, I weighed one hundred forty eight pounds, and I had three weeks to go according to the doctor on April 12th. But Greg saved my bet. About midnight on April 12, 1964, the back pain got more and more severe and I couldn't sleep.

We were getting nervous because it was too early; we thought first babies always came late. We called the doctor a couple of time. He said, not to worry, it was too early, go to sleep, and call him in the morning.

At four in the morning, April 13th, I decided the doctor was wrong and Greg had decided to be born on his Grandfather Ferguson's birthday. So I got up. I called Margie (my care study nurse) and told her to stay close to the phone. The sun came up bright, and I noticed that the buds on the trees had begun to turn into leaves overnight. It gave me such a good feeling even though I was really skittish about what was to come; somehow I knew I was to give a wonderful birthday present to my Dad that day. Elvie had fallen asleep because we had been awake most of the night—I remember it like it was yesterday. At 9:00 a.m. I took my shower; the pain in my back was constant by then. I was having trouble standing part of the time, but there were things to do: I watered all the plants, straightened the house, cooked two meals for the freezer, packed my bag for the hospital, put on my makeup, and lay down beside Elvie. He put his hand on my stomach, asked how I was—he said my stomach was really hard. I remember I said—that it came and went. That comment woke him up with a start. He jumped up and called the doctor and told him I was having contractions. The doctor needed to know how often, but I couldn't tell him because I was just having so much back pain that I couldn't feel the pains in my stomach. So Elvie sat with his hand on my stomach for the next hour or so trying to figure out when a contraction actually happened and, in good engineering style, recorded each of the times. I was hurting, so finally, I said, "call the doctor and Margie and tell them I'm on my way to the hospital." Margie met me there; the sun was so bright; I was so tired and excited.

I don't remember much about the labor except what Margie told me; the doctor gave me something called "twilight sleep" to help me relax and I went to sleep—at least my brain did. Margie said I cooperated and did very well, but that I threatened her with never being invited to my house again if she didn't let me up to go to the bathroom. It was just pressure of course, and I remember the great warm relief that came when my water broke and entry was near. Greg was born I'm told, crying and wiggling and full of life—I have no real memory of his birth. Dr. McKnight presented him to me a little later. My first thought was that he was the ugliest thing I had ever seen—he looked just like a bird. I unwrapped him and counted his fingers and toes to make sure he was perfectly healthy.

The second time I saw Greg, I was more awake and more aware of what a new baby should look like, and I thought he might be cute later on. He didn't disappoint me. By the time he was a few months old, he was the most beautiful child I had ever seen. When Elvie and my Dad came into my room they looked as if they would burst with pride—I said Greg was in the nursery although they had already seen him, and then I dropped back to sleep totally exhausted.

When we took Greg home, he weighed five pounds and ten ounces. He was so long and skinny it was amazing. I had been in the hospital for only three days, but when we arrived in our driveway on Rosebury Drive, the tree leaves were in full bloom. My Dad held Greg up in front of the window and introduced him to the world. Greg was his special gift. It was a time of fear and wonder for a young, new mom and dad. Elvie never paid me the $50 to cover the bet about the weight; he said it didn't count because Greg came early. Sometimes when you bet and don't receive the payment you expected, you win more than you could have imagined. What I won was a bright eyed, expressive child that became the center of our families' lives at every gathering for the next three years. He was so loved, and as a young Mother even then I was unsure how to best help him grow. All the attention seemed too much for anyone. My fear grew, but his presence made everyone so very happy. He became the entertainer, and Elvie and I let it continue not knowing what the future had in store.

Patterns were forming quickly and spring turned into summer and life was full! This encounter with this new little life brought with it my first profound knowledge of spiritual connection. I knew with out a doubt that within us it existed.

The House and Family Grows

This part of our life was a time of growing and everything was changing for me as a homemaker, Mother, wife, community activist, and architect of the expansion of Elvie's little brick house. You may have noticed that I said Elvie's house; that is what his family and mine called it, and how I thought of it. It now seems odd that I did not embrace it as my own even in my own thoughts.

Greg was growing into a beautiful little boy and he was so busy. Elvie and I decided it was time to restructure and prepare for more growth. We asked my Dad to help us, and he readily agreed. It was both a stressful and exciting time. As Greg grew, the house grew, and Elvie and I chaired the development of a park in our neighborhood. Elvie became the President of the Huber Heights Jaycees and I became the Secretary of the Jaycee Wives Club. Elvie founded and became the first President of the President's Club; I can't remember all the dates of these accomplishments, but they seemed mine as well as his. Later he went on to serve as a member of the community Trustees. To say the least, we were busy in every area of our life, and life seemed good. I noticed that we didn't spend a lot of time together, but that situation was common among our friends. Most of our friends were involved in the Jaycees, and we worked and played together as a group. Most of us were around the same age with the same set of problems and celebrations.

Greg began to walk and talk and get into things, and my Dad worked steadily on the addition to our home. I came up with the idea that if we knocked out the back sliding glass door and built the addition from the middle of the house it would become "T" shaped and no one could guess it was not the original architectural design. The opening left by the sliding glass door became the entrance into the family room. It was spacious and full of light with burnt orange carpeting; next to that we built a den with lots of bookshelves lining the walls; I loved it. It was intended as a study for Elvie, but it quickly became my hide away to read and recoup from childrearing and homemaking.

During this house project, Elvie and I were showing some signs of stress with each wanting control of the process. It was the first and last time that Elvie completely lost his temper. My Dad had hired an electrician that never showed up when he was supposed to be working and the progress of the building had slowed while we waited. Greg was a toddler and having a construction site in the house was problematic at times. I wanted to fire the electrician, and Elvie was adamantly opposed since my Dad had helped us so much and the electrician was Dad's friend. I was just as adamant and continued to insist—Elvie had had enough and in anger hit the wall in the spare bedroom and his fist went right through the wallboard leaving a big hole. We both were so startled by his behavior that we began to laugh.

Elvie's parents were due that evening for a visit, so we had to come up with a room arrangement that would hide the hole behind the chest. We joked that they would never believe that it was Elvie that had hit the wall since it was so out of character, and they would be just as sure that it had really been me that was the perpetrator of evil doings. The weekend passed and no one knew, but again I could see that "goodness" could be a tool that had the power to control others, even me. I didn't like that I seemed to be acquiring the label of the "difficult" partner in our relationship. And, of course, I was sure I was in the right. The tally of who was right had begun silently and would continue to quietly grow as the years passed. Elvie was a pillar of the community, a wonderful Father, a caring husband—how could I explain that I needed more; I didn't even understand what it was that was missing. Like everyone said, "I should have been the happiest woman in the world." In many ways it was true.

Sometime in 1967 I think, the grand opening for the neighborhood park was held, but the land clearing for the park was a daily event for years as we worked side-by-side with neighbors to bring it into being. The more it looked like a park the more excited I got and the harder I worked to help create it. As I've review my accomplishments in life, it still stands out as my most passionate creation other than my children. I kept a scrapbook; later I noticed that all the newspaper accounts, if I was mentioned at all, reported that Elvie was accompanied by his wife. No one was to blame for this omission; that was the way of the world in those years. Men held positions, went out into the world, and women supported them and smiled and nodded with pride at the just the right moments. It was our job! As the park took its final shape and the work had slowed a bit, I discovered that I was pregnant. I don't remember all the details like I did with my first pregnancy, but I remember the excitement I felt and the deep knowing inside me that this was to be my first, last, and only daughter. We did no testing so I couldn't truly know, but intuitively I knew! The shape of my body was different than it had been in pregnancy before, and the small kicks and rolls felt so different. There is an old wives' tale that says if you hold a string over your pregnant stomach and it swings back and forth, the baby will be a girl. So you see I had all the proof I needed. Elvie's Mom was also excited, because one week before my due date was her birthday, and she was planning to come and stay for a few weeks to assist with the care of Greg while I was giving birth. Since Greg had been born on my Dad's birthday, Elvie's Mom was hoping that this baby girl would arrive on hers.

"The baby" almost cooperated. My labor began on the evening of 23 February—Elvie's Mom's birthday. I remember playing on the floor with Greg and falling asleep. I was so tired that whole day. I woke at midnight with a severe backache and began preparations to go to the hospital. Elvie went to get Sandy, my sister, to stay with Greg—I remember that he looked so tiny sleeping in his bed. For some reason, I remember his tiny hand lying stretched out on the blanket and how it curled up under his chin. It was a cold and blustery night, and I watched the clock until Elvie returned. Like before I couldn't tell when I had a contraction because of the constant pain in my back and being alone for that hour seemed like forever. Just at daybreak we pulled out of the driveway; the trees were bare and the snow blowing across the road was mysterious, beautiful, and serene. I loved winter, and so it seemed like a perfect morning to meet my new baby girl. It never occurred to me that "the baby" could be anything else.

On 24 February 1967, 12:00 noon, twelve hours after her grandmother's birthday ended, DeAnna arrived. She was so small boned and thin. Her limbs were long and her body seemed very short. She had a large blood blister on her head under the scalp that made her head look lopsided. She had dark hair, and she gazed at me from the darkest deepest brown eyes I had ever seen. In the soft light of the hospital, her dark coloring came as a surprise to me. As I gazed back into those eyes, I asked her, "Who are you?" She wiggled and squirmed, put her thumb into her mouth, and her eyes looked into mine and said clearly, "I'll show you later." She was the ugliest and cutest, daintiest and strongest, foreign and familiar little package. Just as I knew before she arrived that she would be a girl, I knew she would keep all those characteristics into adulthood. She didn't disappoint!

We bundled her up in the same small blanket that I had used to carry Greg home almost three years earlier. When Elvie pulled up to the curb at the hospital, Greg was in the car seat eager to welcome her and me. As I sat down beside him, he reached out and put his hand on her blanket. It seemed to have tripled in size in the three days I had been away. I still remember that moment of growth recognition. It was a bright crisp winter day with a hint of promising warmth from the sun; it seemed like a perfect day to hold two children by their hands. So I did—all the way home.

At home, the house seemed full of people, Elvie's Mom, my Dad, and neighbors popping in to see our new wonder! My new family glowed and hummed with color and life. I was happy to be home. A few days later as Erma and I sat on the sofa with DeAnna lying between us, we were amazed when DeAnna flipped from her stomach to her back. We thought it was a fluke, but from that day on she would flip to her back and then cry because she scared herself. Even in those early days, her curiosity and need to observe what was happening around her was a passion.

At DeAnna's six-week check-up, the doctor took one look at her boney little legs and said, "DeAnna has a small problem here." I held my breath as he explained that one of her legs was twisted, and she would need to be put in a cast immediately to straighten it. I had noticed that her feet turned in instead of out, but I chalked it up to how she had curled up in my womb. I drove to the specialist with Greg tired and cranky, me crying, and DeAnna gazing at everything that came into her vision. Her eyes sparkled like drops of coal. How could this be happening to us? Two hours later there she was in a cast from her foot to her hip; it seemed to weigh more than she did, but she was undaunted. Her whole body shook the first time she lifted the cast, and then it was no problem! The doctor changed the cast every week because she was growing so fast, and at the end of three weeks, her leg was straight. It seemed like a miracle. She had to wear a night brace for a year, which required her to sleep on her back. That too was no problem for DeAnna. She learned to stand and rock on her night brace and giggle. We giggled with her, and reflected on her early ability to acquire needed skills, just like flipping over to see the world around her more clearly. Somehow she must have known sleeping on her back was going to come in handy soon.

The first year of DeAnna's life seemed to fly by; we were so busy. She was walking before she was a year old and very mobile after pulling up at six months old. She actually climbed out of her bed with her leg brace on at eighteen months.

In conjunction with the park, Elvie and I, with help from the neighborhood, co-created a bike path. Elvie and I rode the sixteen miles on a bicycle built for two to commemorate the park and celebrate the opening of the bike path. At the end of the day, neither of us could walk very well due to sore, underused, now overused, leg muscles; and we flipped a coin to see who had to chase Greg and DeAnna around for the evening. They were active, healthy, unstoppable, and everywhere at once. I lost the bet, but true to character, Elvie decided to help out by getting on the floor and crawling around with DeAnna and bouncing her on his back. She loved it. All of us together on the floor trying not to move unless we absolutely could not avoid it, is a strong memory of a very happy day.

Even with the addition we had added to the house, our space seemed to grow too small overnight. Our need to move was probably as much about buying a house together as it was a space issue. We wanted our house, not Elvie's house. So we began to build on a street just a few miles away. We were planning and learning, loving, growing, and I began to feel as though we needed to create a spiritual structure for our children even though I had grave doubts about my own. I was baptized into the American Baptist Church, and we began to attend on a regular basis. I taught Sunday school, but found myself unable to teach the "one Path to God" doctrine. So I took each lesson and edited it to teach what I believed was the essence of all spirituality—love and rebirth as I witnessed it in nature. The more I studied Christianity, the more I came back to the same questions I had asked as a young girl. In a diverse world, it simply was not possible or even desirable to believe such a rigid dogma of sin, guilt, punishment, and repentance. I knew in my heart from my own experience that wherever we sprang from, it was a place of love and purity. The fear and guilt I found in traditional Christianity dogma was gradually replaced in total by my own belief of the natural order of things. It would be years before found the language to express this belief with clarity even to myself.

On the Move

The next seven years would bring major moves outside and, more importantly, inside me. In fact, I believe my inner journey toward wholeness began with the choice to move to Troy Crest Court on DeAnna's second birthday. Elvie and I left his life and my life behind, and we began a new life together. With all the ups and downs that our life took, I have never regretted the decision to have him in my life nor have I minimized his contribution to my growth.

It would be easy now to digress into all the lives of all the lives that touched mine in those days: my husband's, my son's, my daughters', my relatives', and my friends and acquaintances. That is not my purpose here. I want to examine my own thoughts, feelings, and choices as they related to all those who co-created with me. Perhaps it's still the middle-child syndrome, which wants to examine the importance of my own existence and how that has contributed to life as I have known it.

I loved the new house and filled it with color—our bedroom had purple carpet, and the living room carpet was burnt orange to match the chair I bought when I first got married. I still have it. It is no longer orange! As my house filled with things we bought together, my life started to fill with interests of my own. I went to modeling school, joined a philanthropic sorority—Beta Sigma Phi—and continued my community work through the Jaycee Wives Club. Elvie was traveling a lot with his job, and I was taking on more and more of the responsibilities of caring for our two small children. It was a joyous time, but also a time of limits on my freedom to come and go. I began to journal and write regularly again. Needlework also became a pastime. I actually thought I would someday write a book; but as life unfolded, I began more and more to write to dispel or express feelings I felt I couldn't share out loud. This choice began a pattern of connecting with my spirit by allowing whatever was troubling me inside to leap from my soul upon the blank page. Sometimes what I wrote seemed to come from somewhere or someone else. I began to trust this source and feel gratitude for its support. Although the connection to this source was strong, I was not sure how to express its origin to others or even to myself.

It was also during this time that my closest connection to other women was created. Through the sharing of the duties of childrearing, sharing an interest in making the world better, and sharing an interest in developing our own life, we met, talked, planned, supported, and shared more intimacies with each other than with our husbands and families. It was through this sorority that I met my closest and life-long friend. Her name was Brenda. We had so much in common. We were almost the same age, had children the same age, and had married older men when we were young. We were both from small towns and both had ambitions to create a different kind of life than the life we had known as children. The main difference was that I had by all accounts a "good" marriage, and hers was a life of emotional abuse and unhappy drama. I supported and advised her, and in those days preserving a marriage was something we did at all costs. Later it was she who supported me through difficult times.

From our new colorful house, I helped launched Greg into school, DeAnna into life, Elvie into economic success, and me into being a person in my own right. We also acquired a nervous cockapooh puppy. She added excitement to our days. She wet on the floor every time someone arrived at the house, she bit the neighborhood children, and she shook with fright or stood motionless in fear. She definitely needed a quieter environment than she found herself in, but we all loved her, especially Greg.

There were so many exciting and memorable experiences that helped me in my discoveries of who I was to become. Elvie dressed up like Santa for parties, DeAnna put a rock in her nose, Greg drove his bicycle into the front of a car and broke his arm, I ran projects and supported community events, Elvie traveled to Europe for two full weeks, my friends needed support as they ran into rough spots in their marriages or with their children, my sister gave birth to her children, and I quietly became an advocate for women to stand on their own even within marriage. I was not out marching and waving flags, I was asserting my own talents and needs, and when possible, making them as important as the needs of others.

I recall with a smile one such event. Greg was six and DeAnna was three, Elvie's job was challenging and time consuming, and I was becoming the "Twiggy" of Dayton, Ohio, as I did fashion shows, photo shoots, and cosmetic modeling. I had this big show and both of my children were scheduled to have their tonsils out. All of this was to happen on the same day. I determined to do it all. Elvie volunteered to transport the children to the hospital while I was doing my show. I planned to meet him at the hospital and be there as Greg and DeAnna were prepared for surgery. Things went according to plan. I don't remember much about the fashion show, which had seemed so important at the time, but I remember clearly the strange looks when I showed up at the hospital in full make up, false eyelashes, my hair in a Gibson Girl up do, and wearing an oh-so-short orange mini skirt.

I'm sure tongues were wagging at my appearance, but that was not my concern. As they prepared my kids for surgery, I was there. DeAnna especially seemed so small; she was a tiny sleeping lump under the sheet on the big gurney they used to take her to the operating room. Greg had already left, laughing, and talking with the nurses and aides.

Elvie and I waited in the lounge, me reading and pretending calm and he smoking and pacing the floor, both anxious about our decision to do both surgeries on the same day. Greg got back to the room first, and he was old enough to understand why his throat hurt and followed instructions to relax and to fall back to sleep. Not so, DeAnna! She came back into the room crying and scratching and trying to climb into my arms from her bed. My heart pounded as the nurses tried to quiet her. Elvie said he couldn't take it and left to smoke. I understood because it was very difficult to watch. What could I do? I asked the nurse to put her back to sleep for a few hours. She agreed, gave her a shot, and all was quiet for a while.

I slept between the children's beds that night in the hospital, false eyelashes and all. It was a long night and I finally fell asleep around dawn. The nurse and Elvie shook me awake and said it was time to meet the doctors and interns for the post-op instructions. I had one problem—maybe more than one. My left eye was stuck together with one of my false eyelashes; my Gibson Girl hair do had tilted into a lopsided, matted, hairspray clump; and my oh-so-short orange mini skirt was even shorter because of the wrinkles from sleeping in it. In summary, of course I was ready! We were late for the meeting and all the other parents were there showered and looking good. I at least was there, and it has been a welcome and entertaining story to relate to my children over the years. I learned that people are more important than appearances, but that I also appreciated looking my best whenever I could. Oh such vanity again and again! The kids recovered quickly, and we were on to the next drama of marriage and childrearing.

We had only lived in our new house for two years, when Elvie was given an opportunity to move to Massachusetts in the early 1970's and continue his work at Hanscom Air Force Base. We had to decide in one week whether to go or stay. Elvie was excited about his opportunity, and I was excited to start an adventure in a new part of the world. We also were a bit nervous about leaving a place where our roots were so strongly attached; mine especially. However, it took us only one hour to decide to change our life forever. We celebrated, told our family and friends, and started our plan to move away.

We had recently bought a large plot of land and had started the construction on our "dream" home in the countryside outside of Dayton, Ohio. The builder had dug the basement and canceling the contract cost us money, but the decision to move to Massachusetts was in place. We were so eager that we didn't think twice about the financial loss. We worked to solve the complications and get on with it. It had become our pattern; face it, resolve whatever needed to be resolved, and get on with it. Elvie and I were both task driven, and sometimes, in hindsight, may not have given enough attention to the human side of change—our children's or ours.

We flew to Boston and stretched our budget to buy our home. We probably decided to buy it because it was burnt orange for I was definitely in my "orange" period. It was a beautiful house nestled in the woods and backed up by thickly wooded common land. In the fall, the house looked as if it had grown there just like the brilliant trees that surrounded it on all sides. In the spring and summer, it was the accent color for all the greenery, and in winter it was a backdrop for the purple barked trees and the bare crooked branches of the woods. And I can't tell you how amazing it looked surrounded by snow with ice hanging from all the trees. Along the back of the house was a long wooden deck and the blue jays would dive bomb our heads when we least expected it. But I'm getting ahead of my story. During this transition, many reactions to our experiences contributed to how my family would interact in the future.

The house on Troy Crest Court sold in two days and was a completed contract in less than a month; way too soon for us to be ready to move, but we called the movers, put our belongings into storage, and got on with it. We had planned to vacation at Myrtle Beach before we left for Massachusetts. Two decisions were made that caused painful reactions within the family, but at the time they seemed insignificant.

The first was a plan to find a new quieter home for our puppy, and the second was the decision to drive both cars and the camping trailer across country pretending that no one had any fear associated with this huge change that was taking place in our lives.

I'd like to talk about the second first as that memory of driving away in solitude, following the rest of my family in a station wagon with our camping trailer behind it, is an unforgettable moment, and yet it is filtered through all the fears I let no one else see. I was about twenty-eight years old and had lived near my birth family all of my life. I was excited for the new adventure, but realized this decision to move would be life altering for us all. My heart ached and my stomach churned, but my face smiled, my demeanor was confidence personified. As we packed up in separate cars, my Mom stood beside me. I could see her fear for me on her face, but the words she chose to express that fear have haunted me until recently.

What she said was, "If one of my children has to move away, it's best that it is you." I knew intellectually that she meant that she thought I had the strength to take care of my family and myself on my own. On that day, however, as her fear mingled with my own what I heard was that she loved me less than the others; something I had always suspected. As our old farmhouse—which had turned gray with age and had grown closer to the roadway as time encroached on its boundaries—receded in my rearview mirror, I could not stop the deluge of tears that rose in my eyes, paused on the brink, and fell soft, warm, bitter, and salty down my face. It was the beginning of a period of aloneness that I chose not to share, especially with my family. It was a shadow that came and went with activities, but was never completely explored. I am the one that chose to move away from my birth family, but inside me it seemed that they had begun to abandon me when I was small, first emotionally, then intellectually, and finally physically. I straightened my back and resolved, "So be it!" My Mother was correct; I could take care of myself. Right?

The departure of our puppy, the decision of a young Mother, which had the intention of lessening the pain of separation for her children, had an unseen consequence. While we vacationed we had placed Blondie, our nervous pooch, with a local kennel that we had used many times. The owner was a good friend and I confided that I didn't think our busy, noisy, moving family could provide a suitable home for this high-strung puppy. The kennel owner agreed. We also agreed that if he could find a home with an elderly couple or a couple with no children, I would consider giving Blondie to them before we left for Massachusetts. As things sometimes do, the decision took on a life of its own. He found the perfect family the following day, and Elvie and I gave our permission to give Blondie to them. The kennel owner gave her away before we returned from vacation. We thought that leaving her behind would be less traumatic for our kids if we waited until after our move to tell Greg and DeAnna that she wasn't moving with the family. We never saw Blondie again, and my children held me and only me totally responsible; first for giving her away and second for not allowing them to say goodbye. It was a foolish fear-based blunder that my son especially found unforgivable. His trust in me diminished at a critical period of transformation for us both. I'll come back to how that lack of trust contributed to our experiences later on.

Massachusetts held many opportunities for growth for the entire family. It was a beautiful place filled with conservative, immobile families. We were transients to them even though we had only moved once. I vowed to find acceptance and began to join community groups at once. Elvie's job continued to take more and more of his time, and I continued to support whatever direction it took him. If he was home, we celebrated. If he was gone, I took charge. We made a good team, and over time, just as we had arrived there in separate cars, we were living together with clearly defined and separate duties. It seemed a good and healthy existence at first.

As time past, I became more dependent in some areas and he became more dependent in others. His life tasks seemed to take him out of the home and mine were more in home or in our immediate community. I felt like I was a little stuck and the aloneness hovered. I decided to take steps to reach out to broaden my world in whatever way I could and still care for and support my family. I reconnected with my Philanthropic Sorority, joined the Methodist church, tutored in Greg's school, planned neighborhood functions, hosted business dinners, and continued to write down my thoughts and read whenever I could find the time. Both children were in school some of each day in Massachusetts and that gave me a lot more time to pursue my own interests. I began to play tennis and golf a few times a week and became more and more active in my sorority. It served as my social connection much as it had in Ohio, and those couples became our closest friends. For the most part, I was happy mainly because I did not allow shadows across my path to stay for long.

When I had more time for myself, I began to study the spiritual teachings of both western and eastern prophets. I began to open to the possibility that the natural order of things was not just something I wanted to believe, but that for me that belief was the most valid source for my own spirituality. I remember a Methodist church retreat where I became very tearful. Those running the retreat were sure it was because I had lost my way within their faith. But somehow, at a very deep level, I knew I was tearful because I could no longer remain in the church and have integrity with myself. It would take me years of continued study and looking inside me before I had the courage to acknowledge first to myself and then to others that my spiritual path did not lie in the dogma of Christianity. I still needed the admiration of my family as well as their approval of my life's choices.

Massachusetts Life and Loss

The years in Massachusetts are a blur of memories and activities all jumbled into a few years. Greg and DeAnna both were off to school for at least part of each day, and I was off to some activity that kept me busy and involved with other people, and Elvie was off to work. As I said before, I was mostly happy, which was different from feeling the joy of living. It was such a time of change for all of us that it is difficult to decide what I want to share here. I've decided to focus on the changes I saw even though most of those memories seemed at the time painful and/or filled with loss. Now as I look back with more wisdom about myself, I can see that each experience was exactly what I needed to learn about my own authentic needs and myself.

My memories are a bit confused after so much passing of time, and I have trouble remembering the order of events, but the events and the impact they had on me are as if they happened yesterday. The first thing I remember is finding just the right pet to replace our puppy. Her name became Heather, and she was a brindle Scottish terrier. I thought she looked and behaved like me, and being Scottish was always something I was aware of within me. She was full of energy and beautiful in an angular, homely, and quizzical kind of way. Her face had a serious and contemplative expression, and her eyes were full of mischief and curiosity. She was partly gray-haired as was I, and she was moody but never shy. She had a mind of her own about what she wanted to do and a playful side that was oh-so-gentle with Greg and DeAnna. From my humble perspective—not my strongest attribute in those days—she was the perfect pet.

If I close my eyes, I can see my Dad in the backyard with her when she was only a few months old. They were just playing and talking. It reminded me of when I was very young and just hung out with Dad. Dad and Mom were visiting us and I had just given Dad an original painting I had created just for him. It was a painting of a stormy sea at night and was in shades of black and white. He said it reminded him of nights at sea when he was in the Navy. Through his interaction with Heather, I saw his gentle spirit that was often hidden under his fear of seeing the people he loved suffer. His fears, of course, are another story for another day. We all fell in love with Heather immediately, and she lived with us wherever we went for the next sixteen years.

Three difficult events happened in only a few months time; I think it was the third year we were in Massachusetts. First my sister's daughter died. She had been ill with a regressive nervous disorder since birth, but the light in her hair and her incredible clear blue eyes were gifts from the divine. It was as if she could see into my soul when her eyes connected to mine. My sister was her legs, arms, and body for some sixteen years, and her death left a really big hole in our family. It is hard to put her contribution to my learning about compassion into words. She could not speak, but she could sing. Mostly it was just Sanskrit sounds, although my Christian family would never have called them that. Her sounds drew me to her, and my heart ached to understand why such beauty would come into physical life without the ability to communicate her joy. As time passed and she died, my answer came. She had communicated with great clarity the need for acceptance of the present moment. Like most of my profound learning's, I had to hear them more than once to incorporate them into my daily life.

A month or two later during the night, my mother-in-law, Clarice, died in our guest bedroom. It gave me the opportunity to touch death in a way that I had never imagined I would. The event began late afternoon. Heather had disappeared and everyone but DeAnna, Dennis (Clarice's grandson who was also visiting), and Clarice were out in cars searching the neighborhood. We all were just crazy with worry. We found Heather walking down the middle of a busy street several hours later. After we brought her home, Clarice said she was having pain in her left arm. We offered to take her to the emergency room to check it out, but she said it was just her old gall bladder acting up again. She laid down to rest, we had dinner as usual and went to bed.

Around midnight, Elvie's Dad came into our room and said Clarice was ill and could we come. I jumped out of bed and ran to the bedroom where she had been sleeping. It is another moment that remains crystal clear in my memory. The room was decorated in black and white bold designs and moonlight covered the bed. Clarice lay on the pillow; her eyes opened with a startled look in them. Her left arm was reaching out as if to hold on to life. But the warmth and spark of life was already gone. I felt for a pulse and found the beginning of coldness within her. She had died. I turned to see

Elvie and his father at the door; their faces contorted in pain. I turned back to Clarice and closed her eyes as gently as I could. We called the coroner's office and waited for him to arrive. It took several very long hours.

We used the time to call Clarice's other children who were on the road vacationing. Elvie's parents lived in Michigan and arrangements were needed to take Clarice's body back for burial. Clarice's family began to arrive later that day including children and pets; it was chaotic to say the least. I felt I had done everything just right, but later learned that moving DeAnna and some of the other children into the room where Clarice had died was a mistake. For months afterward, DeAnna would ask me to come into her room and feel her heart to see if it was still beating. It was another young Mother's mistake that altered our interaction in an unforeseen way. Later she would share with me her discomfort and fear of sleeping there so soon, but I couldn't change the past.

The entire family traveled by car caravan with Clarice's body back to Michigan. We took care of each other as best we could, but it was a difficult task. When I arrived back home, I realized that I had hardly slept for ten days. I gave in to the exhaustion and went to bed. Afterwards, I took down the black and white wallpaper and redecorated the room. It's funny, but I can't remember what the room looked like after that even though I sewed in it almost every day.

A month or so had passed and the family had begun to heal, and we were getting back to routine living. I went off to play tennis in the late afternoon. When I returned, Elvie's face was grim with an expression I recognized. Something was wrong. He told me my Dad had died. I reacted with anger and told him that was not funny. He said it was not a joke; that Dad had choked to death on the roof of his house. My mind could not believe it; Dad was only fifty-five. He and Mom were due for a visit to Massachusetts in two days. We silently packed up the children, our clothes, put Heather in the dog kennel, and began our eighteen-hour drive to Ohio.

We had hardly left the driveway, when my tears began. It was a flood that could not be damned. I thought it was about Dad and it was. But, it was also the tears of sorrow I had not shed for Pamela and Clarice, because I had felt being tearful was a sign of weakness and would not support those with real sorrow. The tears flow unimpeded until we arrived at my parent's home, and then they stopped as quickly as they had begun. The façade of strength in times of crisis returned; there were things that needed doing. I found my Mom lying on the sofa, drugged into confusion with prescription medications by well meaning family members. The entire family and many friends surrounded her as she went through financial papers. It was heart breaking to see her in such a state, but my Dad's death had come as a shock, and the family felt she had been hysterical, and they had done what they felt was best.

The story as I remember it being told to me was that Dad had just consumed a large heavy dinner, when he noticed a piece of roofing flapping in the breeze. Since my parents were planning on traveling to Massachusetts in a few days, he felt he should climb up and repair it. Dad was a heavy smoker and had a deep rattling smoker's cough. Once he was on the roof, he began to cough. He regurgitated his dinner and when he sucked in to cough again, food particles went into his lungs. He suffered an immediate cardiac arrest—he died face down on the roof.

That is where my Mother found him. She had flagged a driver down as he passed her house and begged for his help. She could see Dad's purple swollen face, but could not reach him. The driver was a paramedic and took charge. All this was happening while I was playing tennis, it seemed as if I should have had some kind of inner message, but I had not. I faced my Dad's funeral with a stoic determination I had learned from him; I did not, could not cry! My Dad's death came suddenly and way too soon from my perspective, and there were papers to file and plans to put into action. So I stayed with my Mother and sent my husband and children back to Massachusetts. It was as if I was someone else, and my Dad had been someone else's Dad. It remained that way until I board my flight to return to Massachusetts.

As I flew into Boston, the fall foliage had arrived, and I remembered how much my Dad and I had enjoyed the change of season and how now he was gone. The flood of tears began again. I got off the plane and there stood Elvie, Greg with a broken arm, and DeAnna looking so tiny and beautiful. I put a smile on my face and went to meet them. Later I sat on a mountaintop and grieved for my Dad. I was angry with him for leaving me too soon; I was not ready to be the elder. I didn't know how I would meet the challenges of my life; he and I had always faced our family's challenges together. Now I felt sorry for myself and believed that now I was all I had. The question kept repeating, "How could he have left me?" I wasn't sure that just "me" would be enough, but I picked myself up, put my anger on hold, and began life without him. How differently my grieving could have been if I had had the courage to ask for support, but that was not the choice I made then and certainly not for a very long time afterwards. As I look back from here, I believe that was when my numbing-out began for real!

Unconscious Growth and Change

After that year of loss, the needs of raising children and supporting Elvie in his efforts to support our family financially became my full-time job, most of which I loved. Again looking back, I have few specific memories of the everyday happenings during that tremendous time of growth for all of us. Mostly I remember the big events and/or dramatic changes in my own perspective of what I needed to happen from time-to-time. The children's adjustment to the neighborhood in Massachusetts was not without difficult experiences. Both of the children made friends quickly, but there also seemed to be an element of meanness in the neighborhood children. Perhaps this is true of all neighborhoods and is simply part of the growing up and learning how to care for oneself.

Greg and DeAnna were sensitive to the actions and reactions of others and displayed hurt feelings when they were teased or threatened. When that happened—another child said something mean or a bully showed up in school—I was not always sure of what to do or what not to do. As a young Mother, I believed that teaching children to be independent was my most important job. From this place looking back, I can see that I sometimes hid my caring heart and instead of offering them the compassion they sought, I energetically taught them to "suck it up and get over it." I still believe that independence in thought and action are very important lessons, but my method of cultivating that in my children could have looked very different. I could have added, "Examine it, feel it, learn about yourself and then move into the present moment." I have often hidden my gentle and tender side, seeing it as weakness. My stoic stance may have contributed to a pattern of stifling their feelings or may have contributed to a feeling within them that it is not okay to express authentic feelings appropriately.

I also remember sewing Halloween costumes, watching basketball and soccer practices, staying up into the night with illness and injuries, working for days to prepare food for an office party, baking cookies, helping to deliver the Sunday papers, cooking meals, keeping schedules, shopping for clothes, kissing boo boos, dealing with emotional upsets, packing up and moving to Virginia for a year, packing up and moving back to Massachusetts, and packing up again a year later to make a permanent move to Virginia. My job was encouraging everyone in every way that I could find or was capable of seeing. It is important for me to remember these successes, collectively if not specifically, and how much laughter and fun I was able to give to my children and my somewhat serious introverted husband. It was challenging and wonderful, joyful and painful, and I have never regretted the years of my life spent in this way. They were amazing.

We lived in Massachusetts for about five years when Elvie got a prestigious opportunity to attend the Industrial College of the Armed Forces; only one civilian from Hanscom Air Force Base was chosen for this honor. My reaction was, "No problem!" A month later, we had rented our house, packed up our furniture and moved to a townhouse in Springfield, Virginia. We all adjusted to this change quickly, and we had an exciting year of exploring the Washington DC area and just having fun.

Elvie graduated with honors and we discussed moving to Virginia permanently, but we owned a home in Massachusetts and the job Elvie was offered was a lateral move and would not increase his salary. We decided that kind of move would not be in the family's best interest. So at the end of the year, we packed up again, people, pets, and belongings, and made the best of moving back to Massachusetts. We all loved Virginia from the beginning, but the decision was made, and we just left! I'm not sure why, but leaving that small community and small townhouse left me with a heavy heart and a feeling that it might be a mistake. It could have been that the year in Virginia was without stress and continual commitments and somewhere inside me that was appealing. I also discovered that I had a talent for teaching and held a part-time job teaching sewing for Stretch and Sew Fabrics. It was creative, fun, and challenging, and it was just for my own entertainment.

One year later to the day, Elvie was offered a promotion back in the Washington DC area, and we began to build a new home in Burke, Virginia, while we sold our house in Massachusetts. That move preparation time gave me some of my happiest days in Massachusetts. I was eager to leave the house where my mother-in-law had died for one thing, but I also think it was more. A few years earlier, I had celebrated my thirtieth birthday in Massachusetts with friends and family. As I drove DeAnna to school, the carpool children sang, "Mrs. Gardner's thirty, Mrs. Gardner's thirty." After they got out of the car, tears streamed from my eyes and I didn't understand why. When I got back home, my friends had used black paper to decorate the garage door; the sign said, "Happy Black Monday." It was their idea of a joke about getting older, but inside me, it was no joke. I had learned to play golf and had won a tournament, I had learned to play tennis and won more than I lost, I was a good wife and mother, I had served successfully on many community committees and boards, I knew I had a talent for teaching, but deep inside me I was beginning to wonder what if anything was my "real" purpose in life. Many years later, I still felt something was missing, something of me that I couldn't define. Elvie and I were getting older, the children were getting older, and I felt like my life definitely needed a kick start. When we decided to move back to Virginia it felt right and good, and I set the intention to make it my kick-start to rediscovering me. It was 1979.

The peculiar thing about growing unconsciously is that you can't see that it is happening. Life changed, I changed, life changed again, and I changed again, and the pattern continued. I had adopted the philosophy that I would quietly adapt to life's changes just as I witnessed the change process in nature. The object was to survive! So I made that my goal and accomplished it. I began to get back to writing more, reading more, and studying philosophy more. I took on every task with energy and enthusiasm. For the most part, the tasks were rewarding and successful. The children continued to grow more and more beautiful and more and more independent. Elvie and I continued to grow more and more in different directions. It isn't that we stopped supporting each other's growth; it was more that our own growth was done without seeking collaboration with the other. I began to see my life as belonging to just me, and I feel he often felt that way about his own. Our life together was losing its luster, but the changes were subtle as we unconsciously moved toward separate lives.

Although for years, we continued to behave lovingly towards each other, I feel my true intention in the early 1980's was to raise my children and then leave the relationship. I have experienced many times since, that whether a true intention is conscious or unconscious, the Universe supports it without judgment. The opportunities for choices came, and my choices made in the moment co-created what I truly wanted. I so wanted to be on my own, see the world, and learn, learn, learn about life; mine in particular! I didn't see that as a possibility within my marriage.

The early years of the 80's were the years of my greatest joys and some of my deepest wounds. After we moved to Burke, Virginia, I took a part-time job as an orthodontic surgeon's office manager. I took up racquetball and began distance running to build up stamina for racquetball tournament play against much younger players. I began as a beginner, and eventually evolved into a racquetball instructor for beginning and intermediate players. I loved teaching; next to writing it's what I most loved to do.

My most remarkable learning came from three deaf students that wanted to learn how to play racquetball. At first, I didn't know how to go about it, but slowly they taught me how to communicate without words. After that, the next hurdle was to always have a visual contact with them and to teach myself how to anticipate the flight of the ball without the benefit of sound so that I could show them. Although I was their teacher from an outsider's perspective, it was me that improved not only my racquetball but also my ability to relate to others. I utilized that ability later to teach sewing to people who had never sewn, to teach my children a skill they didn't have; and more importantly, to teach myself how to relax in order to run long distances without tiring.

To be able to see an experience from the perspective of someone else or to shift my perspective about my own abilities also came in handy a few years later when I began to play competitive soccer. I could visualize where the ball was going, anticipate the movements of my opponents, and pass to space, knowing just where my teammate was headed. I discovered just how fast my foot speed actually was. When I was a child I competed in a small environment and won, but in Northern Virginia I was running against younger, bigger, and cream-of-the-amateur athletes, and I was still winning. I was an accomplished distance runner so my stamina could match anyone's I played against, which sometimes came as a surprise to them. It was heady stuff during those years. My ego was soaring. I was earning my own money, competing in racquetball and soccer, and distance running, and I was Good!

Other parts of my life were not quite so good. Greg, my son, was beginning to show signs of addiction. First with alcohol and later I discovered that he was smoking heavily. Within me, out of a feeling of helplessness to control his behavior, I blamed his best friend's influence, and told myself all young men drink beer. He attended college for one year and then dropped out to go to community college and finally just to go to work. His demeanor began to change and he seemed less open and happy than he had been, but he had a job with a lot of responsibility and good pay. He seemed to be gaining focus, but my intuition told me something was not quite right.

DeAnna, my daughter, was growing up and excelling in her own activities and preparing to go off to college. My previous ways of Mothering were changing drastically, and in many ways my main job became less interesting as the children's needs diminished. DeAnna complained that I wasn't like other Mothers. Instead of greeting her with cookies, as she thought other Mother's did for their children, I was out running, teaching racquetball, or playing soccer. I felt she was becoming a young woman and I was letting her. She didn't really come to understand that until she actually went off to college. Once there, she wrote me a beautiful letter expressing her gratitude for my ability to let her make her own decisions without hovering, but before that our relationship was trial and error. She created the trials and attributed all the errors to me. My feelings were much the same in reverse. I remember those anxious nights of waiting on the stairs for her to arrive, grounding her or yelling at her in relief once I knew she was safe. Then one night it dawned on me that once she was late she knew she was in trouble, and her logical mind decided if she was already in trouble she might as well stay as long as she wanted too; and so she did. This great parental insight into teenage behavior permitted me to drop all deadlines and just ask her to be home at a reasonable time. She was excited at the new responsibility, and she almost always arrived home about the time that had been her imposed deadline earlier. When she couldn't make it, she called. That power struggle ended. No one was more pleased than me. Like I said—trial and error—big time.

As I began to spread my wings outside the home, Elvie and I grew farther and farther apart. I left my part-time job and decided to take a full-time job at Northern Virginia Community College. The job in the Office of the President quickly led to another job. I became the Officer Manager for the Public Relations Department, a busy and creative place. I fell in love with reading, studying, and learning all over again.

One of the perks of my new jobs was that I could take courses at the College for a reduced tuition, sometimes for free. So I added two courses to my busy schedule of Mother, Wife, Homemaker, Athlete, Teacher, and Worker. I was rarely home and when I was, my relationship with Elvie was tense. Most of the time at home was used to support the needs of my growing children. I remember one Saturday morning, I got up and there were so many things on the calendar for the family to accomplish collectively and individually that I had been forced to write around the outside edges to get everything on it. I stood for a moment and made a decision that changed our lives; I threw the calendar away. I declared that if something was not important enough for us to remember, then I wasn't going to track it. The family freaked, but I felt so free. We each had full responsibility for our own activities, and it liberated us all. Surprisingly enough, we rarely missed an event for each other or ourselves. More trial and error!

Elvie and I continued our support for the family, but often we did it in angry silence or with verbal blaming. The relationship was changing from what had once been a loving one to at best on my part one of indifference. The year DeAnna went off to the University of Virginia, things really began to unravel. Greg had moved away to live with a few other young men, had lost his job, and had taken a job at a gas station to support him. The pay was low and so were his spirits. I rarely saw him without a cigarette in his mouth or a beer in his hand. He was still leader of the pack with his friends and seemed in charge of "fun" while his friends continued their education. Heather, our wonderful Scottie died. Elvie and I were alone for the first time in over twenty years, and I didn't know him. I felt he didn't know me.

We discussed a one-year separation as a temporary experiment for me to do what he perceived I needed to do. For me the real question was whether we wanted to spend our lives together, and for me the answer was no, loud and clear no need for discussion. I felt I was at the beginning of new and important discoveries, and he seemed focused on being home and working in the yard. Of course, the problems were much more complex than that simple statement implies, but that's how I saw us then.

In 1985, I took a job with The Center for Naval Analyses, began training and ran my first marathon with co-workers, continued playing traveling soccer, as well as taking even more courses toward an associate degree in business. At some point in the process, I simply decided and then energetically at least left my marriage. I began to enjoy the attention of other men. They seemed younger and happier and time with them was more appealing than going home. My marriage was in trouble, and I was making unconscious choices that supported a less encumbered life. I wanted to experiment with life on every level and felt I could not do that with integrity while I was still in my marriage and its limited freedom. It was the most difficult and the easiest decision I have ever made.

Elvie and I talked with Greg and DeAnna to tell them I was leaving and getting my own place. It was a thorny time for all of us, but the pull of complete freedom was urgently important to me. I didn't want to miss one more day of life. Also I was naive about the consequences that would come with the decision to leave my home and my oldest dearest friend. We chose to be civil, but he was hurt and I was arrogant and unsympathetic. I just wanted what I wanted, total freedom. What I learned is that there are always limitations and total freedom does not come cheap and has limitations of its own. I just walked away from twenty-five years of marriage with no thought toward reconciliation or counseling. It was the right choice, but an incredibly insensitive act of selfishness.

Six months later, I called Elvie to say I wanted to come home. Without a word of anger or disapproval for the calamity my leaving had created for him, he drove and then hiked through a giant snowstorm to talk and to comfort me. One week later I was back in my home with him. Within days after I arrived, I knew I had made another unwise and thoughtless choice. It had been my home and old friends I had missed, not my husband.

A few weeks later, I told him that I had made a huge mistake, which wasn't about him, but that I could not continue in our marriage. He asked me to stay through the holidays and I agreed. It was a sad and dark season. We traveled to the Rose Bowl for New Year's in the deepest kind of misery. We were two old friends with nothing to say that could help either one of us.

In 1988 I left home again, but I had a much better grasp on reality and the obstacles that I would confront. I had left much debris in my wake. My children were confused and angry, Elvie eyes were red and swollen from lack of sleep and tears of sorrow, friends and family were disapproving, and my schedule of work and activities was overwhelming. But for the first time in a long time, I felt free to make my own choices and strong enough to suffer the consequences. I didn't understand that I still had much to learn. Later when someone I loved left me, I experienced and remembered how much anguish my actions in those weeks had created for Elvie. It seemed then as if karma was balancing the experiences of the past.

I too had suffered. I had lost my home and financial comfort, experienced betrayal of a false friend, felt the anger of my children, faced the judgment of my old friends and family, and had been witness to the deep sorrow of my most loved and trusted friend. It was excruciating, but I knew that leaving was the right choice for me. I went to register for my new classes at Northern Virginia Community College with renewed energy in my step, but also aware that the most difficult and most exhilarating years of my life may have just begun. Spring was in the air and the small tree buds were straining against the cool breeze, the sun was shining, and I was on my way to happiness. It was a moment of Grace without fears of the past or the future; a small sampling of what life in the present moment can be. I can close my eyes and experience it even now over twenty years later. I am profoundly grateful for that moment of authentic power, because the memory of that feeling has sustained me through the many painful and unbelievable consequences that have followed.

Freedom and Consequences

In late spring of 1988, I was flying high, three soccer games a week, multiple dates every weekend, gathering "A's" in all my classes, training for more marathons, reading and studying in every free moment, going out bar hopping with co-workers, getting promoted at work, and running constantly in more ways than one. I was living life as if there was no tomorrow. But late at night, I began to feel the loneliness of the life I was creating. I needed people around me constantly. I had met one long-distance male runner that had become a dear and loving friend. Soon after we met, he discovered he had cancer of the larynx. He faced it with bravery and we supported each other in so many ways. We ran together and he teased me about being "above average in a below average group," and said he, "loved that I bleached my hair only at the roots so they were only visible when the wind blew." I loved him as a friend or maybe more like a brother. He told me that I should date and have fun and live life, and when I was ready, he would be there waiting in the wings. I know that he loved me, but I was looking for excitement not stability. In less than a year, he died and I mourned, but my "mouth only smile" didn't fade. "I was happy." Right?

During those incredible years, I developed four amazing friends, two male and two female co-workers. They became my extended family and were aware of my constant need for activity. I sometimes shared with them that my life was less than perfect, and they supported me everyday with non-judgmental love. Of all the people I've met since 1985, they were and they are the most intimate and most loving relationships that I have ever had. They have celebrated my successes and caught me mid-fall during my difficult and trying experiences. They seemed to love me unconditionally through everything I created. I cherished my family and other dear friends, but they were not with me during my daily journey. Marty, Chris, Clay, and Jack were there. They threw me a rope or blew wind in my sails whenever and wherever I needed their support. As time passed, I needed a rope more and more often.

The need for a support rope began in fear, but I didn't recognize it as fear at the time. I thought I had fallen in love for the first time in my life. The relationship brought me all the things I thought my marriage had lacked. We shared our passions, the love of adventure, the love of books, the love of travel, and the love for drama in our lives. It is a long and complicated story of love, fear, betrayal, forgiveness, separation, and authentic love. The ending has not been written, but it began in unconsciousness and now exists in consciousness. It began as a love story and it began in the spring of 1988.

When I write of it now, this period of my life may appear more painful than it was for I suffered gigantic losses, but it was a time of unprecedented growth and of really deep and needed learning. Often I was lost in my thoughts about how to cope with the past and how to create a more pleasant future. In this moment remembering, I will report to you the essence of what has remained with me most.

Perhaps the greatest of my losses was the loss of innocents and trust. Until this period began, I trusted that I could create my own life, but during this time I saw myself as the victim of other people's failures and the circumstances in which I felt compelled to change. Even the order of these monumental events is cloudy in my mind.

Greg continued to drink and used my divorce as the reason for not speaking to me for four years. By the time he chose to interact again, he was deep into alcoholism. He drank and Elvie, DeAnna, and I rescued and worried. It kept my life in a state of anxiety of what to do to help him recover. At one very low point after I found him curled into a fetal position from drunkenness and dehydration, he went to an in-house rehabilitation program at Fairfax hospital. Watching him recover I was filled with guilt, doubt, pain, and a wish that I could make it better. Nothing I did made it easier for him or for me. His alcoholic behavior was justified through his anger at my perceived injuries. I went to counseling sessions at the hospital, and became angry when Elvie chose to attend only one session. It was a session that seemed to point the finger at him for enabling Greg's drinking; he never went back. My current partner flew in from Texas to support me. I attended AAA meetings for a few months, but the meetings seemed for some a place to vent their addiction to pain. I wanted to move beyond the pain and live my life and support Greg in his bid for wellness. When he was sober and had completed the program, he moved to Florida, and my hopes for his happiness and mine soared. But within a year, he was drinking again. At little at first and then full-blown alcoholism returned.

My current partner and the man I had grown to love like no other misrepresented his marital status to me, and by the time I found out the truth, we had begun to travel the world and see the places I had only imagined. He had had a dysfunctional family and his value systems were much different than mine, and it was clear that his level of integrity had suffered. I so loved him and in his own way, I believed that he loved me as much as he was capable of loving. I chose to make excuses for his unhealthy behavior so that I could share his time and adventures. I was skydiving, spelunking, rock climbing, and traveling. I called it my summer of adventure and freedom. It was both and it was neither. I had played soccer on an all-star team that traveled to St. Louis and almost won a National Championship. I had completed my associate degree in general studies from Northern Virginia Community College and had received another promotion at work. So much of my life was as I had dreamed it that I failed to see the avalanche of trouble I was brewing.

I have always been hesitant to receive love perhaps for fear of losing it, and so of course, I was drawn to this man who seemed incapable of giving it with commitment. It was a perfect match that resulted in periods of ecstatic highs and debilitating lows for us both. A few months after we became sexually intimate, I learned that a few weeks before we had met, he and his wife had conceived a child, a boy. It was an unhappy marriage to say the least, but he was indeed married with a child on the way! I spoke with his wife; told her I would leave him only when he no longer wanted to be in the relationship—our life was not her call. Later I would remember those words and feel shame when her shoe was on my foot.

For better or worse so they say, I chose to stay in his life; he made the choice to keep me in his by continuing to misrepresent his situation. He moved away to a new assignment, and unknown to me, so did his wife. It was an entire year before I knew what he had done. His story was that he didn't want to lose his children or me—I didn't believe his story. I weighed the risk of what I would lose and what I would gain by staying, and I decided seeing the world with someone I loved was worth the risk. He would grow up and his situation would resolve itself, or so I thought. Instead of leaving him, we left together for Spain. It was my first trip to Europe. We saw a bullfight in Madrid, drank orange juice in Valencia, almost got bitten by a large dog at a monastery (Mt. Serrate) turned hotel, visited cathedrals and very old castles, got drunk in Toledo, bought a vase and stole the plate, kissed on a blanket by the Mediterranean Sea, and prayed to the Black Madonna for healing. I'm still grateful I didn't miss those experiences. For that one week, the rest of the world did not exist for me, and it seemed we loved each other with abandonment.

It would be easy to say I should have left and/or he should not have lied. Both, perhaps at first glance seem true. In fairness to both of us, we did from time-to-time end our relationship out of anger, frustration, and/or guilt. The ending did not last, and one of us would reach for the other, and the other would come running. It seemed that we both feared living without the other—we had great passion. We had much in common, and for me I can truly say that he is the only person I have never tired of even briefly. I shared things about myself with him that no one else knew; he listened to me, shared my interests, and I liked it. I loved the energy he brought into my life, and I couldn't imagine not having him in it. But more than that, he had a heart that was so big and so empty and so needy, and I believed that only I could bring him to wellness. I didn't know then that "need" does not heal; it just creates more need and more pain. Nor did I truly understand or recognize my own neediness. My need for him to learn to love and to love only me was powerful and compelling.

After a few years, he retired from the military and came to live with me in Virginia. In the beginning, it was a mix of hope and fear everyday. He was in the middle of a messy divorce with his children hanging in the balance. He loved them; she loved them; and their anger at each other colored their view of a healthy ending to their marriage. Again, I considered my options and I chose to stay, but it was a distrustful and angry truce. I wanted to "fix" him so that I could be happy. I thought that was love and in so many ways, we supported each other's fears.

After a gallant fight with cancer, my former husband, Elvie died. He died without giving consent in sufficient time to validate the paperwork that would have insured me a life-long income. I don't mean to imply that he left me with nothing in the way of financial security for I received some of his life insurance and a large lump sum settlement from his employer. In our divorce decree, we had agreed that I would receive a portion of his retirement income, but we had failed to cover what would happen if he died without retiring. He had not chosen to retire before he died of prostrate cancer at sixty, and even with appeals and the agreement of his employer that he intended me to have the retirement income, legally it was not possible for me to receive the funds. No retirement date meant no retirement funds existed. I took it in stride, but the anger inside me thickened around my heart as I said, "That's life" to my children and family. I gave his eulogy and supported my children during his illness and their recovery from his death. It was most hard on DeAnna, and I chose to be strident with her instead of compassionate. The tenderness I felt for her was as painful to me as my own Father's death, but I didn't have the courage to look at it with her then. Losing my oldest most loyal friend who had fathered my children left me feeling more alone and without a rudder. True to form I said, "That's life," and moved on.

A while later, DeAnna moved to Florida and got engaged to a wonderful young man, named Michael. I wanted her life to be perfect, and Michael seemed like a perfect choice. I felt the joy of a happy ending coming. It was interrupted when I received word that my Mother was fatally ill. She had been a robust woman of eighty-one that walked four miles a day, and suddenly she was dying of a brain tumor. It just made me angry and I felt helpless to influence what was happening to her. She seemed to have done everything right, and still she was dying. I searched for an experimental treatment to buy her a few years, but the attempt failed. I wanted to kick something, but instead with my families' encouragement, I went on a rafting trip to the Grande Canyon. There was nothing anyone could do for my Mother, and the trip had been planned for a very long time. It was probably my most memorable vacation to date, and I had time to accept my Mother's eminent death without scrutiny. Two months after she was diagnosed with a brain tumor, and a few days after I returned from my trip, she died. I miss her still. At first it didn't seem real, but then later that year she visited me in a dream on DeAnna's wedding night to let me know that she had attended the wedding. I already knew she was there, but it was good to actually see her. She looked to be about thirty, a time when I thought she had been her most beautiful.

In December, the deep truth of her death hit me when my birthday card with $50 in it didn't arrive. She had not missed sending me my birthday money since Dad died. When she was dying, I felt like my own life was falling apart piece by piece, but I chose not to share that with my family. I still had hope that I could make a miraculous comeback, but sadness was descending, and I just couldn't seem to stop it.

When my Mom was ill, my partner drove with me back and forth from Virginia to Ohio every weekend. He never complained. When DeAnna needed support, he was the first to give it or support me while I gave it. He used his retired officer's status to acquire a ballroom for DeAnna and Michael's wedding. He loved my family and they loved him. He was to them a brother-in-law. He helped entertain them and planned itineraries and cooked for them when they visited. He shared my tears and my pain as Greg's alcoholism grew worse and worse. He shared my joy when Greg went into rehab during the late stages of alcoholism to attempt to regain some of his health. Again he traveled and shared and worked to support me as I supported Greg's recovery and living expenses for over a year. He never said no even when his money was tight if I expressed an interest in seeing some distant place that called to me. He would drop everything and fly with me to a different city just to have dinner. He grocery shopped and cooked my meals, because he got home earlier from work than I did. I could go on and on. There was so much that was good. We worked so hard to stay together, but our fears were more powerful than our romantic love, and we didn't know that we could create a deeper kind of love with other choices. Neither of us really understood the meaning of intimacy; we seemed to fear vulnerability more than we loved each other.

The years passed so quickly. I worked; I saw the world; I loved; I grew in fear, sadness and anger; new life came into the family; people left and died; and I mourned in solitude. I rarely laughed and almost never sang. Things were not good, and it was up to me to make them better. Of course, right?

I attended lectures seeking guidance for the changes I sought in others. But what I discovered was that I was the one that had co-created my life with my choices, and I was the only one I could change. I had to learn that receiving love and giving love are the same dynamic. To create a more joyful and meaningful life meant changing my choices, and it was the most frightened I have ever been. Sadness overwhelmed me, and I wasn't sure I had the courage to really examine my life let alone drastically change it, but that's the next chapter.

The decision to change my perspective about whom and what I could change presented a picture of a new vision of living, and that picture was how I wanted to live. I knew there would be consequences and I wasn't sure of what they would be. I also knew that the joyless existence I was living had to end one way or another. Let me tell you how it came about.

Discovering "Authentic Power"

For the last twelve years, I have been on a journey of discovery; a journey described to me by Gary Zukav, and later by Linda Francis, as an inward journey toward "Authentic Power," a power that can not be taken away, an internal power. It began when I discovered a book called *Seat of the Soul*, which Gary Zukav had written several years earlier. I was in a bookstore browsing to see which book would choose me on that day. Again and again *Seat of the Soul* drew my attention, but I would pick it up and then put it back on the shelf. You see, I viewed myself as someone who didn't need "self help" books. As I waited in the checkout line, I had a knowing that if I didn't buy that book my life would somehow be different. Little did I know at that time, that the choice to buy that book would be the catalyst to a deep and enduring change of how I saw myself in the world.

That choice and many others since have uncovered much pain, but that choice and many others have brought me back to the source of my own joy as co-creator of my own life. As I settled down to read *Seat of the Soul*, I felt a divine Presence. It seemed the same divine Presence I had felt when I walked in the woods and touched a tree, heard the cry of a small baby, held my own children at their births, or viewed the magic of a rainbow at the end of a stormy day. It seemed to put into words, my own belief of the connection, through a shared energy, of all living things. The book spoke to me of my ability to create my own life, and when I had read the book through, I read it over again, and again, and again.

Time passed, but I returned over and over and over again to *Seat of the Soul* for inspiration. It both comforted me and disturbed me, and I wasn't quite sure why. Perhaps it was because more and more, I was allowing the fearful part of my personality that saw itself as a victim to surface. I didn't know it then, but it was this core fearful part that had controlled a big part of my life and experiences and was most in need of healing.

The next few years would bring many changes and many dramatic and then calming experiences. Within this span of time, I began to feel as if I had lost control of my own life. Nothing was as it should be from my perspective. I was divorced and my former husband and oldest friend was ill and eventually died of prostrate cancer, the man I loved lived far away physically or emotionally and he seemed to lack integrity, my only son was an alcoholic, and my Mother died suddenly from a brain tumor. The only area of my life that felt okay was my success at work. I had become a vital and necessary part of a team that was changing the focus of our defense-based business and co-creating a domestic-focused entity within it. It was new, it was satisfying, and I was working longer and longer hours. It was at work that I seemed to have control so that is where I focused almost all of my energy.

Also during this time, DeAnna and I were planning her wedding to a wonderful young man that she had met at graduate school. She was healing from the loss of her Father and Grandmother, and changes in her life were creating the necessity for my attention. I was grateful, because it allowed me to ignore the growing sadness that at that time "was my life." When I see pictures from that period, when I look closely, that sadness is not hard to see. The man I loved had moved into my small apartment a few years earlier and our relationship was filled with passion and volatility as he transitioned out of the military. In short, we loved each other, but there was little respect left between us. With so many other parts of my life in turmoil, I clung to the thought that I could change him and me so that we would eventually be "happy." Even then I knew we were in deep trouble and were in a cycle of hurting and needing each other. I blamed him for our situation and I worked harder.

As I planned for DeAnna's wedding and tried to "fix" my relationship, I decided the problem was not enough space for all that was about to happen. So without consulting my chosen partner and while he traveled home to visit his children, I bought a larger condominium. He was not truly committed to our future together, so he reacted in fear that resulted in some very destructive choices on his part. I was committed to our future so long as he behaved, as I wanted him to behave. It was a recipe for disaster, but we were too busy working and planning to be truly aware of what we were co-creating. I was not aware that I was feeling more and more a victim of circumstances. In fact, I viewed myself as courageous to take the blows and remain standing. I also didn't notice that I rarely felt anything in my life; I had gone numb, the ultimate pain.

Greg's alcoholism was reaching the dangerous level. He was never without some amount of alcohol in his body, and I feared he would not show up for DeAnna's wedding. That entire summer as we worked toward the wedding, I was consumed with the fear of losing control and dropping into deep sadness from which I might not recover. Since I could not let that occur, I worked harder at work, harder at home, harder within myself to resist the sadness. My friends began to notice that I rarely sang and/or smiled as I had before. They began to ask what was wrong.

Only my closest friends knew what was happening in my life. I hid behind a façade of what I considered at that time to be bravery. Over time, the new apartment got remodeled, the wedding got completed, the partnership vacillated between getting better and getting more troubled, and Greg's alcoholism intensified. I worked long hours, worked out several times each day, avoided my friends and to some degree my family, and tried to make the best of all the things I perceived were happening to me. I confided in one friend that I had sought counseling, because I had begun to tear-up at work for no reason, and I was scared. My counseling sessions lasted for about a year, but each session ended with me leaving the session in anger—adamantly complaining that I was not "angry," I was just "sad."

Again and again, I reread *Seat of the Soul,* and began to see my life from a different perspective. I had stopped tearing-up in public so I thought I was getting more control back into my life. Things were better with my partner, but I didn't sing very much and rarely smiled except in social occasions were it was expected. Life still seemed heavy and grime most of the time. I kept reading, writing, and working on learning about myself. Matthew my first grandson was born, and he was so precious. The pure love I felt for him was overwhelming, but I did not judge myself to be filled with the joy that should have come with such an event. I was beginning to doubt that I would ever by happy, but I felt my unhappiness was the result of Greg's drinking and my partner's lack of integrity. Greg was in treatment for his alcoholism again, but critically ill with liver disease. My partner and I seemed to be reaching out to each other again. If I could change both of them, everything would turn out all right in the end. Right? I worked harder on all of us. Soon instead of feeling sad, I was deeper into feeling nothing at all—no anger, no sadness, no passion, and certainly no joy!

I accepted my life as it was for the most part. I put on a happy face in public and felt exhausted at the end of each long and busy day. Then another happy event occurred. DeAnna gave birth to my second grandson and named him after me, Thomas Reed. I felt deeply honored. I went to care for Matt and DeAnna's family for several weeks at Tom's birth. DeAnna and Mike, her husband, didn't have anyway of knowing that their gift of a small butterfly pin, representing my spirit that arrived for a few weeks of support for them and then was gone, gave me the first true feeling of joy I had experienced for a very long time. In that moment, I knew that my perspective on my life had begun its transformation, and I was going to change me. With that intention to heal, I went home.

After I arrived home, I turned on the television. Gary Zukav and Linda Francis were on public television discussing their book, *Heart of the Soul: Emotional Awareness.* They showed clips from a recent workshop and mentioned that they had a website. I was intrigued to say the least. My first act at work the next day was to go to the website. I found they were having a workshop in Orlando the same weekend I was returning there for a short stay with DeAnna's family. I called my partner to see if he was interested. He said that we should wait until that evening to discuss it. I couldn't wait! I signed up for the workshop, and my day immediately seemed lighter.

The workshop was focused on learning to recognize when I was being controlled by a fearful part of my personality by scanning my energy centers to locate whether or not I had pain in them. I couldn't feel anything, but I cried constantly for the entire two days of the workshop. I thought I must be losing my mind, and I viewed "being a tearful woman" as a weakness greater than any other, but I seemed to have no control. I needed help!

Gary and Linda offered me the opportunity to apply for a three-year program of study with them. I was so controlled by fear that I could not open my throat enough to say I wanted to accept their offer. With gentle understanding, they gave me the application; I filled it out, and waited to hear whether or not I would be accepted. I told myself it didn't really matter—one way or the other, I was going to get control back into my life. However, when the call came, and I waited to hear the result, my heart was nearly beating out of my chest. My entire body was filled with pain. When I was told I was accepted, the tears of relief came for hours. I was scared of what would come next, but I was committed to changing my life. I had no idea how much pain and intensive inner work would be required to do that. That call came about six years ago. My journey toward Authentic Power has been a bumpy one. With the beginning of emotional awareness, came my resistance to learning about my deeper and core emotional pain. For a long time, I preferred the pain I felt in my body as sadness to an unknown pain I might discover. My feelings of sadness had become so painful it had overwhelmed me, and I feared that looking at the feelings of anger, jealousy, and victimization would be more pain than I could bear. So I learned intellectually about Authentic Power, but held my fearful parts at a distance to remain safe.

More painful experiences arrived at my doorstep as I resisted going into the awareness of my core fears. My son eventually died from complications of alcoholism. But for a year and four months, I supported him toward wellness of spirit. He did not die an alcoholic; he did not die with something to hide; he did not live without intimate love, and he did not die alone. Our experience together taught me the meaning of acceptance, the strength in non-judgmental support, and the true essence of compassion and tolerance. It would not have been possible without the inner acceptance of my own pain and a genuine knowing that he and I had co-created our experiences in order to heal the core issues we had come to physical life to heal. His physical life was short, he died at thirty-nine; but the essence of who he was is still resident in everyone he touched, especially those he touched during the last few months of his life. He had a gift of creating laughter that he rediscovered as he healed, and he gave it freely to friends, family, and strangers alike. Greg, DeAnna, Michael, my partner, and I faced his death with courage and love for each other, and I let him go with the knowledge it was time for him to start again. That new beginning, as a consequence of his previous choices required that he leave his physical body to perhaps find another. I felt at peace when the nurse came to me after he died and said she had opened the window of his room so that his spirit could depart. It felt just right! He had been on loan to me and I was letting him go. I felt the same closeness to my spiritual source as I had when he first came to me.

A week later as I traveled home alone carrying his ashes, the sadness of not ever seeing him physically again settled back down over me. He had made me laugh! It was a snowy wintry day and evening. Cars were sliding off the road and a big truck had overturned in the medium strip. I was tense and I turned on the CD that he had left in his car. A song titled, *Thank You for Loving Me*, filled his car and my tears began to flow. I knew he had intended for DeAnna and me this last message, and I just wanted to hear his laughter one more time. That of course could not be in this lifetime except in memory.

Days, weeks, and months passed. My partner was spending less and less time at home, and I was working hard to not give in to the sadness I felt returning. I was comfortable with Greg's death, but I had so much sorrow about the way he had chosen to live and how I had contributed to those choices. I didn't understand that I had not forgiven either of us. I was new to creating Authentic Power and had acquired some emotional awareness, but there were layers to come that I could not have imagined then.

Seven months after Greg's death, my partner of many conflict-filled years, chose an action that I could not accept. It was filled with drama, departure, pain, and fights for control of what we had shared. During this time, I had many thoughts of revenge, and I made choices that prolonged the painful experiences we were co-creating. I did my best, with the help of friends, family, and my spiritual partners in the Authentic Power program, to understand what was happening in my life and to continue to learn how I had helped to create these experiences of pain. Unfortunately, I also made sure I kept the story of victim running in my mind and shared it with others. This complete awareness did not really come until recently. My intention to heal all the fearful parts of me created my awareness of so much pain—first of sorrow, then of anger, then of my core feeling of being a victim of my own life, and finally a deep and painful discovery of my feeling of powerlessness and unworthiness of being upon the Earth in physical form. I've learned through experiences with others working toward wholeness, that fear of unworthiness is the universal fear of humans living in duality as we attempt to reconnect with our spiritual source—our collective soul.

I had set the intention to let go of the past and come into the present. At times I had periods of grace that allowed me to see what life could be like without fear, and then the fear would come rushing back. Sometimes it appeared through a different fearful part of my personality, and I greeted it from the healthiest part of me I could find—sometimes not all that healthy. But I began to ask for guidance from my non-physical guides on a more regular basis and to listen for answers instead of indulging my active fearful parts. I began to see my life as a series of choices that had truly created my experiences, and I began to make different choices, and my life became interesting again. I also noticed as I faced the fearful parts of me, that I began to experience the joy of just watching a butterfly flutter and land upon a flower. It seemed to be its purpose, and I began to know at a deep level that I would not be in physical form if it was not part of the Universal plan, and my healing through spiritual growth was indeed my purpose.

The world of nature I knew in my childhood began to call to me more loudly. I sold my condominium on the seventeenth floor of a city high-rise because I had a longing to live nearer the Earth. I chose to retire from a job with long hours and to move into a small quiet mountain resort community. The process took two years, but once I decided to build this new way of life, the Universe backed my choice at every decision. I watched in awe how authentic power manifested in my life once my intention was clear, and I began to trust. That is where I find myself now, nestled in the peaceful valley at the foothills of the Blue Ridge Mountains of Virginia. A view of the mountains surrounds my little blue house, and a golf course runs behind me. There are small creeks running down from the mountains everywhere. I am surrounded with people who seem to have found contentment in their place in the sun. I have time to write, read, review my life, plan my future, hike in the woods, watch the sunrise and the moonlight shine through my windows, and I simply do what feels most important to me each day.

My old relationships have a new intimacy, my new and old relationships have less drama, and my connection with my divine source and myself is what gives sustenance and nourishment to my life. I do not mean to imply that I have no fearful parts anymore; I have many. Sometimes their subtle influence creates circumstances that result in painful experiences. Lately, I have been led by my need to examine the true meaning of compassion for me and for others. Within me the fearful part that judges is still often too much in control of my reactions, and I cannot always see my true intentions clearly. The exciting part about that is that I am grateful and excited about another opportunity to learn about yet another part of me that these experiences bring into my deeper awareness.

For many years, I have "tried" to be forgiving of the actions that others in my life have taken as well as action I've taken. The part of me that continues to sit in judgment makes forgiveness a struggle for me at times. A few days ago, I discovered something new about forgiveness as I looked at my growing capacity for compassion. I no longer believe that I can just think and then choose to forgive. That is not how forgiveness works for me. What I've learned is that when I can truly see beyond the actions others or I take when we are consumed with our fears, I can see our divine Presence and forgiveness is no longer needed—peace is just there and there is nothing to forgive. I can see that each of us is in the process of connecting with our authentic selves and co-creating our experiences of learning. My connection to that divine Presence that guides my writing is gaining strength as I allow it to be the guidance for actions in other parts of my life.

My fearful parts are well practiced and clever at controlling my reactions, but through an intention to heal completely, my healthy parts are more and more coming forward to choose what action I will take. It has taken a long time for me to forgive myself through the creation of emotional awareness and conscious responsible choice, but my intention to make my spiritual growth the most important thing in my life continues. I have had an amazing transformation and a new perspective is now possible. I now understand my role in choosing my experiences and how they have assisted me on my journey to Authentic Power. I am so grateful for all those who have touched my life, co-created my experiences, and supported me on this journey. For me the journey has taken me inward, and I have discovered that I can trust the Universe to support my choices, and that if I am conscious in each moment, I can make responsible choices that result in a healthy and productive existence upon the earth. My experiences of late have reflected that amazing discovery, and I am blessed with the knowledge that I am connected to all living things.

As I write this, I remember a time when I was very young, when I hugged trees, and ran through fields of grass, and sang to the birds; a time when I was in awe of all life, a time when my fearful parts had not been quite so strong within me. It was an extraordinarily joyous time of freedom. Maybe what I have been experiencing the last six years is not transformation at all, but simply a return to the knowledge that I came from a divine source and this process of remembering and allowing it to guide my physical life is my purpose. Once again I choose Life and choose to share it with you.

Namaste and Happy 41st Birthday DeAnna
February 24, 2008

AFTERWORD

Whoever you are, live your life completely. If you are a plumber, be the best plumber. If you are a saint, be the best saint. If you are common, be common. If you are extraordinary, be extraordinary. People only err when they try to be who they are not.

Deng Ming-Dao

Stones in Harmony

Small Steps – Huge Changes

Change is constant and we cannot stop it. An intention to make the healthiest choice possible in each moment can support us in making the huge changes needed for a joyful life. Each of my experiences described in these pages has been written at a different time throughout my life. Although they are placed in an order that seems meaningful to me, they are not necessarily in chronological order. Each word picture represents my thoughts and feelings at the time of the writing even though my perspectives may have changed over the years. It has been an amazing journey that has brought me this far, and it continues.

It is December 2010, and this chapter of my recorded experiences is complete. It is my intention to continue to live authentically in each moment knowing that to be human is to create more opportunities for learning and spiritual growth. It will not be easy and at times it will be more challenging that I can imagine now! Amazingly, each moment's challenge is exciting instead of frightening, which is a huge change of perspective that adds to the joy of living. What remains strong within me is my intention to continue to record and to share my experiences through my writing. It is one of my gifts. It is very personal and yet it seems important to give it openly without attachment to the outcome so others who have like-kind experiences may find it supportive. Although sharing creates a feeling of vulnerability within me, it also creates a feeling of appreciation. All of us have had joyful experiences and have chosen to celebrate. Many of us have suffered difficult experiences and have simply responded to the call for learning and renewed health! Together we have rejoiced, laughed, cried, fallen down, gotten up, forgiven, disappointed, loved, suffered, healed, rejoiced, taken small steps, made huge changes, and chosen over and over again to live as co-creators with a wise and compassionate Universe!

Understanding what is occurring all the time is not possible, but trusting that all experiences are designed to support our own spiritual growth and/or the spiritual growth of others is necessary to co-create responses that bring balance to living. To me it is clear that it is not what happens that matters, but how we choose to respond to what happens that is "Life" re-creating itself.

Many have supported me in making small steps toward wholeness and this more balanced existence. Grace has given me time and strength to explore the essence of my soul, to connect with the divine source of my being, and to discover how to change what is no longer wanted as a controlling factor in my life. My feeling of connectedness to all living things humbles me and supports my belief that each connection serves the whole. I am filled with wonder when a butterfly touches me gently, and I am filled with amazement when the sun rises over the mountains. It is a huge change to finally know that gratitude is the feeling that trumps disappointment, that anger can be healed with compassion and understanding, and that the fear of powerlessness can be transformed into a personal power from within that cannot be taken away. Yes, it requires small steps, hard work, self-knowledge, emotional awareness, free will, wise choices, facing deep fears, an opening of the heart, and a trust that the Universe is friendly. It is my precious life; only I have the power to choose what energy will create it! Within your life the choice is the same.

Now in this present moment, my small steps have brought me to the completion of this written collection of a lifetime of thoughts and feelings about my extraordinary, ordinary life. It is my gift to you and to myself. May you recognize and/or find comfort for your extraordinary life within our common experiences, may you know that each of us has the potential to become a courageous explorer, and that it is no accident that we are here together at this time, in this place, and in this way!

Our divine connection will remain constant whether or not we notice, and the choices we make in each moment will support all of humanity as it evolves toward a more collaborative existence. This moment is our time to take one small step and then another and then another. *May all beings find a deep and abiding peace; may all beings awaken and be free. May all beings choose Love!*[10]

Namaste
Phyllis Reed

---

10   Buddhist Metta Prayer

ABOUT THE AUTHOR

Phyllis "Reed" Ferguson Gardner has been writing for as long as she can remember. She writes about the people, places, thoughts, feelings, and experiences of her "ordinary, extraordinary" life. She feels there is a "wiser woman" that speaks through her writings, a "spiritual presence" that has existed in difficult and joyful times. She has come to believe that it represents the soul's essence of her maternal Great, Great Grandmother "Reed." She has never met this grandmother, has never even seen her photograph, but she has been a non-physical teacher and guide since childhood. Phyllis Reed was given her name at birth. In the beginning, she thought that her middle name was strange, but as she began to publish her work, it was Reed that seemed to identify her best. It is through her connection to this grandmother that she has a true "knowing" of the continuity of the human web of existence of which she feels a part.

Phyllis lives in the foothills of the Blue Ridge Mountains of Virginia where she gives her time and passions to creative writing, improv theatre, volunteering, and learning about nature, including her own. She loves the outdoors and spends her leisure time visiting her family, hiking, biking, playing tennis and golf, dancing, and photographing nature.